STAYING
CLOSE

STAYING CLOSE

STOPPING *the* NATURAL DRIFT
TOWARD ISOLATION IN MARRIAGE

Dennis & Barbara Rainey

THOMAS NELSON PUBLISHERS®

Nashville

A Division of Thomas Nelson, Inc.
www.ThomasNelson.com

Editor's Note: One technical point to make reading this book less cumbersome: any use of the personal pronoun *I* will mean that Dennis is speaking. All of Barbara's comments are found in chapters 15 and 16.

Copyright © 1989 by Dennis Rainey
Repackaged edition 2003.

Published in Nashville, Tennessee, by Thomas Nelson, Inc.

Unless otherwise indicated, all Scripture quotations are taken from the HOLY BIBLE, NEW INTERNATIONAL VERSION®. Copyright © 1973, 1978, 1984 by International Bible Society. Used by permission of Zondervan Publishing House. All rights reserved. Scripture quotations noted NKJV are taken from THE NEW KING JAMES VERSION. Copyright © 1982. Thomas Nelson, Inc. Used by permission. All rights reserved. Scripture quotations noted PHILLIPS are taken from J. B. Phillips: THE NEW TESTAMENT IN ENGLISH, Revised Edition. Copyright 1958, 1960, 1972. Used by permission of Macmillan Publishing Co., Inc. Scripture quotations noted RSV are from the REVISED STANDARD VERSION of the Bible. Copyright 1946, 1952, 1971, 1973 by the Division of Christian Education of the National Council of the Churches of Christ in the U.S.A. Used by permission. Scripture quotations noted TLB are taken from *The Living Bible*, copyright © 1971. Used by permission of Tyndale House Publishers, Inc., Wheaton, Illinois 60189. All rights reserved.

An effort has been made to locate sources and obtain permission where necessary for the quotations used in this book. In the event of any unintentional omission, modifications will be gladly incorporated in future editions.

Library of Congress Cataloging in Publication Data

Rainey, Dennis, 1948–
    [Lonely husbands, lonely wives]
    Staying close : stopping the natural drift toward isolation in marriage / Dennis Rainey.
      p. cm.
    Previously published under title: Lonely husbands, lonely wives.
    ISBN   0-7852-6168-0
    1. Marriage—religious aspects—Christianity. 2. Intimacy (Psychology) 3.
    Communication in marriage. I. Title.
    [BV835.R347 1992]
    248.8'44—dc20
                                   91-37199
                                    CIP

Printed in the United States of America

07 QW 8 7

We would like to dedicate this book to our friends

Don and Sally Meredith

who gave this ministry a great start and a great message.
Thanks for your impact in our lives and in millions of
families around the world.

CONTENTS

PART
ONE

....

The Threat of Isolation

....

HOMEBUILDERS
PRINCIPLES

If you and your mate aren't living according to God's plan,
you're destined to experience the disease that causes
marriages to die: *Isolation*.

1

MARRIED BUT LONELY

Getting married is easy.
Staying married is more difficult.
Staying happily married for a lifetime
would be considered among the fine arts.
—AUTHOR UNKNOWN

When the letter came to me, I cried as I read it. Tragically, it represented what is happening with increasing regularity in our country. My friend Dave Johnson is a police officer in San José, California. He often answers that dreaded call: "4-15—Family Disturbance." His letter to me, now published in his book, *The Light Behind the Star,* described what happened when he received one such call and arrived on the scene:

I could see a couple standing in the front yard of the home. A woman was crying and yelling at the man, who was standing with his hands in the pockets of his greasy overalls. I could see homemade tattoos on his arm—usually a sign of having been in prison.

Walking toward the two, I heard the woman demanding that he fix whatever he had done to the car so she could leave. He responded only with a contemptuous laugh.

She turned to me and asked if I would make him fix the car. The other officer came forward, and we separated the couple to find a solution to the problem.

I began talking to the man, who told me his wife was having an affair and was leaving him. I asked if they had gone for counseling, and

1

he said he wasn't interested. He said he was interested only in getting back his "things," which he said she had hidden from him.

I asked the wife about his things and she said she wouldn't give them to him until she got one of the VCRs. She said she wanted only one of the three VCRs they owned.

The other officer walked over to the wife's car and looked under the hood to see if he could fix the trouble. The husband walked over, took the coil wire out of his pocket, and handed it to the officer. He then told his wife that she could have a VCR if he could have his things. She finally agreed and went into the house. (I found out later that his "things" were narcotics he was dealing in.)

As the wife entered the house, I noticed two little girls standing in the doorway, watching the drama unfold. They were about eight and ten years old. Both wore dresses and each clung to a Cabbage Patch doll. At their feet were two small suitcases. My eyes couldn't leave their faces as they watched the two people they loved tear at each other.

The woman emerged with the VCR in her arms and went to the car where she put it on the crowded backseat. She turned and told her husband where he could find his things. They agreed to divide their other possessions equally.

Then, as I watched in disbelief, the husband pointed to the two little girls and said, "Well, which one do you want?" With no apparent emotion, the mother chose the older one. The girls looked at each other, then the older daughter walked out and climbed into the car. The smaller girl, still clutching her Cabbage Patch doll in one hand and her suitcase in the other, watched in bewilderment as her sister and mother drove off. I saw tears streaming down her face. The only "comfort" she received was an order from her father to go into the house, as he turned to go talk with some friends.

There I stood . . . the unwilling witness to the death of a family.[1]

As I put that letter down, I asked myself, "Why did this family die?" Was it drugs? The husband's criminal background? Anger and hatred? All

2

these may have been involved, but the look on the little girl's face said it all.

What Dave Johnson saw was the pain-filled eyes of a little girl who over the years had watched a creeping separateness distance her parents from each other. That family died from a disease that infects millions of marriages today, a disease called: *Isolation*.

WHAT IT MEANS TO BE ISOLATED

The dictionary will tell you isolation is "the condition of being alone, separated, solitary, set apart," but I like what my daughter Ashley said once when she slipped into my study to ask me what I was writing about.

"Isolation," I explained. "Do you know what that means?"

"Oh," said our blue-eyed, blonde-haired, freckle-faced, then-ten-year-old daughter, "that's when somebody excludes you."

I may be a bit prejudiced, but I believe Ashley's answer is a profound observation on human relationships. Husbands excluding wives and wives excluding husbands is exactly what happens when loneliness and isolation infect a marriage.

When you're excluded you have a feeling of distance, a lack of closeness, and little real intimacy. You can share a bed, eat at the same dinner table, watch the same TV, share the same checking account, and parent the same children—and still be alone. You may have sex, but you don't have love; you may talk, but you do not communicate. You may live together, but you don't share life with one another.

If there's one thing worse than a miserable, lonely single, it's a miserable, lonely married person. The irony is that no two people marry with any intention of being isolated from each other. Most of them feel that marriage is the *cure* for loneliness. The phrase "lonely husbands, lonely wives" would, for them, contradict what they think marriage is all about.

Isolation is like a terminal virus that invades your marriage, silently, slowly, and painlessly at first. By the time you become aware of its insidious effects, it can be too late. Your marriage can be crippled by boredom and apathy, and even die from emotional malnutrition and neglect.

The drift into isolation can be seen in what one clever observer of marriage called "The Seven Ages of the Married Cold." As we trace the reaction of a husband to his wife's cold symptoms during seven years of marriage, we might hear the following:

The first year he says: "Sugar dumpling, I'm worried about my baby girl. You've got a bad sniffle and there's no telling about these things with all this strep around. I'm putting you in the hospital this afternoon for a general checkup and a good rest. I know the food's lousy, but I'll bring your food in . . . I've already got it arranged with the floor superintendent."

Now, the second year: "Listen, darling, I don't like the sound of that cough. I've called Doc Miller to rush over here. Now you go to bed like a good girl. Please, just for your honey."

And the third year: "Maybe you had better lie down, sweetheart. Nothing like a little rest when you feel punk. I'll bring you something to eat. Do we have any soup?"

The fourth year: "Look, dear, be sensible. After you feed the kids and get the dishes washed, you'd better hit the sack."

The fifth year: "Why don't you get yourself a couple of aspirin?"

The sixth year: "If you'd just gargle or something instead of sitting around barking like a seal, I would appreciate it."

The seventh year: "For Pete's sake, stop sneezing! What are you trying to do, give me pneumonia?"

Of course, it doesn't always take seven years for intimacy to fade and isolation to enter. Sometimes it can happen in seven months! In other marriages, the twenty- to twenty-five-year mark is the danger point. But the isolation process never ceases.

Unless husband and wife work together to keep it at bay, they face the real possibility of someday knowing the discouragement, anger, and pain that was expressed by a woman who attended one of our FamilyLife Conferences.

The lady opened her letter by wondering what century I was speaking about when I had the unmitigated gall to say wives were tired but their husbands were "mentally tired." She reminded me this is the twenty-first century, when many wives work out of need, and then she gave me her daily schedule, plus the rest of a big piece of her mind:

5:30—rise and start getting myself ready and put coffee on.

6:00—start breakfast and get bag ready for child day care.

6:30—get kids, hubby up, fed, and dressed for school.

7:00—wash dishes.

7:15—send kids on bus and finish dressing.

7:30—leave for day care center and off to work with coffee for breakfast.

8:00—eight hours' work.

4:30—back to day care, sometimes need to pick something up for supper.

5:15—home, start supper, load washer, help kids with lessons, listen to their tales of school. Fold clothes, wash dishes, run sweeper, bath for kids and me, flop in bed to rest for next day.

Saturday—clean house you neglected all week. Clean up kids and go to store and do weekly shopping. Same meals, same dishes.

Sunday—Get kids ready for church, come home and do usual things around house. Holidays no different. If company comes, all I can see is more work and I'm already tired.

This doesn't include trips to dentist, doctor, shoes and clothes for kids, PTA meetings, school programs. Where is hubby all this time? Glued to the paper or stuck on the TV.

You need to take off your rose-colored glasses and look at life as it really is for women. You could help marriages if you would tell men if we're helping them, they should pitch in. I can't see how men can be so self-centered and not want to help. It's not hard to resent your husband after years of this. All you can see is another mouth to feed, his extra pile of clothes to clean, his dishes to wash. It's pretty hard to want to make love to a glob that finally unsticks himself from TV when I am semiconscious and look and feel like I've been drug through the brush backwards. Thanks for your help.

P.S. My dream is to be single again and come home from work, grab something for supper on the way, and walk into a clean home, pick up my feet and do *nothing!*

I wish this frustrated wife had included her name and address, because I wanted to write and apologize for sounding unsympathetic and insensitive. Her words are those of someone experiencing the worst kind of loneliness and isolation. Isolation has set her at its mercy.

Because of the alarming number of good marriages unaware of this problem, this book is based on a single premise: *Your marriage will naturally move toward a state of isolation.*

Unless you lovingly and energetically nurture and maintain your marriage, you will begin to drift away from your mate. You'll live together, but you will live alone.

In 1976 we began the Family Ministry, which is part of Campus Crusade for Christ. We've now held hundreds of FamilyLife Conferences in over fifty major metropolitan areas here in the United States and in a dozen foreign countries. From the comments we've received, it's obvious to us that isolation is the number-one problem in marriage relationships today.

HOW YOU WILL BENEFIT FROM THIS BOOK

What every marriage, no matter how good, needs is *the* plan to defeat isolation and experience oneness. This book will give you that plan to gain the intimacy you hoped for when you first married. It will help you understand one another, become a better balance to one another, and rebuild trust that may have broken down.

As you read you will also be *equipped* to take your marriage into the twenty-first century. You'll be better equipped to handle conflict, work through sexual difficulties, and express forgiveness. You'll learn the strength that comes from being accountable to one another. This book will enable you to make that good marriage better and help a struggling marriage recapture intimacy. Most chapters end with a practical project that will ask probing questions to help stimulate you and your mate into a deeper understanding and application of the principles taught. I'd even suggest, if possible, you read the book a chapter at a time with your mate.

Finally, I want to *enlist you* to leave a legacy of changed lives. I want to challenge you to pass these concepts on to others who need them—people in your neighborhood, your church, your community, and most important, your own children.

Let me help you defeat isolation first. From my counseling experience and from speaking to hundreds of thousands of people on the issues elaborated upon in this book, I'd estimate that well over 95 percent of all married couples are oblivious to isolation and how it works. In the next chapter, we will see just how destructive isolation can be—and what can be done about it.

HOMEBUILDERS
PRINCIPLES

The choices you make determine the oneness you enjoy.
Isolation is Satan's chief strategy for destroying marriage.

2

THE SUBTLE DECEPTION

We are a nation of strangers.

—VANCE PACKARD

A woman related the following story that expresses how my wife, Barbara, and I feel many days:

> My husband works a night shift, while I work days. Thus our cars always pass going in opposite directions on a street just a few miles from our house. When we pass, we both yell, "I love you!" One day, after our rush-hour rendezvous, a man who had obviously witnessed this scene several times pulled up beside me at a stoplight. "Hey, lady," he said, "you two seem to like the looks of each other pretty well. Why don't you stop and introduce yourselves sometime?"

Like that couple, many of us have become so busy that we don't even stop and consider how isolated and lonely we may be.

Loneliness. It's been around since the beginning of creation. In the last twenty to thirty years it's been sung about, written about, and researched. But it seems to be gaining momentum as we race from year to year on a sphere teeming with five billion plus inhabitants. A veteran member of the Billy Graham Crusade team told me recently that the number-one need Dr. Graham addresses is loneliness.

The term that sums up how so many people feel today in our fast-paced society is "crowded loneliness." Even when surrounded by people, we feel alone, detached. The person who coined the phrase, Dr. Roberta Hestenes, president of Eastern College in St. Davids, Pennsylvania, said,

9

"Today we are seeing the breakdown of natural 'community' network groups in neighborhoods like relatives, PTA, etc. At the same time, we have relationships with so many people. Twenty percent of the American population moves each year. If they think they are moving, they won't put down roots. People don't know how to reach out and touch people. This combination produces crowded loneliness."

Dr. James Lynch, a specialist in psychosomatic diseases at the University of Maryland, wrote a book, *The Broken Heart: The Medical Consequences of Loneliness,* based on the premise that heart disease is connected with a lack of human companionship. "Almost every segment of our society seems to be deeply afflicted by one of the major diseases of our age—human loneliness," he wrote. "The price we are paying for our failure to understand our biological needs for love and human companionship may be ultimately exacted in our own hearts and blood vessels."[1]

But the soul was not created to live in solo. We yearn for intimacy. And marriage is where most people hope they'll find it. The tragedy is that few couples achieve it. Some experience intimacy to a degree, and some live with their cup full but not knowing they could have still more. For many, marriage becomes what filmmaker Woody Allen cynically described as "the death of hope."

Throughout our culture symbols of isolation can be found. Here are a few symbols I've observed in different marriages over the past twenty years.

SYMBOL #1: "NO TRESPASSING"

Paul and Michelle's marriage has steadily grown during their twenty years together. They communicate well and have worked through several difficult problems. They are relaxed around one another and are considered by many to have a model marriage.

But over the years they have become alienated from one another because of an unsatisfying sex life. Too proud to seek counsel, they find they can't discuss the subject anymore—the area is declared off-limits—and "NO TRESPASSING" signs now replace welcome mats.

Unfortunately, neither knows how to uproot the "NO TRESPASSING" sign, so they decide to ignore it. Each night they fall asleep facing in different directions.

SYMBOL #2: A TICKING CLOCK

Near retirement, Ben and Mary have raised their family and now they are proud of their new grandchildren. Their marriage of thirty-five years has withstood the test of time. But neither of them realize that silence has crept into their relationship.

Their children know about it, though.

Growing up they felt the loneliness between their parents at points of unresolved conflict and misunderstanding. They've seen Dad give his life to his job and Mom pour her life into her kids. And now when they come to visit, it's evident there isn't much of a relationship, much less partnership, between the two.

Instead, the silence in their home is broken only by the occasional squeak of a rocking chair and the *tick, tick, tick* of a clock. And the children separately resolve never to see their marriages end up in small talk like their parents.

SYMBOL #3: CROWDED CALENDAR

Steve and Angela are both aggressive professionals, actively involved in civic responsibilities and their church. But ever since they started their family, they've noticed a difference in their marriage.

Those walks and late-night talks that they used to enjoy have disappeared. They're too whipped—they now live for the weekends. Fatigue is taking its toll and has left little energy for romance.

Now with their children adding their own set of escalating "priorities," they feel even more pried apart by their driving lifestyle. In spite of their apparent successful life, their lives only touch at points—when their paths cross. Their bulging calendars are fed by endless activity and an attempt to overachieve. Sheer exhaustion has left this couple as a lonely husband and a lonely wife.

SYMBOL #4: LOCKED DOORS

Bill and Teresa have been married only six months, but they have already hurt one another deeply. The dream and hope of intimacy is already fading in the darkness behind locked doors where they have withdrawn.

Bill was able to open up during their engagement, but now he finds it difficult to share his feelings. He feels trapped within the limitations of his personality. Teresa craves intimacy and desperately wants to be his partner in life. She can't get in and he won't come out.

SYMBOL #5: EXCESS BAGGAGE

Because both Bob and Jan came from broken homes, they were determined their marriage would be different. After watching many of their friends divorce after the seven-year itch, they felt a good amount of success in their twelve-year marriage.

Although they have talked many times, neither has grasped the impact their parents' divorce had on them. Not having a model embedded in their minds, they have made great progress in their marriage but are unaware of how much excess baggage both really carry. Fear, anger, and feelings of insignificance all surface occasionally, but they are quickly stuffed into over-loaded bags. Neither really knows how to help the other process their feelings, so heavy bags continually suppress the intimacy of their relationship.

SYMBOL #6: THE TV DINNER

Walter and Jeanne both work some distance from their suburban home, so when they arrive home they have fought rush-hour traffic after a long work day. Both become mesmerized by a steady diet of TV dinners or take-out food, eaten during the evening news and digested with the weekly sitcoms.

Without realizing it, they are beginning to shut one another out of their lives.

Their five-year marriage isn't in trouble, but later after they start having children she'll feel she's become a widow to a seasonal selection of football, baseball, and basketball—not to mention his hobbies of golf, fishing, and hunting. She's lonely. And he doesn't even know it.

SYMBOL #7: A DIVIDED HIGHWAY

Sue and Tim are in their eighteenth year of marriage, and it looks great to all on the outside. But they are going in different directions while attempting to raise their teenagers. They lack oneness.

One is too lenient—the other too strict. Their differing styles have always been a struggle, but adolescence has furthered the distance between them. One is a perfectionist, the other is not. One tends to be critical, the other too patient—avoiding conflict at all costs. And both are overcompensating for the other.

Now that they have teenagers, intimacy is even more difficult to achieve. She is caught up in all the emotional struggles of their two emerging adults, and he secretly resents how much their needs tug and pull at their marriage. There's so little time for just the two of them to talk. And there's a growing distance between them.

SYMBOL #8: BLUEPRINTS

When Robert and Sherry were engaged, they spent hundreds of hours and thousands of dollars preparing for their marriage ceremony. But neither spent much time preparing for making marriage work.

When they married, they assumed they had the same plan for achieving oneness. But in reality they had no plan at all for building their home together.

Bliss turned to burden as they struggled through everything from how to handle finances, to how to spend a Saturday afternoon. They had no idea when they married that crisis after crisis would come their way—a lost job, poor health, a financial setback, and the loss of their parents. Now they are both lonely, and although neither has told the other, secretly they wonder if their marriage is going to make it.

TELLTALE SIGNS OF ISOLATION

As it did for these married couples, isolation starts when husband and wife slowly drift apart in ways not recognizable at first. Signs of isolation include:

. . . a feeling that your spouse isn't hearing you and doesn't want to understand.

. . . an attitude of "Who cares?" "Why try?" "Tomorrow we'll talk about it—let's just get some sleep."

. . . a feeling of being unable to please or to meet the expectations of your spouse.

. . . a sense that he's detached from you.

. . . a feeling that she's going her own way.

. . . a refusal to cope with what's really wrong: "That's *your* problem, not mine."

. . . a feeling that keeping the peace by avoiding the conflict is better than the pain of dealing with reality.

THE EFFECTS OF ISOLATION

Isolation can fool and trick its victims. Solitary seafarers have told tales of hallucinations after weeks of isolation and stress. Bombardiers flying at high altitudes for long periods of time have "seen" monsters land on the wings of their aircraft. NASA is presently researching the effects of isolation as the agency works on plans to put a space station into orbit.

Writing about the power of isolation in *Psychology Today,* Dr. Philip Zimbardo, professor of psychology at Stanford University, said: "I know of no more potent killer than isolation. There is no more destructive influence on physical and mental health than the isolation of you from me and us from them. Isolation has been shown to be the central agent in the development of depression, paranoia, schizophrenia, rape, suicide and mass murder."[2]

And, he goes on to add: "The devil's strategy for our times is to trivialize human existence and to isolate us from one another while creating the delusion that the reasons are time pressures, work demands, or economic anxieties."[3]

I believe Dr. Zimbardo has identified Satan's chief strategy for destroying marriage—isolation. Barbara and I were married in 1972, and we have felt its diving tug in our relationship when we have had disagreements and misunderstandings. Our busyness has repeatedly inserted its presence into our marriage. Even our children have attempted (unknowingly) to isolate us by their seemingly never-ending needs. And while attempting to give our children what they want, we can sometimes fail to give each other what we need.

Isolation can also create a "marriage mirage." The dictionary defines *mirage* as "anything that appears to be real." Many couples look at their own marriage and feel they have it all together. Unfortunately, these couples won't realize until the end of their lives that they have deluded themselves.

KEEPING HOUSE, PLAYING MARRIAGE

Couples put on a happy façade—going to church, work, and play—their lives filled with packed schedules that give the appearance to family and friends that all is well. They keep house and play marriage while real needs go unmet.

In his book *His Needs, Her Needs*, Dr. Willard F. Harley Jr. contends that meeting each other's needs is the key to making your marriage happy and affair-proof. Harley, who directs a network of mental health clinics throughout the state of Minnesota, has had more than twenty years of experience in counseling hundreds of couples. He writes: "Once a spouse lacks fulfillment of any [basic] needs, it creates a thirst that must be quenched. If changes do not take place within the marriage to care for that need, the individual will face the powerful temptation to fill it outside of marriage."[4]

Unmet needs indicate isolation's presence in a marriage. Ironically, slipping into a state of isolation seems to offer protection and a certain kind of self-preservation. A person finds safety in solitude. The peace of avoidance is better than the pain of dealing with reality. Silence feels like a security blanket, but it is perilously deceptive and ultimately destructive.

THE CHOICE IS YOURS

Isolation is the result of the choices couples make. Every day each partner in the marriage makes choices that result in oneness or in isolation. Make the right choices and you will know love, warmth, acceptance, and the freedom of true intimacy and genuine oneness as man and wife. Make the wrong choices and you will know the quiet desperation of living together but never really touching one another deeply.

In marriage, the most intimate of human relationships, isolation has reached epidemic proportions. In addition to more than a million legal divorces each year, isolation saps the strength from millions of marriages that still appear to be intact. In fact, the divorce decree is only the final sorry scene of a drama that began long before when the husband and wife became emotionally isolated from each other.

HOMEBUILDERS PROJECTS

TO THINK ABOUT INDIVIDUALLY

1. Have you ever thought of "isolation" as a threat to your marriage? What other words might you have used instead?

2. Every marriage is going in one of two directions: toward intimacy or toward isolation. Which path are you and your partner on? Is this by conscious or unconscious choice? Are you making a conscious effort to direct it toward oneness? How?

3. Review the following areas of your marriage and separately rate your marriage on a continuum of 1 (isolated) to 10 (intimacy). Then get together and compare your ratings.

	Isolated								Intimacy	
	1	2	3	4	5	6	7	8	9	10
Spiritual growth										
Finances										
Problem solving										
Rearing of children										
Goals for our marriage										
Physical intimacy										
Emotional intimacy										
Resisting stress and pressure										

FOR INTERACTION TOGETHER

1. Discuss your individual answers to questions 1 and 2. How do your perceptions of how you are doing agree or differ?

2. Compare your individual ratings from question 3. In what areas do your ratings differ strongly? Why?

HOMEBUILDERS
PRINCIPLES

Divorce is the death of hope and the final product
of prolonged isolation.

3

COMBATIVE ISOLATION

*To feel completely alone and isolated leads to mental disintegration
just as physical starvation leads to death.*

—ERIC FROMM

Marriage begins with a man and woman wanting to be together to
share life. But when the bride and bridegroom walk down that wedding aisle, they fail to see the dangers. They're like soldiers walking blindfolded into a field filled with land mines and booby traps. Psychologist
Judith S. Wallerstein said it well: "Nobody goes to a wedding today without somewhere in the back of their mind wondering how long the marriage
is going to last."

I've watched too many couples wander into these marital minefields
and wind up shell shocked in a divorce court. In every case I've observed,
isolation was the major cause leading to their final parting of ways.

A classic example of the final effects of isolation appeared in a San
Francisco Bay newspaper:

> FOR SALE: 1984 Mercedes, 240 SL. Loaded.
> First fifty dollars takes it. 868-5737.

Not believing his eyes, a man called the number to see if the "fifty dollars" was a misprint. A woman assured him it wasn't. She was indeed
selling the car for fifty dollars, and there was absolutely nothing wrong
with it.

The man rushed to her home, gave her fifty dollars in cash, and as she handed him the title to the luxurious automobile he asked the obvious question: "Why are you selling a Mercedes for fifty dollars?"

"Well, my husband just phoned me from Las Vegas. He's there with his secretary, and he said he's leaving me. He went broke gambling and he asked me to sell the Mercedes and send him half of what I get for it."[1]

This wife got what she thought was "sweet revenge." When seeking vengeance, we justify our actions because we have been taken advantage of. The other person deserves what he gets, because accounts need to be "evened up." Getting even or getting back at the other person is characteristic of a dying—or dead—relationship.

At this point, divorce is the last despairing resort. In growing numbers, couples crowd into courtrooms to abolish the vows they didn't keep. The demographers dutifully record the devastating statistics: One of every two couples joining in holy wedlock eventually ends up in holy deadlock. This union eventually becomes totally unlocked. With the marriage dissolved, each partner is left to deal with the pain of total rejection by the other person.

DIVORCE ANNOUNCEMENTS ARE IN VOGUE

Many try to put on a brave front. A phenomenon of recent years is a "divorce announcement" sent by the couple or sometimes by parents to let friends and acquaintances know a marriage has died. In a column headed "Happy Divorcees Make Their Own Announcements," Abigail Van Buren shared some examples of divorce announcements (with names changed, of course):

SPLIT

After Six Years
Lester and Betty
Have seen the light
Married November 8, 1966

Divorced November 6, 1972
Both are happily back in circulation.
Call Lester: 555-6500 (after 9 P.M.)
Betty: 555-1155 (anytime)

WITH HAPPY HEARTS

Lionel and Jane announce with pleasure
the severance of all legal
and/or other bonds that may have
existed between their daughter
Janet and That Boy.
With the new month of August
Janet enters into a new and
beautiful single life.
As for That Boy—May the
Great Honcho in the sky love him and
Keep him—someplace else.[2]

These announcements of marriages that have died might be called clever, if they weren't so tragic. In some cases I suppose the people involved may truly feel relieved, but in most cases they are covering up hearts that are broken and scarred.

I asked a forty-year-old divorced man how he was dealing with the breakup of his marriage: "The divorce didn't hurt at all," he claimed. "I was already gone. I left emotionally and mentally over two years ago."

Many marriages go on for years, enduring a sort of armed truce in which competition replaces cooperation. Punishment replaces romance. Ugly reality dashes the dreams of hope. Authenticity is assassinated by fear of ridicule and rejection. Conflict unravels the fabric of love and concern. Broken hearts stain pillows with bitter tears. Cursing words and stares jab at the heart.

Many couples literally "stay together for the sake of the children." In one case, an eighty-nine-year-old husband sought to sever their marriage. The astonished judge asked, "Why, after all these years, do you now want a divorce?"

Their answer: "We wanted to wait until the children were dead."

THE END OF THE ROAD

Isolation seems to suck life from its victims. In 1915, H. D. Chapin studied the infant mortality rate of ten U.S. hospitals that cared for newborn children who had not been adopted. In testimony before the American Pediatric Association it was estimated that 90 percent of the "unwanted" infants died in their first year in the Baltimore hospitals. It was also stated that the remaining 10 percent were probably saved because they were taken out of this sterile institution.

The problem? In sterilizing the children's surrounding from germs, the children themselves were insulated from any human warmth, love, and care. Mentally, emotionally, and, finally, physically, they were isolated. And that isolation choked the life out of these newborn babies.

A marriage is not unlike these unfortunate babies. In its infancy the relationship knows little of the hazards of life. Fragile and vulnerable, it needs nourishment and care if it is to grow to maturity. It needs protection from dangers and diseases that could stunt its growth or prematurely terminate its life. Otherwise it will die.

THAT'S THE WAY IT GOES SOMETIMES

Dr. James Dobson, author of many outstanding books on the family and host of the popular "Focus on the Family" radio broadcast, tells the story of a daughter's dramatic description of the day her dad left. Looking back on that day she wrote:

When I was ten, my parents got a divorce. Naturally, my father told me about it, because he was my favorite.

"Honey, I know it's been kind of bad for you these past few days, and I don't want to make it worse. But there's something I have to tell you. Honey, your mother and I got a divorce."

"But, Daddy—"

"I know you don't want this, but it has to be done. Your mother and I just don't get along like we used to. I'm already packed and my plane is leaving in half an hour."

"But, Daddy, why do you have to leave?"

"Well, honey, your mother and I can't live together anymore."

"I know that, but I mean why do you have to leave town?"

"Oh. Well, I got someone waiting for me in New Jersey."

"But, Daddy, will I ever see you again?"

"Sure you will, honey. We'll work something out."

"But what? I mean, you'll be living in New Jersey, and I'll be living here in Washington."

"Maybe your mother will agree to you spending two weeks in the summer and two in the winter with me."

"Why not more often?"

"I don't think she'll agree to two weeks in the summer and two in the winter, much less more."

"Well, it can't hurt to try."

"I know, honey, but we'll have to work it out later. My plane leaves in twenty minutes and I've got to get to the airport. Now I'm going to get my luggage, and I want you to go to your room so you don't have to watch me. And no long goodbyes either."

"Okay, Daddy. Goodbye. Don't forget to write."

"I won't. Goodbye. Now go to your room."

"Okay. Daddy, I don't want you to go!"

"I know, honey. But I have to."

"Why?"

"You wouldn't understand, honey."

"Yes, I would."

"No, you wouldn't."

"Oh well. Goodbye."

"Goodbye. Now go to your room. Hurry up."

"Okay. Well, I guess that's the way life goes sometimes."

"Yes, honey. That's the way life goes sometimes."

After my father walked out that door, I never heard from him again.[3]

The saddest words in this story are "That's the way life goes sometimes." But isolation and divorce *do not* have to be the way life goes. Yes, there are tough situations in many marriages. For many there is pain involved in staying in the relationship—pain and hard work to try to make the marriage go. But for those who succeed, a priceless legacy of love and commitment is left behind for all to share.

TO THINK ABOUT INDIVIDUALLY

1. Why do you think 50 percent of all marriages end in divorce? Under what conditions, if any, would you consider divorce as a viable option for a couple experiencing marital problems? Would you ever consider divorce as an option for you? Why or why not?

2. How do you think having a divorce as an option affects the way two people treat one another in marriage?

3. Are there any areas in your relationship with your mate where you feel isolated, distant, or unknown? Why?

FOR INTERACTION TOGETHER

1. Pick a time when you and your mate can talk openly and without distractions. Be sensitive to hear what each has to say.

2. In your answer to questions one and two in the previous section, do you agree or disagree? How? Why? How does this affect your marriage—positively? Or negatively?

3. Share your response to question three of the individual section. How can both you and your mate create an environment that fosters communication and acceptance and leads to oneness?

HOMEBUILDERS
PRINCIPLES

We begin the process of establishing oneness in marriage as we
agree on the purpose, direction, and plans for our lives.

4

IN PURSUIT OF INTIMACY

The very heart of intimacy is reached when two people are neither afraid
nor ashamed of being possessed by love, when in fact they give themselves
freely to the pure joy and liberty of owning and being owned.

—MIKE MASON

A s one of our FamilyLife Conferences drew to a close, one husband
slipped me a letter. It summed up the despair of isolation and the
hopes of oneness so clearly:

> We have both been "born again" Christians for many years. We plan to
> celebrate our twentieth wedding anniversary next February 14. But
> despite this "seniority" and an unbelievable amount of knowledge about
> the subject of marriage, we arrived at the conference with lots of scar tis-
> sue from emotional and spiritual warfare that had resulted in DESPAIR
> in capital letters.
>
> The Lord has blessed both of us as individuals, but we have never
> grown as a couple spiritually. We have read books about marriage,
> attended other types of marriage conferences, and had numerous
> Christian marriage counselors without making any lasting or meaning-
> ful progress. My wife has even worked as an administrative assistant for
> two different Christian counselors.
>
> What is my point in telling you all this? Very simply, your presen-
> tation (presented with practical examples and humor) has been the most
> penetrating personal experience with God that I have ever had. . . . We
> are leaving with the hope of Christ renewed in our relationship.

Personally, I have this hope because you have helped me to identify the need for a written plan of application.

That husband made a profound discovery: God has a plan that offers hope in marriage. He found the hope that comes when husband and wife commit to build their marriage from the same set of divine blueprints. No matter how far a couple has traveled down the road to isolation, they can still start on a road that leads to a "Oneness Marriage."

A TENDER MERGER

A Oneness Marriage is formed by a husband and wife who are crafting intimacy, trust, and understanding with one another. It's a couple chiseling out a common direction, purpose, and plan. A Oneness Marriage demands a lifetime process of relying on God and forging an enduring relationship according to His design. It's more than a mere mingling of two humans— it's a tender merger of body, soul, and spirit.

Oneness in marriage has been compared with a pair of scissors: two components joined, never to be separated. Scissors blades frequently go in different directions, but they are most powerful when coming together.

THE FOUNDATION OF A ONENESS MARRIAGE

There are three foundational components of a Oneness Marriage. King Solomon spoke of the mortar of the marriage merger in Proverbs: "By *wisdom* a house is built, and by *understanding* it is established; and by *knowledge* the rooms are filled with all precious and pleasant riches" (Proverbs 24:3–4 RSV, emphasis added).

Before we look at these three fundamentals, look at the above verse and note the results when a marriage is built, established, and filled according to God's plan: There's no room in this house for isolation—it's been renovated and firmly fixed, and the richness of its value and the pleasure of its enjoyment fills every room. This is a portrait of a Oneness Marriage.

1. A Oneness Marriage Needs Wisdom. Wisdom is skill in everyday living. It means that we respond to circumstances according to God's design. A wise home builder recognizes God as the architect and builder of marriages. As we ask God for wisdom and search the Scriptures, He supplies the skill to build our home.

One of the most critical issues a husband and wife must settle in their life together is: *Who will be the builder of our marriage?*

King David warned, "Unless the LORD builds the house, its builders labor in vain" (Psalm 127:1). For many, the architect and builder of the marriage is "self." It's no wonder so many marriages fail.

Recently I met a husband and wife who had been married for fourteen years, but because they hadn't grown in their relationship over the years, one might say they had been married for one year, fourteen times! The builder of their home was clearly "self."

Their lives were outwardly successful, but privately their home was riddled with conflict; they harbored resentment and withheld affection. They attended a FamilyLife Conference and fought all weekend. But later at home, they committed their lives to Christ and asked Him to be the Architect and Builder of their marriage and family.

A year later they came back to one of our conferences and shared their story with me. The signs of the Master Builder in their marriage were evident as they told how they had led their seven-year-old and ten-year-old children to Christ. During the last year they had been building their home with wisdom. In fact, they had changed the day they celebrated their wedding anniversary to the date of their first conference! And now when asked how many years they've been married they say, "Since 1988." God does renovate and build homes.

2. A Oneness Marriage Needs Understanding. Understanding means responding to life's circumstances with insight—a perspective that looks at life through God's eyes. Understanding your mate from God's perspective results in acceptance of his or her differences and beginning to learn how God made that person to complement you. Understanding produces compassion for your partner. It will give you insight to lead wisely or to follow prudently.

A handsome husband and wife in their thirties recently shared with me how they finally understood the way their differences complemented one another. The husband explained, "My wife is a prosecuting attorney. I felt like she *prosecuted* from eight to five and persecuted from five to eight!

"In the year and a half we have been married I found out she is a strong woman. I had hoped I could pressure her to change—if I persevered, I might be able to beat her down. But I have finally understood that I don't have to compete with her. I can let her be who she is, and not feel insecure about who I am."

What that husband found was an understanding of how he and his wife balanced each other. He realized he could lead her even though she might challenge him at times, but that it was good for him.

Understanding builds oneness by "establishing" the relationship on a foundation of common insight.

3. A Oneness Marriage Needs Knowledge. Ours is an informational culture. We worship information. But information without application is an empty deity.

Every Sunday morning there are thousands of preachers who present polished gems—sermons filled with outstanding biblical knowledge. But what do we, the parishioners, usually do? At 11:55 the preacher finishes, we dutifully sing a song, there's a prayer, and we promptly leave at 12:00.

Where's the time to assimilate into our lives what we've heard? Do we take even five minutes to look back over the biblical text and *decide* what we're going to *do?* No, instead we gather up the kids and the Sunday school papers, grab a bite to eat, and begin our Sunday afternoon routine.

The point here is that Solomon was talking about a knowledge that fills homes with "precious and pleasant riches." It's more than mere information—it's a knowledge that results in convictions and applications. It's a truly teachable spirit that applies God's blueprints amid the raw reality of life.

Many of us need accountability in order to apply what we've learned to our marriage. We need someone who will break through our self-built fences and our crowded loneliness and ask us if we are applying what we're learning in our marriages.

At our FamilyLife Conferences we encourage people to use both their mates and their friends for that accountability. Many people have found that our HomeBuilders Couples Series groups, which are home-based Bible studies used by laypeople and churches across the country, help them apply biblical truth to their lives. It is in these small groups that they find the accountability they need.

GOD PUT THEIR MARRIAGE BACK TOGETHER

One woman wrote to tell us of how a HomeBuilders group had been ". . . very instrumental in rebuilding a relationship that I thought was forever torn apart. My husband and I were married twenty-nine years and ten months before our divorce. Yet, our life together had become practically nonexistent. We no longer communicated unless it was to growl at one another. I hardened my heart toward him and he closed his mind toward me."

The letter went on to tell how the family was ripped apart at the seams by divorce and, even though the children were all grown with families of their own, they were devastated. Trying to escape all the pain and memories, the woman moved across country and later her son and his family followed to give her help and support at this critical time in her life.

In a new city she began a new career as a registered nurse and also began attending a Christian church, where she eventually gave her heart to Christ. Still struggling with hurt and anger, she agreed to attend a home Bible study and, on the first evening she was there, a HomeBuilders Couples Series was introduced. She wrote:

Well, it (the series) knocked my socks off! I was still so very angry over the way my marriage had ended and with my life in general, but something was beginning to happen inside of me.

For the first time in thirty years I was able to understand what was missing from our marriage. We did not have a personal relationship with Jesus Christ. The seed was planted that night, but I still fought against the idea of getting back with my husband.

Through the HomeBuilders Series, the woman read the Bible and understood it in a way she had never experienced before. After she wrote to her husband to tell him what she was learning, he immediately called her and they talked for the first time about what God wanted to do in their marriage.

The next week he flew out and attended one of the HomeBuilders Series lessons. They read the Bible together and answered as many questions in the study material as they could. That weekend they put their lives in the hand of Jesus Christ, and when he asked her to remarry him, she said, "Yes!"

YOU CAN HAVE A ONENESS MARRIAGE

Like most of those who read this book, you have already started your journey of marriage. You started by wanting the best, and thoughts of becoming isolated and lonely never entered your mind. You were probably quite sure that your marriage would not even be affected by disillusionment or mediocrity.

Now, perhaps, symptoms of isolation are becoming apparent, or you may realize you have been living with it for years. The good news is that isolation can be defeated. Its disease can be cured if you are willing to make the right choices and then put the necessary effort into building oneness.

On the pages that follow are proven principles that our Family Ministry teams have shared with thousands of men and women. We've seen these truths stop loneliness and isolation in their tracks, save marriages, and bring husbands and wives closer than they ever dreamed possible.

This plan has been researched and produced by a team of men and women with a cumulative total of over four hundred years in practical ministry and theological training. The plan is a workable set of blueprints for building a Oneness Marriage that defeats isolation.

The rest of this book is devoted to giving you this plan and explaining how to achieve and maintain oneness:

In Part Two I will look at *seven threats to oneness* of which most people are unaware.

In Part Three I'll outline *God's design for oneness*—His purposes, His plan, and His power. Please read these chapters slowly and thoughtfully. They are foundational to intimacy and oneness.

Part Four covers the sensitive area of the *husband's and wife's responsibilities for oneness.* I hope to clarify a lot of the confusion over words such as *headship* and *submission.*

Part Five will share with you *how to communicate for oneness*—how to be transparent, how to listen, how to deal with conflict, and how to have a fulfilling sexual relationship.

And, in a final challenge, I want to talk about *how your marriage can make the difference* in a world where couples are dying from isolation.

Throughout this book, I want to help you analyze just how isolation might be affecting your marriage and to what degree. Above all, I want to help you avoid its snares and learn how to build oneness and lifelong intimacy with each other.

As one writer put it so perfectly:

Love isn't an act, it is a whole life. It's staying with her now because she needs you. It's knowing you and she will still care about each other when sex and daydreams, fights and futures are all on the shelf and done with. Love, well, I'll tell you what love is. It's when you're 75 and she's 71, each of you listening for the other's footsteps in the next room, each afraid that sudden silence, a sudden cry could mean a lifetime's talk is over.[1]

The oneness marriage knows this kind of love—the kind that lasts until death bids you to part. If you are interested in regaining, building, or keeping a oneness marriage growing, read on!

PART TWO

The Seven Threats to Oneness and Intimacy

PART TWO

HOMEBUILDERS
PRINCIPLES

Your marriage is deeply influenced by the culture in which you live, and much of that influence does *not* encourage marital oneness.

Most couples have not adequately prepared for the gravitational pull of difficult adjustments on the marriage relationship.

5

WHY IT'S SO HARD TO KEEP ALL THOSE PLATES SPINNING

The second most difficult thing in life is getting involved in the process of living and growing with another human being.
The most difficult thing is to live alone.
—HENRY STACK SULLIVAN

Back in the early fifties, TV had just become a black-and-white reality. There were no color sets then—actually, our picture came out kind of pale pink, but I didn't mind. I was just a young boy and one of my favorite shows was hosted by a serious-looking man with a stiff neck who kept talking about his next "really big sheeew."

I watched countless acts on the *Ed Sullivan Show,* but the one I'll never forget was the guy who spun plates on sticks.

Perhaps you also remember watching this performer walk out on the stage with a stack of porcelain plates. He set the stack on a long table, took one of the plates, and somehow started it spinning on a stick that was about two feet high. Then he moved down the table and started another plate spinning on another stick. In a few seconds he had six, seven, even eight plates merrily spinning away.

But as he moved to the end of the table and got his last plate going, the first one would start running out of steam and begin to wobble. I remember actually wanting to leap through the television screen and catch that wobbling plate before it crashed in a million pieces on the floor.

37

Somehow, at just the last moment, he seemed to hear me screaming from my living room, and he'd look back to see that teetering plate. He would dash to that end of the table and give the plate a spin to get it going again. Then, of course, the next plate would be wobbling and he'd give that one a new spin too. Then the next would need attention, and the next, and the next. Back and forth he would dash, catching up to precariously wobbling plates at just the last second and somehow keeping them all going.

Finally, when I was sure he couldn't keep it up any longer because of sheer exhaustion, he would start at one end of the table and collect each teetering plate until he had the entire stack safely in his hands. That plate act had more built-in suspense than three episodes of *Perry Mason*. I just knew one of those plates would fall and shatter, but none ever did.

THOSE PLATES ARE STILL SPINNING

Ed Sullivan's "really big sheeew" is gone now, but in a very real way the plates still spin in your home and mine. Picture the starry-eyed couple as they walk up the aisle and say, "I do." They start at the end of the table and spin that first big plate called marriage. They're madly in love and it's "just wonderful," playing house, keeping that plate spinning.

But then the inevitable happens. They discover there is more than one plate. They have careers, and perhaps they move to a different community and make new friends. They join a church and become involved in their neighborhood. All those plates need spinning too, and so that first plate called marriage begins to slow down a bit.

Then some little saucers come along and things get interesting, indeed. The average number of saucers is somewhere around two, but some of us (who apparently don't know what produces saucers) wind up with as many as six. Husband and wife are pulled their separate ways—meeting deadlines, scratching off "to-do" lists, putting in fourteen- to eighteen-hour days, and falling into bed exhausted. Time for each other becomes a memory, and inevitably, that first big plate suffers neglect. Isolation starts taking its toll and oneness begins to waver.

Every marriage must move in one direction or the other—toward oneness or toward isolation. Avoiding isolation by maintaining oneness is the critical issue of any marriage. But, as we shall see, many of us find our marital plates teetering off balance because of unseen forces and factors that continue to threaten and undermine intimacy.

In this chapter we will look at the first two of these seven threats to oneness: 1) a complex culture; 2) the difficult adjustments couples have to make, particularly in the first years of marriage.

These threats seldom subside, and if they are not met with commitment, determination, and a plan, isolation will extract its price.

THREAT #1: A COMPLEX CULTURE

WHATEVER HAPPENED TO THE SIMPLE LIFE?

Rare is the couple that doesn't grapple with friction caused by the complexity of modern life. Even a brief look at the culture of our present day will tell you there is little about it that encourages oneness in a marriage. In fact, there is much that is driving the wedges of isolation deep into relationships between husbands and wives. The chart on page 41 contains an abundance of insight into why oneness is so elusive.

Most people today do not realize how deeply we have been influenced by the sociological changes of the last hundred years. The chart graphically portrays a strong cultural current that has swept the family far from its moorings of commitment and stability. Our culture has come to think of the family as a risk, not the harbor and haven it used to be.

Perhaps the most important observation to be made from this chart is that one hundred years ago family members *had* to depend upon one another. If they did not function as a team their survival was at stake. Standard of living was not an issue except among a much smaller percentage of the population living in cities. The pressure to survive fused families together.

But today selfishness is eroding the cement of commitment—causing marriages to crumble. Divorce is even advertised as an option today. But only a century ago, families might have starved or frozen to death if one of the mates chose to bail out. Divorce was not an acceptable alternative.

In the 1800s, life was fairly simple. The economy was basically agrarian and most people lived on farms, working eighty-hour weeks to grow their own food and make most of their own clothes and furnishings. In 1859 the U.S. population was twenty-four million people, with 75 percent of them located in rural areas. These cultural islands offered natural protection to marriages and families because there was little opportunity to make comparisons between what you had and what was available elsewhere.

Today, however, 75 percent of the more than 245 million Americans live in cities. We are urban, mobile, and constantly tempted to compare what we don't have, with those who appear "to have it all." These comparisons can be one of the most lethal forms of poison for any marriage.

How do we make comparisons? Picture the typical morning as a man gets up and starts his day. He may kiss his wife good-bye and head out the door, but more than likely she will head out the door with him—or ahead of him! They may ride to work together or each take a separate car to far different destinations.

As he rolls down the freeway, the husband drives by two or three beautiful women who beckon seductively from billboards. One is dressed in slinky black velvet, and the others aren't dressed in much at all. Hubby walks into his office building and inhales a blend of Obsession, Passion, and Giorgio Red as he rides in an elevator full of pretty secretaries, accountants, and lawyers. He greets his own attractive secretary, who is beautifully dressed in an aerobically honed size seven, with perfect hairdo and flawless makeup. And why not? She has plenty of time for all that because she's single.

That evening our hero arrives home and flips on the tube to relax. There it is—a rerun of his favorite show. More beautiful women falling into bed with the main characters. Then up pops a commercial, selling beer, cars, or shampoo—with even more perfectly shaped young things blessed with glistening hair, perfect white teeth, and flawless skin.

THREATS TO ONENESS

There is little in our society today that encourages marital oneness. The chart below illustrates how the family is at the apex of sociological change.

	The home is at the apex of sociological change	
	1800s Simple	**1990s Complex**
Economy	**Agrarian Economy** Jobs and roles changed very little 80-hour work week	**Information Economy** Jobs and roles changed often 40–50 hour work week
Society	**Rural**–immobile–24 million 75%–1859 **Cultural Islands**–Natural protection, little comparison	**Urban**–mobile–245 million +75%–1990 **Melting Pot**–Comparison destroys the natural protection
Family	**Closely Knit Family** Responsibilities clear Home–the influence	**Diffused Family** Function stripped by pressures Irresponsible adults and children Home–one of many influences
Children	**An Economic Asset** Producers	**An Economic Liability** Prestige
Recreation	**Participative** Home ⟶ **Creativity Demanded** Community minimal	**Spectator** Outside Home ⟶ **Creativity Stifled** Television
Religious Life	**Home-Developed** Church on Sundays	**Church-Developed** Several meetings a week
Pattern of Authority	**Patriarchal**–Authoritative	**Democratic**–Man a nominal head Rights pushed to extremes
Working Women	Worked on farm and in home Necessary for **Survival**	Works in industry and business Goals are usually standard of living, security, and fulfillment
Marriage	**For Security** Partner chosen from among acquaintances **Permanent**–Divorce frowned upon Roles clear	**For Social Purposes** Partner chosen from any source **Temporary**–Divorce acceptable solution Roles less distinct

Credit: Dr. Howard Hendricks—Christian Home Class—Dallas Theological Seminary

Our modern warrior glances over at his harried wife. She is cooking dinner as two screaming kids with runny noses cling to her legs like small anchors. More than one hair is definitely out of place, the baby has spit up on her blouse, and she smells more like broccoli than cologne. And hubby begins to think, *What's happened here? How did I end up with this?*

Of course it's easy to reverse the picture, particularly in this day of the working wife and female executive. She can go through the same kind of comparisons, complete with billboards full of Greek gods displaying glistening muscles, washboard stomachs, and no love handles. She can spend the day in offices full of dynamic, well-dressed account executives, and when she returns home at night, she can flip on the tube to channel surf and watch any number of handsome hunks. She glances over at her slightly balding, somewhat paunchy companion and thinks, *This is having it all?*

The point is, *we do compare.* It's unavoidable. And our mates are usually no match for the competition, whether it's at work, on a magazine cover, or even at church. Even if your spouse is still slim, trim, and attractive, there is always somebody *more* attractive who pops up on TV, a billboard, or maybe across the back fence.

The basic problem with comparisons is that they are based on fantasy games played from a distance. The beautiful people on TV don't look quite that good up close and personal at 6:00 A.M. It's always easy to think the grass is greener on the other guy's lawn, until you look closely and see all the dandelions and crabgrass.

A hundred years ago, however, comparison games weren't played as much because most people were too busy with another game called survival. A man got up at 4:00 or 5:00 in the morning, fed the stock, milked the cows, and then had a hearty breakfast with his wife. Later, he didn't gaze at billboards on the way down the freeway. Instead, for the next twelve hours or so he plowed furrows, gazing at the south end of a mule headed north. And when he came in at night, there was no TV. Instead, he saw his wife. And after his day in the fields, she looked pretty good! His marriage had a natural, built-in protection, one that is missing today.

The bottom line on this brief sketch of sociological change from the last century to our present day is this: *Your marriage is being deeply influenced by the culture in which you live, and much of that influence does not encourage marital oneness.* Instead our culture fosters isolation.

THREAT #2: DIFFICULT ADJUSTMENTS

As you look at all those spinning plates (and possibly saucers) in your life right now, take an inventory: How many are there, and how are they spinning? Our problem is that we repeatedly underestimate the energy it takes to spin them. And, just as importantly, we don't anticipate the adjustments that come with marriage and with each plate we add.

Most couples have not adequately prepared for the gravitational pull of these adjustments on the marriage relationship. We have difficulty making the adjustments in the following areas: differing backgrounds, financial pressures, job demands, religious differences, children, sexual performance, personality differences, etc.

Barbara and I were no exception. Perhaps the biggest adjustment we faced early in our marriage grew out of our differing backgrounds. Barbara grew up in a country-club setting near Chicago and later in Baytown, Texas, a suburb of Houston. I grew up in Ozark, Missouri, a tiny town in the southwestern corner of the "Show Me" state. Barbara came into our marriage a refined young lady. I was a genuine hillbilly. It took me several years to learn that shoes were a required part of the dress code when entertaining guests!

It was as though we came from two different countries with totally different traditions, heritages, habits, and values. The differences became apparent even before our wedding. As the day approached, we had to select our good china, our everyday china, our good silver, and our everyday flatware. I wasn't sure where "good china" was. I looked on a map and simply couldn't find it. I found China, but I couldn't find good china.

Barbara chose a silver pattern called "Old Master." Hoping to make everyone believe I had it all together, I got a friend of mine to accompany me on a trip to the May Company department store in Denver. At the silver department I walked up to a very distinguished elderly clerk and said, "I'd like to see 'Old Master' by Towle."

"Of course, sir," said the woman. She showed me a setting of Old Master, and I had to admit it was pretty.

"Ahh, that's really interesting. How much is it?"

"It's $59.95," she replied.

"Did you say $59.95? That's not bad for eight place settings of silver."

At this point the lady became somewhat ruffled. She pushed her glasses back, looked at me a bit condescendingly, and said, "Son, that's for one place setting."

I'm sure what I said next could be heard throughout the entire third floor of the May Company. "Fifty-nine ninety-five for *one* place setting! Lady, do you realize how many plastic knives, forks, and spoons that will buy? I'm your basic functional person. Why would I want to spend twenty dollars on a knife? We don't even own a table!" (Today I'd probably have a coronary—that same knife now costs over $100.00!)

Later, I called Barbara. I tried to be tactful but, secretly, I was trying to discover if she was losing her mind or not. She assured me that the silver was, indeed, a bargain and that's how things were done when you got married. So, her basically functional fiancé followed along dutifully and we registered for Old Master by Towle.

ETHAN ALLEN VS. K-MART

There was also the matter of furniture. Where do you think a hillbilly from southwest Missouri would want to shop? For me, Sears was first class, but Barbara leaned more toward places like Ethan Allen.

She had an Ethan Allen dream book and she was always looking at it. It was full of things made of solid cherry, solid walnut, solid mahogany. It was nothing for chairs to cost $189.95—per leg!

I didn't understand why she wanted to go buy this kind of stuff when, in southwest Missouri, you could go to K-Mart, wait for the "blue-light special," and get a Formica table with chrome legs and *six* chairs! And for a lot less than $189.95. You can eat off that kind of table for years, and it will never show any wear.

So, how did we compromise? We bought an antique and I was expected to refinish it. So another major difference in our backgrounds surfaced. Barbara's father was an engineer. He is mechanically gifted, can fix anything, and actually enjoys it. I'm convinced he could fix a nuclear reactor. He's a genius, especially with his hands.

My dad had a background in sales. Fixing things was not his idea of fun. If bailing wire or a little duct tape didn't work, he usually called the plumber or whatever repairman was necessary.

When I joined the staff of Campus Crusade for Christ, I was given a vocational test. When the counselor checked my results, she looked across the desk and smiled in a knowing way: "Dennis, you're joining the right group. Did you realize that you are in the lower 2 percentile of all the people in the world in regard to working with your hands?"

And so there we were, just married, with an antique table that needed refinishing. I went at it obligingly, and my "2 percent hands" bled all over the place as I sanded and rubbed, but I got it done. In some ways it saved our marriage in the early going.

DOES GOD BELIEVE IN YARD WORK?

Different values come out in literally dozens of ways when you get married. For example, it was amazing how Barbara and I looked at yard work. She believes that grass and flowers are meant to be tamed and made to grow beautifully in front of white picket fences that are always painted, where children play with smiles on their faces.

I developed a much different philosophy. My dad discipled me in the fine art of avoiding yard work. He would let the yard die a slow death in July so he didn't have to mow it the rest of the summer. He believed if God had intended for leaves to be collected, He would have had them fall in plastic bags to begin with. After all, he didn't want to disturb the delicate balance of nature and break the ecological chain.

It's no coincidence that our present home sits back on a heavily forested hillside that overlooks a beautiful lake. We enjoy the sunsets; but you won't find much of a lawn. I'm trying to compromise. Recently the kids and I surprised Barbara by hauling a ton or so of rocks and outlining some trails and flower beds around the house.

There are many other ways in which backgrounds can differ. Barbara and I did not have a great deal of trouble with differences in religious background, but many couples do. You can ask some people, "What's your church preference?" and they'll answer, "red brick." Put a husband like that together with a wife who grew up in the same "Methobapterian church" attended by her parents and her grandparents, and you'll have problems.

SOMEHOW WE KEPT THAT BIG PLATE SPINNING

Barbara and I have worked through many of our background differences. Some were funny; others were not. We had some lively discussions over dinner, but we always managed to reach a compromise.

Actually, what we were doing was keeping that first big plate spinning and not letting all the other plates pull our marriage down. The reason the marriage of the Ozark hillbilly and the lovely, cultured girl from Texas survived was that we spotted these first two threats early. We realized we had a choice: isolation or oneness. *Our relationship became more important than our individual values and we built our home on new values that we hammered out together.*

But it wasn't easy. We had to realize that our different backgrounds brought us into marriage with totally different expectations. We'll look at what expectations can do to a marriage in the next chapter.

HOMEBUILDERS PROJECTS

To Think About Individually

1. What do I do to keep the "big plate" (our marriage) spinning? What other "plates" threaten to take too much of my time and energy?

   _____ Job _____ Children _____ Outside activities
   _____ Church _____ Other _____

2. What plates could I put down for a time or even eliminate to allow me to concentrate more on my marriage?

3. How do our differing backgrounds affect our marriage?

4. What adjustments have I made in our marriage?

   _____
   _____

5. What adjustments has my spouse made?

   _____
   _____

6. In what areas are we still making adjustments? Why?

   _____
   _____

For Interaction Together

1. Share with your spouse your answers to questions 1 to 6. Prepare notes on what could make your marriage plate wobble. How can you work together to avoid this?

2. Talk about adjustments you have made to each other. List some areas where adjustments may still be going on. How can you help each other make these adjustments?

HOMEBUILDERS
PRINCIPLES

The Bible teaches a 100/100 Plan of unconditional acceptance, which builds oneness and intimacy.

6

"I EXPECTED HIM TO MEET ME HALFWAY, BUT . . ."

The spouse who says, "I'll meet you halfway, dear,"
is usually a poor judge of distance.

When two people get married, they have expectations of how the relationship should work. An unspoken assumption on the part of both of them is that the other will "meet me halfway."

When Barbara and I received premarital counseling from our friends and mentors, Don and Sally Meredith, they warned us that we had been thoroughly trained in society's plan for marriage. They called this the 50/50 Plan, which says, "You do your part, and I'll do mine." This concept sounds logical, but couples who use it are destined for disappointment.

Don and Sally went on to explain that many Christians get married with a "Christianized" version of the 50/50 Plan. They weave in a few threads of Christianity and tack on a few Bible verses, but they still have the idea, "You do your part, and I'll do mine."

The Merediths did their best to teach us how to recognize what the 50/50 Plan looks like when it starts to creep into marriage. But we had to experience it to really learn how defective the world's plan really is.

THREAT #3: THE 50/50 PLAN

We spent the first year and a half of our marriage in Boulder, Colorado, where the winters are cold and electric blankets are standard equipment for survival. I can recall how both of us enjoyed sliding into those toasty-warm sheets after the electric blanket had thawed them and done its duty. For some strange reason, however, neither of us could remember to turn out all the lights. We would snuggle in and Barbara would say, "Sweetheart, did you remember to turn out all the lights?"

So I would hop out of our comfy bed and run barefoot through the fifty-five-degree apartment, turning off light after light (that Barbara had turned on). It didn't happen that often, so I didn't mind—until one night when I dropped into bed totally exhausted. Just as I slipped into the third stage of anesthesia, Barbara gave me a little poke and said, "Sweetheart, aren't you going to turn out the lights?"

I groaned, "Honey, why don't *you* turn out the lights tonight?"

Barbara replied, "I thought you would because my dad always turned out the lights."

Suddenly I was wide awake. It dawned on me why I had been suffering occasional minor frostbite for the past few months. And I shot back, "But I'm not your dad!"

Well, we stayed up for a long time, discussing *expectations*—what Barbara expected me to do (because her father had always done it) and what I expected her to do (no matter *who* had always done it!).

As we saw in the last chapter, a marriage is under pressure from a complex culture and the difficult adjustments partners need to make to each other. Each partner brings a certain set of expectations into a marriage. When expectations are not met, the drought of disillusionment dries up the dialogue in the streams of our conversation.

Soon there is no dialogue at all because the world's 50/50 Plan leads us straight into conflict. As the couple fails to communicate and make necessary adjustments so expectations can be met, loneliness and isolation are almost inevitable.

WHY THE 50/50 PLAN FAILS

The expectations we bring to marriage set us up nicely for buying into the 50/50 Plan for a "happy marriage." Barbara was sure that I would do my part and meet her halfway by always getting up to turn off the lights. On the night I flatly refused to get up and turn out the lights, I was pushing her to do her part and meet *me* halfway. It seemed so logical, particularly when I was so tired and already out cold.

Without realizing it, we had fallen into the trap of the 50/50 Plan. Our disagreement revealed its biggest weakness: *It is impossible to determine if your mate has met you halfway.*

Because neither of you can agree on where "halfway" is, each is left to scrutinize the other's performance from his or her own jaded perspective.

Thomas Fuller said, "Each horse thinks his pack is heaviest." That certainly is true in our marriage. So many times in a marriage, both partners are busy, overworked, tired, and feel taken for granted. The real question isn't who put in the hardest day's work or who had the most pressures or the most hassles. The real question is, how do we build oneness here instead of waiting for the other person to meet us halfway? Or by always keeping score to see who did his fair share?

The 50/50 Plan is destined to fail for several other reasons:

- *Acceptance is based on performance.* Many marriage partners unknowingly base acceptance of the mate on his or her performance. Performance becomes the glue that holds the relationship together, but it isn't really glue at all. It's more like Velcro. It seems to stick, but comes apart when a little pressure is applied. What a marriage needs is superglue—but more on that later.

- *Giving is based upon merit.* With the "meet-me-halfway" approach, I would give affection to Barbara only when I felt she had earned it. If she kept the house running smoothly and met my expectations, I would drop her a few crumbs of praise and loving attention. Barbara would show me affection and praise only when I would hold up my end by getting home on time, keeping the house in a reasonable state of repair, or working in her garden.

- *Motivation for action is based upon how each partner feels.* During the engagement or those first few honeymoon months, it's easy to act sacrificially because the heart is pounding, the blood is racing, and romantic feelings fuel us to perform. But what do you do when those feelings diminish? If you don't feel like doing the right thing, perhaps you don't do it at all. I didn't feel like turning off the lights—so I didn't.

- *Each spouse has a tendency to focus on the weaknesses of the other.* Ask most husbands or wives to list their mate's strengths in one column and their weaknesses in another, and the weaknesses will usually outnumber the strengths five to one.

It's uncanny how we tend to focus on weaknesses rather than strengths. We log them and categorize them in the computers of our minds. We remember those times when our mate let us down or disappointed us. Those memories are stored in our minds in neon lights, always ready to remind us of the mate's weakness, idiosyncrasy, or bad habit that is irritating, disgusting, or even maddening.

I had one woman come for counseling concerning marital problems. As she rehearsed weakness after weakness in her husband and catalogued all the reasons why he irritated her and how he hurt her, I tried to take another tack and see if she could think of anything positive about him. Perhaps she could think of one or two strengths he had that she might concentrate on instead of all his flaws and defects.

"Why did you marry your husband?" I asked.

After a long silence she finally responded: "I guess it was because he ran the 100-yard dash so fast."

That was the answer of a bright, well-educated young professional! She had so concentrated on all his weaknesses that she had lost perspective on any of the things that attracted her to him when they first dated. He had evidently disappointed her numerous times. Now she was suffering from a paralysis that kept her from remembering anything good about her husband and from "doing her part in her marriage."

She decided, "Why bother? It isn't worth it. I don't see him changing. I'm not doing my part because he isn't doing his." The romantic feelings that were supposed to have fueled their relationship had faded and slipped out under the door.

Their relationship was a vivid picture of how the original 50/50 agreement became 40/40, then 30/30, and finally 10/10, as two people had resigned themselves to a mediocre marriage. And she had resolved she was not going to be like many wives, who wind up giving 80 percent or more toward a marriage, while hubby gives 20 percent, or less.

As a result, she and her husband had retreated into a state of isolation where neither was giving the other much of anything. They were married, but they might as well have been living alone.

WHY UNMET EXPECTATIONS LEAD TO DISAPPOINTMENT

Expectations go unmet in marriage for at least three reasons:

1. Sometimes you don't know what your mate's expectations are.

2. If you do, you may not be able to meet them.

3. There are times when you may know what your mate wants, and be perfectly capable of doing it, but *you just don't want to.*

One of our early struggles was caused by our differing expectations about food. Back in Ozark we almost always had meat and potatoes for supper. But Barbara's family would have fancy casseroles, finger foods, and quiche for lunch and dinner.

When we were married, I *expected* meat and mounds of mashed potatoes with butter cascading down the sides. Alas, it was not to be. I recall one of the first meals Barbara fixed—an exotic tuna casserole made with millimeter-sized flakes of tuna and lots of other things I could not begin to identify. Having been married for more than three decades, I believe we've had mashed potatoes only a handful of times.

Now who's right in this case? Barbara or me? It all depends, doesn't it? It depends on *your* expectations and how *you* see it.

BIRDS AND BEES IN A TOPLESS BAR

Expectations can also affect how you express love for each other. And it's in this area of sex that the 50/50 Plan can be especially divisive.

A friend who is now a physician once told me how he received his sex education at age twelve. His dad came home from work one day and said, "Son, be ready at four o'clock tomorrow afternoon. Have on your best clothes. We're going to the big city."

The next day they drove two and a half hours to "the big city" where there were plenty of bright lights and the kind of place that his father was looking for. They walked into a bar and for the next few hours they ate supper together and watched a topless dancer do her thing.

As he recalled the incident, my friend said, "Around ten o'clock, my dad and I left and we drove back home. He hadn't said a word to me all evening, and he never said a word all the way back to our house. We walked in about midnight and my mom met us. He looked at her and said, 'There, I did it,' and then we went to bed. That was all I ever 'heard' from my parents about sex."

While my friend's experience may be a bit unusual, it isn't that different from the way many people learn about sex—from the wrong sources. Sexual images and innuendo permeate our media today, and whether you're a youngster or an adult, you can learn erroneously that sex is a performance, not a relationship. It's 50/50 personified: She does her part and he does his part. There's no emphasis on sacrifice and the giving up of oneself to achieve oneness.

The classic problem with sex in marriage is that the woman wants her husband to meet her halfway with tender affection and touching, and he wants her to meet him at the door in a negligee . . . every night! When neither seems to make the other feel that halfway point was reached, both retreat instead of building oneness.

50/50 MUST BECOME 100/100

The biblical plan for marriage states, "I will do everything I can to love you, without demanding 'an equal amount' in return." This is a 100/100 Plan of unconditional acceptance, which builds oneness instead of isolation. I'll share more about the detailed blueprints for this plan as we look at its basic principles in Part Three of this book.

If marriages are to succeed and become havens of oneness rather than dungeons of isolation, Christians must do more than simply "add a few Christian touches" to the world's 50/50 Plan. The 100/100 Plan calls for a total change of mind and heart, a total commitment to God and one another. This is the plan, the superglue, that holds a marriage together no matter what pressures may come.

But, to make the 100/100 Plan work, you need to be aware of another potent killer of intimacy—selfishness. At the center of all threats to oneness is our tendency to be self-centered, especially in relationships. Barbara and I have found that marriage is one of God's finest tools for routing self-centeredness out of our lives. In the next chapter we'll take a closer look at our self-centeredness and learn how to keep it from destroying a marriage.

HOMEBUILDERS PROJECTS

TO THINK ABOUT INDIVIDUALLY

1. The 50/50 Plan says, "You give 50 percent, I'll give 50 percent, and we'll meet in the middle." In your opinion, what is the real ratio in your own marriage? How far does each of you go?

   MYSELF

   MY SPOUSE

2. What expectations of your spouse did you bring to marriage? Which ones were met? Which were not?

3. List five of your spouse's weaknesses and five strengths. Which are easier to think of and why?

FOR INTERACTION TOGETHER

1. Discuss how the two of you match up according to the 50/50 Plan. Who feels he or she is doing more to keep the marriage going? What areas of responsibility particularly stand out?

2. Share your "unmet expectations" with each other. Perhaps you will learn things about each other you never knew before!

3. Share your lists of weaknesses and strengths. How can you help each other with weaknesses? How can you enhance each other's strengths?

4. What steps can both of you take to bring the 100/100 Plan into full operation in your marriage? Keep in mind that reaching the 100/100 goal is not done in a day or even in several years. It is a process. What changes do each of you need to make to begin that process? How will you measure your progress?

HOMEBUILDERS
PRINCIPLES

The only way to unity, oneness, and a successful marriage is
through mutual dependence on Jesus Christ and each other.

7

YOU CAN'T BE SELFISH IN A THREE-LEGGED RACE

Self is the only prison that can bind the soul.
—HARRY VAN DYKE

Some of my favorite childhood memories are of the family picnics our family held every summer. I played all kinds of games with my cousins, including everyone's favorite, the three-legged race. Moms, dads, aunts, uncles, and grandparents gathered around to watch all of the children pair off.

To make the game more interesting, partners were often tied together so one faced backward and the other forward. The starter gave the signal and what happened next would best be described as chaos. Everyone would cheer as the forward-facing participants would half drag, half carry their backward-facing teammates toward the finish line. There were always plenty of grass-stained knees, piercing screams, and roars of laughter.

But occasionally we would run the race in a different way. Instead of facing in opposite directions, each pair would face in the same direction. Even then, the three-legged race was difficult, but at least some partners could work together. Locked arm in arm, and stepping in unison, they could make rapid progress toward the finish line. They might still stumble and fall along the way, but they always got there much faster and more efficiently.

LOOKING OUT FOR NUMBER ONE

Marriage is a lot like the three-legged race. You can run it facing in the same direction and try to stay in step with your partner, or you can run it facing in totally different directions. I've counseled couples where the wife was headed south at sixty-five miles an hour and the husband was going north at ninety miles per hour! When that happens, it means pain, difficulty, troubles. And it also means isolation.

To this point, we have looked at three formidable threats to oneness in marriage: 1) a complex culture; 2) the difficult adjustments couples have to make, particularly in the first years or their marriage; and 3) the 50/50 Plan. This chapter focuses on another threat to oneness that the prophet Isaiah pinpointed over 2,500 years ago when he described basic human self-ishness like this: "We all, like sheep, have gone astray, each of us has turned to his own way" (Isaiah 53:6).

Obviously, Isaiah couldn't have been reading my mail, but it certainly sounds like it. I want to go my own way . . . do my own thing. I want to have it my way or not at all. I'm really your basic, self-centered person— just like you. We all instinctively look out for Number One.

THREAT #4: SELFISHNESS

Harmony in human relationships has always been difficult to achieve. The greatest test of harmony is marriage, where two imperfect creatures seek to defeat isolation and become one. Two people going their own selfish, sep-arate ways can never hope to experience the oneness of marriage as God intended it.

SOCIETY FEEDS OUR SELF-CENTEREDNESS

In 1979, Christopher Lasch wrote *The Culture of Narcissism*, a book that *The New York Daily News* called "a biting new study of present day society." Lasch's book became a national bestseller because it struck a chord with readers who instinctively knew he was right. Our narcissistic society continually feeds our ravenous appetite for self-satisfaction. Indulgent toward our own needs and indifferent toward the needs of others, we have become in great part a society that knows little of true self-sacrifice and self-denial.

If you doubt Lasch's thesis, consider the basis of most of the advertising messages that bombard our senses twenty-four hours a day. The commercials stridently shout their slogans: "We do it all for *you* . . . Have it *your* way . . . Looking out for *Number One* . . . *Get* the best a man can *get* . . . You deserve the best" and on and on. As Lasch observed, "Advertising serves not so much to advertise products as to promote consumption as a way of life . . . The modern propaganda of commodities and the good life has sanctioned impulse gratification. . . ."[1]

MAYHEM IN THE GAS LINES

People like to think they are generous, loving, and well-meaning, and much of the time they can play the role rather convincingly. But every now and then some kind of crisis or event brings out the real human nature.

Few of us who drive cars could forget those long gasoline lines that occurred during the oil crisis in 1973–74.

Naturally, some greedy people wanted to cut in line to get ahead of others. Newspapers carried stories about everything from profanity and lawsuits to stabbings and shootings as people fought for their places in line to get gas.

In one case, a man cut in on an elderly woman. Incensed, she got out of her car and started beating him about the head and shoulders. She finally slugged him, knocked him under her car, and then started to drive off. She dragged him about ten feet while he held on for dear life. Fortunately, she could go no farther due to the traffic jam and he managed to escape.

Another woman cut in front of a motorcycle. The cyclist slowly got off his bike, took off his helmet and glasses, and proceeded to let the air out of all four of her tires while she sat helpless, caught in the line!

But the most creative was a young man who got cut off and retaliated by getting out of his car, unlocking the gas cap from his own vehicle, and walking up to the car that had squeezed in ahead. He unscrewed the gas cap from the other fellow's car, replaced it with his own locking gas cap, walked back to his car and proceeded to drive off, with the key to the gas cap in his pocket!

Selfishness is possibly the most dangerous threat to oneness that any marriage can face. As we saw in Chapter 6, both partners enter marriage with all kinds of expectations, many of which are not met because the other partner is unaware of what is expected, or is incapable of doing it, or unwilling to do it. Caught in an impasse, the marriage is swept into the swift current of self-centeredness and slips into isolation.

One woman shared how selfishness had invaded her marriage by saying, "My husband and I have been married for twenty years. There is nothing he wouldn't do for me and there is nothing I wouldn't do for him—and that's exactly what we do for each other, nothing."

This woman is not exactly describing the bliss of oneness; isolation has claimed two more victims.

Christopher Lasch is right when he observes that our culture has had a corrosive effect on marriage and the family. Three of his observations deserve careful noting:

> Institutions of cultural transmission (school, church, family), which might have been expected to counter the narcissistic trend in our culture, have instead been shaped in its image . . . .[2]
>
> . . . [In our narcissistic culture] satisfaction depends on taking what you want instead of waiting for what is rightfully yours to receive.[3]
>
> To live for the moment is the prevailing passion—to live for yourself, not for your predecessors or posterity.[4]

Lasch's words aptly describe what has happened to America during the final decades of the twentieth century. All too many of us get caught in the rush to the shallow well of self-satisfaction, which appears satisfying but never can quite quench our increasing thirst. There is no question that as we head further into the twenty-first century, we are in the "age of individualism." This thing called individualism, personal freedom, or self-actualization can strangle any marriage.

How Independence Kills a Marriage

One illusion married couples fall for in this new age of liberation is the belief that they can both be "independently successful" and still have a great marriage. A few couples *seem* to make it work, but most do not. Isolation is never defeated when each spouse operates totally independent of the other. The only way to unity, oneness, and a successful marriage is through *mutual dependence*. If each partner doesn't control "self" and subject it to the Creator of marriage, the marriage dies.

As I have counseled and spoken across the nation, I have seen the corrosive effect of selfishness and independence in marriages. Men stubbornly ignore the needs of their wives. They prefer going to the club to play golf, or even spending an extra hour or two at the office. I once met a pastor who frequented Christian bookstores and libraries with the sole purpose of avoiding his wife. And I have counseled women who spend countless hours shopping, not for their families but to avoid responsibilities at home and to gratify themselves.

Often these self-styled independents spurn counseling. They don't want any help or, if they do concede to enter the counselor's office, they defy being taught anything by anyone. Arms crossed, head held high, they refuse to hear anything their mate or the counselor has to say. They are miserable, lonely people, and so are those who have to live with them.

Before the Wedding We Wear Blinders

But marriages frozen in the isolation of selfishness didn't start out that way. People get married with "stars in their eyes." They don't see reality when they're dating or during the engagement. They wear blinders equipped with special lenses that filter out all the unpleasantness. Some are so desperate to love and be loved that they deny reality.

Engaged couples are in love with romance because things are going their way. It's a special time. They don't want to be bothered with the truth or obvious facts that suggest there could be some problems down the line. Instead, they want to experience this thing called "love."

Many couples think marriage promises fun that will never end.

Nothing in the world arouses more false hope than the first four hours of a diet or the first day of the honeymoon.

Then reality sets in. Comedian Benny Fields said it well: "The glances over candlelight that seemed so sweet do not seem so amorous over shredded wheat." The lovely person who, during the engagement, was an ideal now starts to become an ordeal. Selfishness begins to rob the relationship of its romance in tiny but significant ways.

Humorist Sam Levenson summarized the problem when he said: "Love at first sight is easy to understand. It's when two people have been looking at each other for years that it becomes a miracle." I can recall how little Barbara and I knew about each other when we married. We were both selfish in our own ways, and we had to discover what those ways were.

SATURDAY'S HERO—THE GIANT AMOEBA

It didn't take Barbara long to learn about my genuine, fourteen-carat tendency to be lazy, which was closely linked to my enjoyment of television. Early in our marriage I thought Saturdays were "my day" to thoroughly enjoy doing as *I pleased*. Just as my dad had always done, I would get Cokes and chips, and crawl into *my* chair and settle down to watch hours of baseball, football, tennis, golf—it didn't matter. I just wanted to become a giant amoeba, a block of molecules with flat brain waves mesmerized by hours of gazing at the boob tube.

Wasn't it Erma Bombeck who suggested that if a husband watched more than three football games a weekend, his wife should have him declared legally dead and have his estate probated? I understand where Erma was coming from—now. But back then I felt I was within my "rights." It took me several years to realize that my problem was selfishness. There were things that Barbara needed help with, and today—with six kids—her "to-do" list has grown even longer. Actually, it isn't *her* list anymore—it's become *our* list.

Marriage offers a great opportunity to do something about selfishness. So many people say, "There is no hope. I can't get him to change," or, "What's the use? She'll never be any different." Barbara and I know there *is* hope because we learned to apply a plan that is bigger than human self-centeredness. Our marriage has grown and continues to grow toward more and more oneness because of a certain book that is the bestseller of all time. The Bible is alive, and it is the most practical guide to successful human relationships ever written.

We have seen the Bible's plan succeed in our lives and we're still seeing it work daily. Barbara hasn't changed me, nor have I changed her. But God has changed both of us, and most of what He has taught us has come from His Book.

THE PARABLE OF THE PORCUPINES

It's ironic that one of the things all of us need the most is a relationship with another person who accepts us as we are and doesn't reject us. But the closer I get to Barbara the more she becomes aware of *who I really am*—and the possibility of her rejecting me grows even greater.

A well-known story catches the pain of the human dilemma when it compares relating to each other to a predicament of two porcupines freezing in the winter cold. Shivering in the frigid air, the two porcupines move closer together to share body heat and warmth. But then their sharp spines and quills prick each other painfully and they move apart, victims once more of the bitter cold around them. Soon they feel they must come together once more—or freeze to death. But their quills cause too much pain and they have to part again.

Many marriages are just like that. We can't stand the cold (isolation) but we desperately need to learn how to live with the sharp barbs and quills that are part of coming together in oneness.

Is there a way to have oneness without the pain driving us apart? I believe there is—in fact, I *know* there is. The best answer is in the Person and teachings of Jesus Christ. Instead of wanting to be first, we must be willing to be last. Instead of wanting to be served, we must serve. Instead of trying to save our lives, we must lose them. We must love our neighbor (our spouse) as much as we love ourselves. In short, if we want oneness, we must: *Give up, Give in, and Give All.*

The alternative is isolation, the sworn enemy of love and intimacy. Much of our selfishness is driven by fear. We fear the risks and pains of love because it means giving of ourselves, giving up ourselves, giving in to another. C. S. Lewis describes the impact selfish isolation has on a human heart:

> Love anything, and your heart will certainly be wrung, possibly be broken. If you want to make sure of keeping it intact, you must give your heart to no one, not even to an animal. Wrap it carefully around with hobbies and little luxuries; avoid all entanglements; lock it up safe in the casket or coffin of your selfishness. But in that casket—safe, dark, motionless, airless—it will change. It will not be broken; it will become unbreakable, impenetrable, irredeemable. The alternative to tragedy, or at least to the risk of tragedy, is damnation. The only place outside heaven where you can be perfectly safe from all the dangers and perturbations of love is hell.[5]

Lewis was saying you can protect your heart. You can keep your heart from breaking by wrapping it carefully in tissue paper, sealing it in a box, and putting that box in a dark corner of your closet. Let it remain there for ten, twenty, or even forty years. Then open the box and find your heart. It will be perfectly preserved but atrophied. It will be shrunken because it has neither loved much or hurt much. It will be a shriveled memorial to a life wasted in selfish isolation.

If we live our lives for ourselves, thinking only of our selfish desires and interests, in the end God gives us exactly what we wanted: *Ourselves.*

Marriage provides the opportunity to live life for someone besides yourself and to avoid the terrible judgment, "All I've got is me. I can't depend on anyone else."

The key to solving selfishness is learning you have to depend on someone else because you really have no other choice. To experience oneness and intimacy you must give up your will for the will of another. But to do this you must first give up your will to Christ, and then you will find it possible to give up your will for that of your mate.

Unless you can come to this "giving up of the wills" and learn to depend on one another, selfishness will cripple or destroy your marriage as you face the inevitable difficulties that are bound to occur. In the next chapter, we'll see why the storms of life pose another serious threat to oneness.

HOMEBUILDERS PROJECTS

TO THINK ABOUT INDIVIDUALLY

1. How are you and your spouse doing in the "three-legged race" called marriage? Are you running together—in the same direction?

2. How seriously does selfishness threaten your oneness? Which of you is more selfish? (Try to be objective!)

3. How much do you depend on each other? Think of some specific examples. . . .

FOR INTERACTION TOGETHER

1. Sit down, face each other, and take turns completing the following statement: "The times I feel most selfish—needing to have somebody serve me or do something for me—are . . ."

2. Next, take turns completing this statement: "The times I feel you are the most selfish are . . ."

3. Talk together about what each of you perceives as selfishness. Are those perceptions always accurate? What can each of you do to treat each other with more consideration and caring?

HOMEBUILDERS
PRINCIPLES

**If you do not tackle your problems together
with God's help, you will fall apart.**

8

DEATH, TAXES, AND TROUBLES

When we think about people trouble grows;
when we think about God trouble goes.

—AUTHOR UNKNOWN

Lloyd Shadrach is a good friend, a leader in our ministry to families, and he is sensitive to the lessons God has for him to learn. Recently he told me how he had taken a walk after a fierce thunderstorm rumbled through Little Rock. As he walked down a road that was lined on both sides by massive, towering oak trees, he had to step over dead limbs that had been blown from those mature trees. Decaying branches—once lodged amid the greenery above—now littered the landscape below.

Lloyd shared, "It was as though God was giving me a personal object lesson of what 'storms' can do in our lives. In the middle of the storm when the wind is gusting, the lightning is popping, and the storm clouds are getting darker, it's difficult to believe that our troubles are purposeful. But God may allow a storm in our lives to clear out the dead wood so that new growth can occur. And isn't it interesting," Lloyd concluded, "how fresh the air feels after a storm is over? Sort of unused."

As Lloyd shared his parable with me, I couldn't help but think back and reflect on the dead wood, several cords of it, that has been blown out of my life. One of the most important things Barbara and I have learned from these storms is that God is interested in our growth. He wants us to trust him in the midst of the storms and to grow together as a couple and not fall apart. And yet, I've seen oneness uprooted and marriages die from these periods of suffering:

- A child drowns in a swimming pool, the mother blames herself, then abruptly turns on her husband.

- A husband's lost job and subsequent financial disorder cause a wife to stop believing in him. Their disappointment in one another causes them both to retreat from meeting one another's needs.

- An unplanned pregnancy and increased pressures at work provoke a husband and wife to begin to question their commitment to one another.

THREAT #5: TRIALS, TROUBLES, AND TRIBULATIONS

What most couples don't realize is that trials represent an opportunity for them to sink their roots deeper and gain stability in their relationship.

Scientist Lord Kelvin was lecturing his students on an experiment that failed to come off as planned. He said, "Gentlemen, when you are face to face with a difficulty, you are up against a discovery." As inevitable storms rumble through our lives it is imperative that we turn *to* one another and not *against* one another.

We know. We've experienced the temptations that come with trials and troubles. From July 1976 to June 1977, Barbara and I endured a twelve-month period that was a real test for us.

DISASTER STRIKES IN RISING STAR

It all began when I had my fifth job change and sixth move in five years. That summer we sold our home in Dallas and planned to move to Little Rock, Arkansas. First, however, we had to spend seven weeks on the road speaking as well as attending training sessions that would equip us to conduct a new family ministry for Campus Crusade for Christ.

So there we were, on the road again with Ashley, our two-year-old daughter, and Benjamin, age eight months. Traveling with two small children in diapers was challenge enough, but our real trouble had yet to begin.

In the sprawling West Texas metropolis of Rising Star, my billfold and Barbara's purse were somehow relieved of our presence. Our identification as well as most of our money and credit cards were gone.

It was 5 P.M. on Friday and our children were getting whiny and hungry. Fortunately, I had a few loose bills in my pocket. That got us a hotel room for the night. The next day we snacked on crackers and other junk food as we drove out of Texas into Colorado. By nightfall, temporarily short of funds, we had no choice but to camp out with our toddlers in a campground near Durango, Colorado.

A deluge of rain camped with us and transformed our tent from a shelter into a funnel. We tried to keep dry with massive applications of Pampers placed at strategic locations to soak up the minor flash floods that poured into the tent. Somehow we survived the night even though Ashley had an asthma attack and wheezed during most of the predawn hours.

That summer was bad. Really bad. Barbara and I were not getting along very well—just nibbling and picking at each other over everything. Our sexual relationship was at an all-time low. And when we arrived in Little Rock and moved into our new home, it was so filthy it took days to clean it up. Only later did we discover that in purchasing the home we had been cheated out of several thousand dollars.

AND THEN THE PHONE RANG . . .

By now our troubles were starting to pick up speed like the rain that had fed the streams in Durango that night. It was August and after being in our new home three weeks, we got a call one Sunday just before leaving for church. My brother's voice said, "Dennis, Dad died this morning."

I couldn't believe it. My dad had always been one of the strongest figures in my life. That morning he had gotten up as he always did to go to church. He walked into the kitchen and asked Mom for a glass of water and some coffee. Complaining of heartburn, he said he'd lie down in the bedroom for a moment. It took several minutes for my mother to boil the water for instant coffee, and when she walked into the bedroom, my father was dead. A sudden heart attack had taken him at the age of sixty-six.

And so I packed up my family once more and we all moved to Ozark for three weeks of living out of suitcases and trying to help my mother get through the funeral and her initial time of grief.

We arrived back in Little Rock and, two weeks later, began receiving "short paychecks." Anyone who has worked for a missionary organization is familiar with that term—if you don't have enough funds raised, you don't get paid your full monthly salary.

At the same time I needed two thousand dollars worth of dental work. Then in early January, another phone call came from Ozark saying my brother had suffered an apparent heart attack. So in the middle of one of the worst winters in history, I got on a plane and traveled to Ozark to run the family propane business.

Was It My Turn for Heart Trouble?

What I encountered in Ozark was like a war zone—streets frozen solid with sleet and snow—a windchill factor of twenty to thirty degrees below zero—and people desperate for fuel. I was working long hours trying to keep all the bases covered, and one night as I lay in the same bed where my father had died, I suddenly felt my heart beating at an unusually rapid rate. The more it raced, the more frightened I became. I was finally rushed to the hospital where my brother had already been admitted.

For a while they thought I might be having a heart attack too. But it turned out to be a reaction to all the stress and pressure. The same was true for my brother.

In February I returned home to learn that my son Benjamin needed major abdominal surgery. He came through fine, but the financial stress was beginning to weigh on me.

Barbara's Crisis

Fortunately, the spring months passed quietly. Then in June, Barbara was doing her morning exercises. For some reason, I hadn't left for work at my usual time and I was still there, admiring her energy as she did sit-ups. Suddenly she stopped and put her head between her knees. I said, "Sweetheart, what's wrong?"

"I feel faint."

"Well, can I help?"

"I think my heart is beating fast."

I said, "Well, maybe you have the same thing I had. They told me to just get up and try to walk it off. Let me help you to your feet."

I tried to help her walk it off. We got exactly three feet and she collapsed on the bed, nearly passing out. I checked her pulse and her heart was racing so fast I couldn't discern the number of beats. I called the ambulance and they rushed Barbara to the hospital.

Throughout the morning, Barbara's heart raced at 280 to 300 beats a minute. That amounts to five beats a second. Her blood pressure dropped alarmingly low.

Just before noon, I began to despair. I had just lost my dad; was I going to lose my wife too? I called Kitty Longstreth, a widow who had become one of our good friends in Little Rock. As I explained what happened, I asked, "Kitty, would you please pray for Barbara?"

"Of course I will, Dennis. I'll start right now."

Kitty began praying around 1 P.M. Back in the waiting area outside the coronary intensive care unit I prayed also. The doctors hadn't been able to slow down Barbara's heart at all.

Around 2 P.M. the doctors told me Barbara was experiencing an asthma attack, and her lungs were filling with fluid. Asthma is treated with adrenalin, a stimulant, but they couldn't give her a stimulant because her heart was beating too fast. Her blood pressure was dropping, the fluid was rising in her lungs, and Barbara was in imminent danger of developing pneumonia and suffering cardiac arrest.

At 4 P.M. the doctors told me they were going to try to stop Barbara's heart with electric shock and retime it as they shocked it into starting up again. There was no choice. But at 4:05 a doctor came back out and said, "We didn't have to use the shock treatment. Your wife's heart returned to normal before we could get hooked up."

KITTY ALREADY KNEW

Because they wouldn't let me see Barbara, I decided to call Kitty Longstreth and tell her the good news. She said matter-of-factly, "You say they told you that at five after four? That's when I stopped praying. Somehow I knew at that moment that everything was okay. I knew that either Barbara had died and gone to heaven, or her heart had reverted back to normal and she was going to be all right."

For the next thirty days, Barbara had extra heartbeats, I had extra heartbeats, and so did the kids. Then at the end of the month, we discovered that she was pregnant.

That ended our one-year adventure in trials, troubles, and difficulties, but we still faced eight more months of suspense wondering if Barbara would give birth to a healthy baby. Three weeks past her due date, she delivered a nine-pound, five-ounce boy, whom we named Samuel. The Old Testament meaning of the name is "because we asked of the Lord."

All our children are special, of course, but Samuel came out of an absolutely incredible situation. Our marriage had suffered repeated blows of all kinds. During the twelve months of troubles, plus the eight months of pregnancy that followed, sex became a memory, and romance was ancient history. All we could do was hang on to the Scriptures that teach there is a God who is in charge. We had always believed those principles, but now were *living them*.

I realize that what we went through was not the worst possible series of traumas a couple can face. But what our troubles taught us was that without the inner resources to move through your trials, your marriage will suffer. The failure to work through the trials of life will threaten oneness and bring isolation.

HOW COUPLES FAIL TO HANDLE TRIALS

I see two major ways in which families fail to respond properly to adversity. First, and most typically, *they fail to anticipate the trials and problems that will come*. Somehow they think none of that will happen to them, but they are mistaken.

The well-known saying reminds us that nothing is sure except death and taxes. To those two old foes you can add troubles. As I read recently, "The man whose problems are all behind him is probably a school bus driver."

Second, when the troubles do hit, *many couples simply don't know how to respond.* The trauma brought by the problem is not the real issue. The real issue is the response the couple makes to that trauma.

According to studies conducted by Dr. Mavis Heatherington, who works in an organization on the East Coast that helps parents through traumatic experiences, in marriages where a child died or was born deformed, 70 percent of the couples separate or divorce within five years.

Why does this happen? Couples simply have no strategy for living that goes beyond romance. They don't know how to hold their relationship together and even make it stronger during that desperate period of suffering and pain.

Part of the strategy for facing troubles is to realize that God allows difficulties in our lives for many reasons. I'm not saying He causes difficulties, but I do believe He allows them. Malcolm Muggeridge wrote:

> Contrary to what might be expected, I look back on experiences that at the time seemed especially desolating and painful with particular satisfaction. Indeed, I can say with complete truthfulness that everything that I have learned in my 75 years in this world, everything that has truly enhanced and enlightened my experience, has been through affliction and not through happiness.
>
> In other words, if it were ever to be possible to eliminate affliction from our earthly existence by the means of some drug, or some other medical mumble jumble, the result would not be to make life delectable, but to make it too banal and trivial to be endurable.[1]

GRASP GOD'S PERSPECTIVE TOGETHER

The problems Barbara and I faced that year brought us to a crossroad: Would we share our difficulties with one another and give the other person room to process the problem? I remember feeling tempted to think that Barbara was silly for being so introspective during the months that followed her heart episode. I had to fight the urge to discount her emotions. After a few days I had the typical noncompassionate male response: "Snap out of it, dear. Everything is going to be fine." I wanted her to flip a switch and move on. But Barbara wanted to share her fears with me. She needed me just to listen—offering no profound advice—only my two eyes and ears.

The temptations to withdraw from one another are greatest during these periods. By doing so we can become extremely "self" oriented (in reality, a very lonely existence). The married couple who learns the art of facing storms together by seeking God's perspective can develop a spiritual oneness that makes them inseparable.

I was just ending a FamilyLife Conference in Dallas when a trim, well-muscled gentleman came up to greet me. He was a Green Beret.

I had touched a nerve when I talked about having a plan to face problems, because he said, "Dennis, in the Green Berets we train over and over, and then over and over again. We repeat some exercises until we are sick of them, but our instructors know what they are doing. They want us so prepared and finely trained that when trials and difficulties come on the battlefield, we will be able to fall back upon that which is second nature to us. We literally learn to do things by reflex action."

I realized I'd just heard a great illustration of how Christians should face marriage together. They should be so well trained in God's plan that their reaction to crises and difficulties will be an automatic reflex, not a panicky fumbling around. If you wait until a crisis hits and then turn to the Scriptures, you won't be as prepared—and you'll be more susceptible to the enemy.

THE BEST WAY TO HANDLE TROUBLE

During our year of incredible troubles, Barbara and I learned a simple principle for handling problems. It contains only five words: *"Give thanks in all circumstances"* (1 Thessalonians 5:18).

This isn't a simplistic excuse to put your head in the sand and ignore reality. On the contrary, I believe it's the key to dealing with the storms life can bring your way—and that includes the little things as well as the big upheavals and challenges.

If we want to really practice giving thanks in everything, we have to ask ourselves, *Is God really involved in the details of my life? Could God possibly want to teach me something through a flat tire, a kid's runny nose, or a toy-strewn floor? Does He really want to be part of every moment of my day, or is He willing to settle for the 9:30-to-noon slot on Sunday mornings?*

Giving thanks in all things expresses faith. Those five little words express our belief that *God knows what He is doing.* And that He can be trusted. As Martin Lloyd-Jones put it: "Faith is the refusal to panic."

WE TEMPORARILY LOST OUR PERSPECTIVE

During that summer we moved to our new home in Arkansas (and lived out of suitcases for seven weeks on the road while doing so), it definitely was not easy to give God thanks in everything. After losing billfold and purse and having to stay one night in a leaky tent in the middle of a thunderstorm, we arrived in Fort Collins, Colorado, for a training conference. At this point, we questioned whether the Lord really wanted us to start a ministry to families.

Then, a couple of days later, a flash flood swept through Big Thompson Canyon, just a few miles from our training site. It was the worst flash flood in Colorado's history. More than one hundred people lost their lives, including seven fellow Campus Crusade for Christ staff women. Twenty-eight other Campus Crusade women narrowly escaped a twenty-foot wall of water by going up the side of a canyon in total darkness.

As the news of the disaster sank in, we realized we really didn't have any problems at all. We had our lives and the privilege of serving the King of kings and the Lord of lords. We understood that God has all kinds of ways of teaching his children valuable lessons. No matter what the circumstances might be, there is always something to be thankful for.

HOMEBUILDERS PROJECTS

TO THINK ABOUT INDIVIDUALLY

1. Take inventory of your marriage. Have there been any major trials or troubles? Did they result in stronger oneness or in isolation of some kind? Why or why not?

2. How well do you follow Paul's exhortation to "Give thanks in everything"?

   _____ I do it all the time.

   _____ I do it most of the time.

   _____ I do it some of the time.

   _____ I seldom, if ever, do it.

3. When is it easiest for you to give thanks? When is it most difficult? Does it really make sense to give thanks for problems? Irritations? Catastrophes?

FOR INTERACTION TOGETHER

1. Talk about the trials and troubles you have had as a family. Which ones stand out and why? Which ones brought you closer together? Which ones seem to separate you?

2. Think of ways you can help each other "give thanks in everything." Why not agree to share the "sharp pebbles in your shoes" and stop to give thanks as a couple for what they may be teaching you?

3. What action can you begin to take now that will prepare you for the inevitable truth to come?

HOMEBUILDERS
PRINCIPLES

**When you feel lonely and isolated at home,
you begin escaping from reality by searching
for fulfillment outside the marriage.**

9

THERE'S MORE THAN ONE WAY TO HAVE AN AFFAIR

If any of a spouse's basic needs goes unmet, that spouse becomes
vulnerable to the temptation of an affair.
—WILLARD F. HARLEY JR.[1]

Have you ever played the word association game? You know how it works:

You say, "car," and I say, "breakdowns."

You say, "kids," and I say, "noise."

You say, "house," and I say, "repairs."

If you say, "affair," I could give you typical answers like "adultery," "cheating," or "motel"—things that relate to the extramarital sexual liaisons that we see acted out in so many ways across our land, particularly on television, in the films, and in newspaper headlines.

Extramarital affairs are another major threat to oneness in marriage, and I believe the danger is even greater than most of us imagine. Extramarital affairs are not always what we think they are. An extramarital affair is basically *an escape from reality that begins with feeling lonely and isolated at home and ends with a search for fulfillment of needs outside the marriage.*

THREAT #6: EXTRAMARITAL "AFFAIRS"

It's true that extramarital affairs are often sexual in nature; but there are other types of affairs. How about the one called "career"? Often people escape the reality of their mediocre marriages by pursuing wealth and materialistic desires, or through the affairs called "busyness."

Our desire to escape is prompted by the pressures of the secular culture in which we live. From one end of the country (Hollywood) to the other (Madison Avenue), comes a barrage of advertising, TV programming, films, commercials, and public-relations schemes, all designed to teach us that we should seek self-satisfaction in life.

As a result of all this pressure, it's easy to get an improper perception of reality. We say we know that romance movies and soap operas aren't real, but nonetheless they affect how we perceive reality.

And it's obvious that you bring this programming with you when you get married. As you start comparing your expectations and fantasies with your real life, you can begin to say to yourself, *How come my love life doesn't match up with the one led by my favorite TV hero or heroine? Why can't my mate be that cool, that sexy, that romantic?*

We Question Reality, Not Our Fantasies

From there it's just one short, slippery step to questioning reality. Instead of challenging your fantasies, you begin to look at life and say, "Wait a minute. Why don't we have all that passion and chemistry?" You can begin to compare your relationship with your mate to a fantasy that's been developed with a multimillion-dollar budget and by shooting twenty retakes of every scene. And it's easy enough to be duped into thinking that you deserve exactly what the fantasy on the screen depicts. As the Scriptures tell us, "Although they claimed to be wise, they became fools and exchanged the glory of the immortal God for the world's" (Romans 1:22–23).

It is no wonder, then, that so many people take the next step into an extramarital affair. Instead of finding happiness and fulfillment in the real world with a real husband, real children, and a real God, they bail out and chase after the illusions conjured out of their fantasies. The problem is, if we catch our fantasy it too becomes tarnished with reality. The illusion is transformed by disappointment into disillusionment.

Because love affairs with other persons are such imminent and dangerous threats to marriage, let's look at those first. Once we understand the typical love affair, it's easy to see how the other kinds of affairs can happen as well.

THE CHEMISTRY OF EMOTIONAL ADULTERY

High-school chemistry taught me a very valuable lesson: when certain substances come into close contact, they create a chemical reaction. One day during my senior year of high school, I decided to conduct an experiment. I dropped a jar full of pure sodium into a river and nearly blew up the bridge I was standing on. In my naiveté, I didn't realize how powerful the chemical reaction would be.

I have learned that adult husbands and wives don't respect the laws of chemistry any more than I did as a teenager back in high school. They mix volatile ingredients without giving much thought to the chemical reaction that can happen with someone other than one's mate. I'm not talking about sexual attractions per se. What people fail to grasp is that before sexual indiscretion starts, there is a reaction of two hearts, the chemistry of two souls.

In other words, people commit emotional adultery before they commit physical adultery. Emotional adultery is unfaithfulness of the heart. It starts when two people of the opposite sex begin talking with each other about intimate struggles, doubts, or feelings. They start sharing their souls in a way that God intended exclusively for the marriage relationship. Emotional adultery is friendship with the opposite sex that goes too far.

Let's look at the typical scenario. The busy executive arrives at work still simmering over the argument concerning their finances he and his wife had the night before. It's becoming increasingly difficult to talk to her, it seems, about *anything* without ending up in a fight.

When he walks into work, there is his secretary. She's *always* easy to talk to, he thinks, and she *always* treats him with respect.

One night they both find it necessary to work late together. That report for the home office just has to get out and there is no choice. It's all innocent enough, but as they relax their guard during the late hours they begin talking in ways they never did before—about their lives, their struggles.

They stay and work late again, and he takes her home afterward. Nothing happens. Just a friendly "Thanks for the lift; see you in the morning," and he drives away. But then they have lunch together, and soon they decide that they need to discuss various business matters at lunch at least once a week.

Before long, a mystique develops. The executive knows his secretary is really interested in him—and vice versa.

Meanwhile, back home, perhaps the executive's wife is nagging him to fix the screen door and repair her car. She keeps reminding him of family decisions he has to make, and he begins to feel he doesn't really *need* all the hassle. The responsibility of home feels heavy and restrictive—he'd rather have lunch with his secretary because they have such a great time together, talking, sharing, dealing with things that are new, interesting, exciting, and challenging.

The executive may not know it, but he is already having an emotional affair. And, almost inevitably, the emotional affair turns into a physical one. Meanwhile, his wife senses she is losing her husband. She becomes hurt and lonely, but she doesn't blow up. Instead, she plays it cool and decides she'll go out and find an identity of her own, since she's not finding one at home.

She gets a job and guess who she meets? That's right—the nicest guy who pays attention to her, compliments her, and actually talks to her. Next he asks her to have lunch, and then . . .

ONE AFFAIR OFTEN LEADS TO ANOTHER

A man and woman came to me and that was their story. They were both escaping from problems in their respective marriages. In fact, they were both considering divorce and marrying each other. And they wanted me to tell them what to do!

Because the thought of divorce appalled me, I gave them a brief lesson in reality and fantasy. I told them that no one could stop them from divorcing their mates and marrying each other, but then what? Under the stress and pressure of daily life, there would be many painful difficult adjustments, and what would be their plan to cope? Obviously, they were firmly committed to the 50/50 Plan that already had failed both of them once.

WHAT TO DO IF YOUR MATE IS HAVING AN AFFAIR

- Make your home a haven, not a hassle. You may need to seriously evaluate if you have taken your relationship with your spouse for granted.

- Nurture your "attraction quotient." Don't wear grubbies around the house. Lose a few pounds, smile, be warm. Be an invitation for him/her to come home to.

- Take a hard look at your schedule. You may not be meeting your mate's needs because you're exhausted from a job that is too demanding. Determine where you want to succeed— at work or at home.

- Offer your mate a real relationship—with real forgiveness, real love, affirmation, and encouragement. Become a magnet to draw your mate back home.

- Don't try to cope alone. Get competent counsel and help from your pastor, a counselor, or a therapist. Read *His Needs, Her Needs,* by Dr. Willard F. Harley Jr.

- Pray that God will begin to displace wrong values with His values in your mate's life.

- Get godly counsel.

Would they act selfishly in their new marriage? Definitely, because they started their own relationship selfishly. Would there be trials? Absolutely. They would face alimony, child support and visitation rights, and struggles all the way.

Might there be the possibility of another extramarital affair? Of course there would, because their relationship had been undermined by deceit, treachery, and mistrust.

Today our churches and Christian homes have too many people who are being deceived by fantasies that convince them they must search for the pot of gold at the end of the rainbow. They don't realize that the closer they get to the "end of the rainbow" the more the rainbow vanishes, and the "pot of gold" is seen for what it really is—a fantasy. The real gold, the real pay-off, comes to those who want to dig deeper and deal with reality in their own marriages.

How to Recognize the Danger Signs

Whenever you develop an in-depth relationship with someone of the opposite sex at any level, certain forces come into play that can result in a chemical reaction with that person. Some signs that this reaction is beginning to occur include the following:

. . . You've got a need you feel your mate isn't meeting—for attention, approval, affection—and that other person begins meeting your need.

. . . You find it easier to unwind with someone other than your spouse by dissecting the day's difficulties over lunch, coffee, or during a ride home.

. . . You begin to talk about problems you are having with your spouse.

. . . You rationalize the relationship by saying that surely it must be God's will to talk so openly and honestly with a fellow Christian. You become defensive about the relationship and protective of it.

. . . You look forward to being with this person more than with your own mate.

. . . You wonder what you'd do if you didn't have this friend to talk to.

. . . You hide the relationship from your mate.

Avoiding Emotional Adultery

When you find yourself connecting with another person who starts becoming in even the smallest way a substitute for your marital partner, you've started traveling a dangerous road. So, how do you protect yourself—and your marriage?

Here are some principles many have found helpful:

1. Know your boundaries. You should put fences around your heart and protect the sacred ground that is reserved only for your spouse. Barbara and I are careful to share our deepest feelings, needs, and difficulties only with each other and not with friends of the opposite sex.

2. Realize the power of the eyes. They are the "windows of your soul." Pull the shades down if you sense someone is pausing a little too long in front of those windows. It's true that good eye contact is necessary for fruitful communication, but there is a deep type of look that must be reserved for only one person: your mate.

Frankly, I don't trust myself. Some women think I'm insecure because I don't hold eye contact too long, but that's not it at all. I simply don't trust my humanity. I've seen what has happened to others, and I know it could happen to me.

3. Beware of isolation and concealment. One strategy of the enemy is to isolate you from your spouse, by tempting you to keep secrets from your mate. Barbara and I both realize the danger of concealment in our marriage. We work hard at bringing things out into the open and discussing them. Our closets are empty.

4. Extinguish any chemical reactions that may have begun. A friendship with the opposite sex that is beginning to meet needs your mate should be meeting must be ended quickly. A simple rule of chemistry is this: To stop a chemical reaction, remove one of the elements. It may be painful or embarrassing at first, but it isn't as painful as suffering the results of temptation that has given birth to sin.

Ruth Senter wrote an article for *Partnership* magazine entitled simply, "Rick." It was an incredibly honest examination of a godly wife's encounter and ensuing friendship with a Christian man she met in a graduate class. Her struggle and godly response to this temptation were graphically etched in a letter that ended the relationship. She wrote, "Friendship is always going somewhere unless it's dead. You and I both know where ours is going. When a relationship threatens the stability of commitments we've made to the people we value the most, it can no longer be."[2]

5. Ask God to remind you how important it is to fear Him. The fear of God has turned me from many a temptation. It would be one thing if another person learned I had compromised my vows, but it's quite another thing to realize that God's throne would have a knowledge of my disloyalty to Barbara faster than the speed of light.

It has been said that a "secret sin on earth is open scandal in heaven." My heavenly Father and my earthly father are there right now. Thinking of hurting them keeps me pure.

IF YOU'RE CAUGHT IN AN AFFAIR . . .

What if you have already failed? What if the chemical reaction has occurred but you have told no one? Go to your heavenly Father, confess your disobedience, and let Him wrap His arms of unconditional love, forgiveness, and acceptance around you. The old hymn speaks of "grace that is greater than all our sins." You have no business remembering that which God has forgiven and forgotten.

Should you tell your mate of your indiscretion? If there is any question in your mind about how your mate would respond to your confessions, then it would be wise to seek counsel before dropping any atomic bombs.

In fact, some therapists advise never trying to end an affair by yourself. Dr. Willard Harley is a licensed psychologist and committed believer in Christ who has spent more than twenty years counseling people trapped in the throes of an affair. In his book, *His Needs, Her Needs*, Harley flatly states that you cannot end an affair by yourself. It is not a simple problem; when he starts counseling with a couple whose marriage has been damaged by an affair, he estimates it will take at least a one-year program of hard work and therapy. He writes:

> I set up my absolute iron clad rule that the estranged spouse must stop seeing his or her lover immediately and *never* go back. In explaining this
> I compare a spouse engaging in an affair to an alcoholic. An alcoholic can only hope to separate himself entirely from alcohol one day at a time. In much the same way, the only hope for a person entangled in an

extramarital affair is to crate as much distance as possible between himself and his lover.[3]

Unquestionably, an extramarital affair is a devastating threat to oneness in a marriage. In many cases it is a final blow that leads to the total isolation of divorce. But there are other ways to have affairs. Some of them, in fact, can be part of the situation that leads a husband or wife to stray into someone else's bed.

THE SIREN CALL OF CAREERISM

The caricature of the executive in the crisply starched shirt, tie, and expensive silk suit working long hours to make it to the top has been around for decades, but his female counterpart is a more recent development. Today, both men and women are having affairs with their careers, and the effect on marriage is undeniable.

Magazines carry articles on husbands and wives who pursue careers with brilliance, energy, and drive. Somewhere in the article the wife mentions that she would like to have a child, but her career has been her all-consuming passion. Or she will lament the fact that she has to leave a small baby in some kind of day care situation while she zooms off to catch a jet to the next sales conference. Such articles make these couples sound content, chic, sophisticated, and totally fulfilled. In a word, they seem to have it all.

It's easy to fuel the fires of fantasy down at the office as you escape from reality with a mistress called "career." Few think of it that way, but what is adultery? It is breaking your marriage vows and giving yourself to another.

I see men who are trapped on the corporate escalator, and there seems to be no place they can get off. They must ride it all the way to "the top." Meanwhile, back where the home fires are slowly going out, a family waits dinner for another night. Or, the better half of that family may be out, "caught" on her own escalator.

Perhaps we need to understand that when we exchange wedding vows we are doing more than simply pledging our "troth" to one another. What about the home we are committing to build? Ironically, many people will claim they are true to their wedding vows, but they are pursuing career ambitions that may be undermining and even destroying their homes.

Today, many don't have the conviction to say "no" and get off the escalator. Our addiction to success is a narcotic that numbs us. The bottom line: loneliness and isolation.

I know the pressures are real, because I've felt them myself. In a fast-growing ministry like ours, there is always the temptation to put my work ahead of my wife and family. There is an instant gratification, a "messianic high" in meeting people's needs.

All these responsibilities at work can easily lure me away from my more important responsibilities of husband and father. I don't always make the right choices, but to protect our family Barbara and I talk frequently about our schedules, deciding what we can say no to. She is my anchor who reminds me of my *real* priorities.

HOW TO HAVE A PLASTIC AFFAIR

I believe a lot of people also have affairs with their credit cards. One credit card company wants you to believe you can't leave home without its card because you *need* the privilege of being one of its members. Another credit card commercial suggests that it can bring you the whole world at the flick of a piece of plastic. Analyze the credit card commercials and you soon see they are ploys tempting people to escape from reality through the fantasy of getting whatever they want *right now.*

One of the most powerful strategies advertisers use is to convince people they *need* those possessions to be happy. Ask the average person if he believes he is a materialist and he will say, "Of course not. I don't have all this stuff just because I *want* it. It's just that we *need* it. The kids needed new shoes, I needed the sports coat, and my wife needed a new dress. And last Christmas we definitely needed the new color TV and now it's pretty obvious we need a new car."

As we pursue what we think we need, the real needs of our family often go unmet. Much of what we think we need we don't need at all. We are simply chasing an illusion that doesn't satisfy. We search for fulfillment in things, but as Solomon, the disillusioned preacher of Ecclesiastes, said, ". . . whoever loves wealth is never satisfied" (Ecclesiastes 5:10).

THE PRICE OF FANTASY IS MUCH TOO HIGH

Any affair is an attempt to escape reality by pursuing a fantasy of some kind. And the price of fantasy is always high—much too high. Recently, I received a letter from a woman whose marriage had been shattered by her husband's unfaithfulness. After twenty-seven years of marriage, he confessed having affairs with several different women. While his admission devastated her, they stayed together and tried to put it all behind them.

They made progress by attending a FamilyLife Conference, getting counseling, and having prayer and Bible reading together every morning. But in one of their discussions, it seemed apparent to the wife that her husband still had secret dreams of the last women he was involved with. She wrote:

> I feel so horrible knowing he will always wonder how it might have been with her, especially on those days when I can't quite measure up to the image he had of her, since he only saw her at her faking best, and he is stuck with me, cold cream, curlers, and all. I say "stuck" because, although he says he always really loved me, I also think he had the good sense to see what divorce would do to our children, his parents and family, his reputation, his business, but sadly, I don't think what his unfaithfulness would and did do to me was really of much primary consideration. It is so sad knowing the memory will always be there, and nothing will ever make it go away . . .
>
> At this point, I'm not sure reconciliation is always the best thing. Sometimes things just go too far and hurt too much. Forgiveness is always possible, but how do you put it all back together again, even when forgiveness is present? I have probably read everything written on every aspect of this whole situation, trying to find a way to deal with my feelings of betrayal, inferiority, anger, bitterness, rage, you name it . . .

I thank God every day for the grace to live that day. But sometimes I just can't believe the reality of the horrors of life, and that we are actually going through this. It's like a death in the family and it is real.

This wife asked for my prayers to help the healing process, and she certainly has those. She also has God's love and grace, which will bring healing over time; but, meanwhile, she struggles with the pain her husband brought upon them both. I believe God can heal their relationship, but it will take time, patience, and much soul searching by them both.

RETREATING TO EMOTIONAL SOLITUDE

Escaping reality to pursue fantasy ultimately results in a retreat to emotional solitude. Discouraged and lonely, we stop caring. We've become passive, bored, resigned to mediocrity. And the final step after this emotional withdrawal is divorce.

Another threat that has surfaced in recent years is Internet pornography. For more information on this, check out Stephen Arterburn's *Every Man's Battle*.[4]

There is one final threat that is a major cause of this retreat and divorce—a threat that permeates our lives today. In Chapter 10, we'll look more closely at the pressures of daily living and how being accountable to each other can ensure a Oneness Marriage.

HOMEBUILDERS PROJECTS

To Think About Individually

1. Analyze your relationship with members of the opposite sex other than your spouse. Have you ever been (or are you being) tempted to commit "emotional adultery"? What do you think of the advice not to look too deeply into the eyes of another? Is his advice extreme or wise?

2. What are some other ways you can have an "affair" besides straying away to another person? Have you ever thought of overemphasizing your career as "adultery"? Is this a problem for you or your spouse?

3. What about materialism? Could playing the consumerism game actually lead to seeking satisfaction and fulfillment outside your marriage? How?

4. What type of affair proves the greatest potential threat to your marriage?

For Interaction Together

1. If your relationship is open and strong, talk with each other about possible temptations to getting involved in emotional adultery. Share concerns you may have about what you see your partner doing that could be encouraging someone in the wrong way. (Note: This kind of discussion can be volatile unless you are both willing to be vulnerable and honest. Don't attempt it unless you are both sure you can deal with where it may lead.)

2. Discuss how careers can affect your marriage. If only the husband works, rate his career on a scale of 1 to 10.

1   2   3   4   5   6   7   8   9   10
Not that threatening   Very threatening
to oneness in our   to the oneness of
marriage.   our marriage.

3. If both of you work, rate how serious a threat your careers pose to your marriage.

HIS CAREER:

1   2   3   4   5   6   7   8   9   10
Not that threatening   Very threatening
to oneness in our   to the oneness of
marriage.   our marriage.

HER CAREER:

1   2   3   4   5   6   7   8   9   10
Not that threatening   Very threatening
to oneness in our   to the oneness of
marriage.   our marriage.

4. Have a frank discussion about your budget, expenditures, and consumerism. Can material possessions become an escape for you? In one sense, every American family is trapped in a consumer society that pressures them to spend, spend, spend. Is too much spending threatening your oneness in any way?

5. Having already discussed the possible ways Satan could get a foothold in your relationship and cause isolation, what are some potential steps you can take to help "affair-proof" your marriage?

HOMEBUILDERS
PRINCIPLES

Life's pressures can isolate you
from God and your mate, or press
you closer to them.

By submitting your life to the scrutiny
of another person, you'll gain spiritual
strength, growth, and balance.

10

OVERCOMMITTED
AND OVERLOADED

Time deals gently with those who take it gently.
—ANATOLE FRANCE

Since age thirteen, Larry Walters had dreamed of soaring high into the sky in a weather balloon. His truck driving job never allowed him to make any kind of official flight, so he improvised. One night, he went to his girlfriend's house, inflated forty-five six-foot weather balloons with helium and attached them to an aluminum lawn chair snugly tethered in the backyard.

The next morning, six of Walters's friends looked on as he strapped himself into the lawn chair, equipped with parachute, a CB radio (to call for help, if necessary), and a BB pistol (to pop some of the balloons if he somehow got too high). Walters cast off, planning on only a short flight. But when his main safety rope snapped, he shot into the Southern California sky.

Worried but not panicky, Walters got on his CB radio with a "Mayday!" call. Meanwhile, the Los Angeles International Airport tower started getting calls from TWA and Delta jet liner pilots saying they had spotted a flying lawn chair at sixteen thousand feet! A Western Airlines pilot also radioed to ask if the FAA knew of any skydivers in the area.

The higher Walters got, the colder the air became, and he decided to take action. Taking out his air pistol, he shot out several of the weather balloons in an attempt to get his out-of-control lawn chair headed back toward earth. His nearly frozen fingers lost their grip on the pistol and it fell overboard, but fortunately his chair started drifting downward, controlled only by gallon jugs of water attached to the sides for use as ballast.

As the thirty-three-year-old truck driver neared the ground, his ropes tangled in a power line and he ended up dangling five feet off the earth, shorting out the electricity in a Long Beach neighborhood for twenty minutes.

Safely back on the ground, Walters said: "Since I was thirteen years old, I dreamed of going up into the clear blue sky in a weather balloon. By the grace of God I fulfilled my dream. I wouldn't do this again for anything. But I'd be happy to endorse Sears' lawn chairs."[1]

MILLIONS BATTLE BEING UP IN THE AIR

Walters's adventure is a picture of how so many people live life today—soaring out of control, jerked off the ground by relentless schedules that cause stress and pressure. As we take on more and more, it's like adding another weather balloon to our lawn chair. Sooner or later our safety ropes won't hold and we're soaring out of control! We feel helpless and alone.

The persistent pressures of the pace we keep even make an impact on our health. According to psychologist David Stoop, some forty million Americans suffer from allergies caused in part by pressure. Another thirty million have insomnia, twenty-five million have hypertension, and twenty million have ulcers. In addition, one out of three Americans has a weight problem and all of this can be traced back, at least in part, to stress and pressure.[2]

Every married couple I know of lives under the unending demands of pressures that cause them to be overcommitted, overextended, and overloaded. The hustle and bustle of life turn into a blur of hurried and harried activity. I often hear promises such as: "Well, we're going hard right now, but as soon as this month is over, we're going to slow down."

The trouble is, the "month" doesn't seem to end. I agree with comedian Flip Wilson, who said, "If I had my life to live over again, I don't think

I'd have the strength." Our many responsibilities seem to continually force us into meeting unreal expectations.

THREAT #7: THE UNRELENTING PRESSURE OF A FAST-PACED LIFESTYLE

Pressures always come from two directions: what other people expect of us and what we expect of ourselves. It is so easy to let yourself be driven by the agendas of other people. Externally, their voices form a deafening chorus, incessantly telling us what we ought to do.

Recently I made a list of a few things I am "expected" to do by outside forces. My dentist tells me I need to floss every day and not use a toothpick.

My doctor wants to know how much I weigh, what I'm eating, and if I'm getting any exercise.

My CPA wants to know why I'm not keeping better records, and if I'm staying within my budget.

My creditors want me to pay on time every month, and advertisers want me to become discontent with what I have, buy more, and go further into debt.

My employers and colleagues want me to meet deadlines, do it right the first time and, of course, do it with excellence while doing it quicker, better, cheaper, faster, and always with the right Christian attitude.

My church wants me to be available—faithful in attendance, always willing to serve, spending time on committees, boards, teaching, etc.

Barbara wants me to help with redecorating and remodeling, move furniture, and keep things repaired.

I'm needed to be an understanding father who is a spiritual guide to the family.

I'm expected to spend time and play with the kids, impart values to them, know their friends, and what their parents stand for, be involved at their school, and prepare them for adolescence. And I need a savings plan for their college education.

And then there are our parents, who tell us we're living too busy, too fast, too much in debt with too little in savings. They want us to call and write more often.

Oh, yes, and there is community involvement—invitations and pleas to do more to help the poor, the PTA, civic clubs, and local political parties. And I need to be an informed voter.

Pressure from a list like that can easily isolate Barbara and me from one another. I get pulled one way and she goes another, our lives only touching at points. There is little time or energy for any in-depth relating. We find ourselves reverting to quick clichés like, "How are you doing?" or "Did you have a good day?" Privately, pressure can pry us apart, while creating a mirage of the successful family that is "doing it all!"

PRESSURE CAN BE GOOD OR BAD

Hans Selye, the leading pioneer in the study and treatment of stress, points out that in itself stress is neither good nor bad. It depends on what it's doing to your system.[3] All of us need some stress in order to conduct daily activities. The only people who lack stress are dead.

Selye calls good stress "eustress," and bad stress "distress." Distress occurs when the stressors—the pressures of life—cause stress overload which preys on our weakness and vulnerability. More stressors pile on top of the ones we already are facing and we soon have more overload, more weakness, and still more vulnerability.

Eustress occurs when stressors are seen as opportunities. Instead of a stress overload you have a growth-enhancing reaction. This leads to strength and the ability to resist, and the next time stressors come you are able to continue the positive cycle of growth and strength.[4]

Barbara and I are finding that we need to deal with stress in a way that turns it into opportunities to build oneness, not sources of distress and isolation. It's an ongoing process, because every year the incline seems to be getting steeper and the speed is picking up. That means we have to be smarter about how we handle life. We have found that isolation feeds off our schedules of being too busy, too pressured, and too stressed.

Making Life Manageable

J. Hudson Taylor, the great missionary who served in China for so many years, said this about pressure: "It matters not how great the pressure is, only where the pressure lies. As long as the pressure does not come between me and my Savior, but presses me to Him, then the greater the pressure, the greater my dependence upon Him."

Those words give me the scales I need to balance the pressures of life. As long as our schedule draws us closer to Christ, the stress is eustress (good). If it starts to draw us away from our Lord, then it's distress (bad). There is no such thing as a pressure-free, stress-free life. Perhaps in heaven we'll feel no pressure and be stress free—experiencing only total peace, total contentment. But here and now we have responsibilities, and responsibilities equal pressure and stress.

Because Barbara and I have a large family by today's standards and give leadership to a growing ministry, people often ask us, "How do you do it all?" The answer is simple: We don't. Part of the "all" we never get around to is our social life. We don't go out that often with other people, and don't have that many guests.

This particular season of our marriage finds us with a growing ministry to maintain and a family that needs constant nurture, care, and supervision. To try to do any more than that would lead us straight to burnout. The stress could literally fracture and shatter our family.

Install Your Own Stress Alarm System

One of the tallest skyscrapers in New England is the John Hancock Building, which stands near the famous Freedom Trail in Boston. When this structure of over forty floors was built, there were all kinds of problems with the windows. During the stress of the freezing and thawing of the New England winter, the windows actually popped out of their frames and shattered. People walking on the sidewalk below were showered with glass and businessmen working at their desks suddenly found themselves seated a few inches from nothing, staring straight down at the street.

The architects and contractors got together and finally decided to install a small alarm system in each window. When the windows began to bulge and contract, the alarm system would let maintenance people know, so they could make adjustments that would take tension off the glass before it completely blew out and shattered.

I believe every marriage needs an alarm system that can help the partners take off the tension before something shatters. One of the best alarm systems I know of is to *become accountable to each other.*

Accountability is a scriptural principle that tells us to ". . . submit to one another out of reverence for Christ" (Ephesians 5:21). This means I choose to submit my life to the scrutiny of another person to gain spiritual strength, growth, and balance. Marriage is a perfect arena for this to happen as husbands become accountable to wives and wives to husbands.

Some couples challenge me on this subject, saying that becoming accountable to one another would be like playing policeman, but I explain exactly the opposite is true.

Accountability gives each marriage partner freedom and access to the other. Accountability means asking the other person for advice. It means giving the other person the freedom to make honest observations and evaluations about you. It means we're teachable and approachable. We both need to be accountable to the other because each partner is fallible and quite capable of using faulty judgment—each of us has blind spots.

WHY ACCOUNTABILITY IS HARD FOR MEN

While speaking to men at our FamilyLife Conferences, I often ask: "Are you accountable to anyone? Are you accountable to your wife? Does she have *access* to your life?"

Over the years I have continued to see a number of men and women in the ministry "bomb out" due to sexual sin, materialism, or bitterness. As I read and heard about these Christians, I noticed a recurring pattern: They were all isolated. They had created for themselves walls of unapproachable invulnerability. No one had access to their lives.

For whatever reason, they refused to submit their lives to the scrutiny and advice of others and thereby forfeited the opportunity to be held accountable. Now they have forfeited, for the most part, the privilege of public ministry in others' lives.

As a result, I purposed to lead a lifestyle of accountability. I certainly have much to learn on the subject, but I have resolved to be teachable, approachable, and most importantly, willing to hear what Barbara wants to say to me. The apostle Paul's words have spurred me on: "I run the race then with determination. I am no shadow-boxer, I really fight! I am my body's sternest master, for fear that when I have preached to others I should myself be disqualified" (1 Corinthians 9:26–27 PHILLIPS).

True accountability involves letting another person into the interior of your life. You have the choice to submit to another human being for perspective, advice, or even to be taken to task on something. Solomon says a wise man welcomes a helpful rebuke (Proverbs 9:8). Each of us must choose to whom he or she can be accountable. In some cases it might be a good friend of the same sex.

I know of two men who hold each other accountable each month, asking themselves the tough questions about how they've spent their time in the past thirty days. And the last question is always, "Did you just lie to me?" In many cases, they have to admit to each other that they did fudge a little on the truth, then they discuss where they had slipped up and what they can do about it.

If you can find a friend to help you with accountability, it can make a real difference. But you already have one friend to whom you should automatically be accountable—your spouse. I would strongly encourage you to start with him or her.

ACCOUNTABILITY IN YOUR MARRIAGE

As you and your mate face continuing pressures and stress, it's best to handle life in duet, not solo. As the preacher said, "Two are better than one, because . . . if one falls down [or weakens], his friend can help him up" (Ecclesiastes 4:9–10). Two can always see more clearly than one. Your mate can detect blind spots that you are missing. Accountability promotes healthy oneness as you interact and depend on each other.

Here are some areas where Barbara and I practice accountability in our marriage:

1. Schedules. We try to help each other make good decisions by monitoring each other's workload and schedule. Making good decisions simply means saying yes to some things and no to others.

2. Raising children. Barbara and I also spend time talking over our children's schedules because what one child does affects the whole family. Monitoring everyone's schedule helps all of us not to get overextended.

We also find that we have different parenting styles because of our different backgrounds. As Barbara and I draw on the parenting styles our parents modeled for us, we notice the good and the bad tendencies in each other. By being accountable for our flaws, we complement one another and work out what we believe is the best parenting style possible for our own children.

3. Money and values. Barbara and I constantly compare and check our personal values. What is really important to each of us? Why are we doing what we are doing? What do we dare not lose?

You may have heard the story of the two thieves who broke into a department store. They didn't steal anything, but they spent hours switching the price tags on almost every item in the store. The next morning, the store opened and business went on as usual for four hours before anyone noticed. Customers were buying $500 cameras for $4.95, $1,200 outboard motors for $15.95!

This story sounds incredible, but it actually happened.[5] And in a way, the same thing is still happening today in Christian families. An enemy has broken in and switched our price tags. Many couples decide that pursuit of goals, plans, money, career advancement, and pleasure are all more valuable than building oneness in marriage and rock-solid relationships with their children. They say they value their families above everything else, but their actions reveal that their real priorities lie elsewhere.

4. Fidelity. Some years ago I led a Bible study that included several new Christians. During those studies, Barbara began to sense that one of the men was increasingly friendly toward her. At first she thought she was imagining things. She was embarrassed, so she kept it to herself. It seemed absurd to her that this happily married husband and father could be interested in her.

But as the weekly sessions went on, the man continued to be extra friendly and Barbara began to feel more and more uncomfortable. When she finally confided in me, I could see unmistakable relief spread across her face. What had been a secret she had been carrying alone quickly evaporated as we discussed her feelings together. Fortunately, Barbara's admirer never tried going beyond being friendly, and, when the Bible study ended, he went his own way.

Looking back on that incident, we see that it was a test for both of us regarding accountability. Would Barbara tell me what she thought was happening? Would I respond in jealous anger and suspicion, or with understanding and acceptance? Fortunately, both of us did the right thing and it reaffirmed our commitment to one another as we stood together against a potential threat to our marriage.

GET AWAY AND MAKE THE BEST CHOICES TOGETHER

One reason for so much stress and pressure today is that we want too many of the good choices. But the Christian couple should want only God's *best* choices. To make these best choices, you need to be controlled by His Spirit and not the spirit of the age in which you live.

I often ask myself, *Who is controlling you, Dennis? Is it your job, your neighbors, your friends, your children? Or is God controlling you with your full permission?*

Solomon was right: "Like a city whose walls are broken down is a man who lacks self-control" (Proverbs 25:28). I know that if God isn't in control, my lines of defense will be down. People, schedules, and other forces will break in and control me and my family. It is just too easy to be driven by the needs and demands of others and not be led by the Holy Spirit (see Chapter 11).

It's one thing to vow not to take on too much and let pressures get out of hand. But it's another to keep life in control. I have discovered the only

consistently dependable method is to be dependent upon God and accountable first to Him, next to my mate, and then perhaps a close friend.
Otherwise, life will continually jerk me right off the ground and leave me
dangling helplessly in midair.

BEYOND THE THREATS TO ONENESS

If you have been faithfully working through the HomeBuilders
Projects at the end of each chapter, you and your mate have already begun
the process of accountability. As you analyze each of the seven threats to
oneness I have detailed in the last few chapters you should be able to pin-
point specific areas in which your relationship is affected by the types of
pressures that lead to isolation.

In Part Three of this book I'll cover the most important information of
all: God's purpose, plan, and power for marriage. The next three chapters
cover the absolute bedrock foundation of oneness in marriage. Without
these three elements, the Christian couple is fighting a futile war with isolation. Read them carefully.

HOMEBUILDERS PROJECTS

To Think About Individually

1. Take a good look at your schedule. Where are the pressures coming from? At what points are you choosing to put pressure on yourself because of your own expectations or the expectations of others? At what points are the pressures caused by forces out of your control?

2. List your top five values—the beliefs and practices you feel are most important in life. Do any of these values cause pressure and stress?

3. Pray about how accountable you are—first to God and then to your mate. How accountable are you willing to be?

For Interaction Together

1. Share with each other about what is causing pressure in your lives. Discuss what can be eliminated and what must be kept. Categorize the things you can change and control and the things that you can't. Ask yourselves, "Where must we say yes and where can we say no?"

2. Share your list of the top five values—the things you feel are most important. Where do your values differ? On which ones can you agree? Then compare your schedules and talk about how your schedules can help you accomplish the values that you both agree are most important to your marriage.

3. List decisions that need to be made—by both of you or by either one of you. Remember, sometimes pressure is caused by procrastination. Prioritize the decisions that need to be made, then make them and move on. It's better to make a decision, right or wrong, than to let pressure continue to wear one or both of you down.

4. Pray together often and ask wisdom from God for how to handle pressure (see James 1:5-6).

PART
THREE

··

The Plan, the Purpose,
the Power

··

HOMEBUILDERS
PRINCIPLES

As we fulfill God's purposes for marriage,
we defeat isolation and experience intimacy
through true oneness.

11

GOD'S PURPOSES
FOR ONENESS

A great purpose leads to a great marriage.
—AUTHOR UNKNOWN

Here's an interesting question: Why did you get married? For sex? For romance? For companionship? For security? To have children?

There are good reasons for marriage, and there are childish ones. The following comments, all by boys and girls ten years old and under, reveal their humorous perceptions of marriage.

Gwen, age nine: "When I get married I want to marry someone who is tall and handsome and rich and hates spinach as much as me."

Arnold, age six: "I want to get married, but not right away yet because I can't cross the street by myself yet."

Steve, age ten: "I want to marry somebody just like my mother except I hope she don't make me clean up my room."

Bobby, age nine: "First she has to like pizza, then she has to like cheesecake, after that she has to like fudge candy, then I know our marriage will last forever."[1]

We chuckle at these childish impressions, yet I have counseled couples whose purpose for getting married wasn't much more profound. Seneca, the Roman philosopher, wrote, "You must know for which harbor you are headed if you are to catch the right wind to take you there."

One problem in so many marriages today is that partners have so many and varied purposes for getting married. The result is that husband and wife sign on for a lifetime voyage, but set sail for different harbors. It's no wonder that eventually they end up in different ports, their ships in two pieces—isolated and alone.

WHAT ARE GOD'S PURPOSES FOR MARRIAGE?

What many couples lack are God's blueprints for marriage—a plan that leads to oneness. You can read dozens of books about what man thinks, but since God created marriage we should find out what He has to say. What were His original purposes, plans, and intentions for marriage? I want to examine the foundational basis: God's purposes for marriage. They include:

> to mirror God's image
>
> to multiply a godly heritage
>
> to manage God's realm
>
> to mutually complete one another
>
> to model Christ's relationship to the church

What these five purposes bring to a marriage are a sense of direction, internal stability, and the stamp of God's design.

PURPOSE ONE: MIRROR GOD'S IMAGE

The place to discover this blueprint is in the Bible, beginning in the book of Genesis. After creating the earth and the animals, God said, "Let us make man in our image, in our likeness, and let them rule over the fish of the sea and the birds of the air, over the livestock, over all the earth, and over all the creatures that move along the ground" (Genesis 1:26). And the account goes on to say, "So God created man in his own image, in the image of God he created him; male and female he created them" (Genesis 1:27).

God's first purpose for creating man and woman and joining them in marriage was to mirror His image on planet earth. Center your attention on those words, *mirror His image.* To "mirror His image" means to reflect God, to magnify, exalt, and glorify Him. We are to be God's representatives to a world that desperately needs to see who He is.

Hanging in my mother's bedroom is a photograph of the Grand Teton Mountains. I gave her that eight-by-ten enlargement after photographing the Tetons from the edge of Jenny Lake. Anyone who has been to the Jackson Hole area of Wyoming knows that when the waters of Jenny Lake are still, you can see these snow-capped peaks mirrored on the surface.

The morning I took that picture, Jenny Lake was like a mirror. If you take the photo and turn it upside down you can't tell which is the reflection and which is the real mountains. Jenny Lake perfectly reflects those mountains and their grandeur.

Because we're created in the image of God, people who wouldn't otherwise know what God is like should be able to look at us and get a glimpse. For example, we're never more like God than when we love one another or forgive one another.

But what happens if you toss a stone into that perfect reflection? My good friend and colleague, Dave Sunde, one of the founders of Family Ministry, told me he had also visited Jenny Lake on that same kind of clear, still day. Dave watched a small boy skip a small rock across the placid water, and immediately the perfect reflection of the mountains was distorted. The mountains did not change, but the image did.

A stone breaking a perfectly still reflecting surface is a picture of what happens when we go our own way and decide, *I'll do it myself.* The shattered image illustrates sin, a word that is not popular and understood today. Sin, which is going my own way, distorts the image of God in our lives and in our marriages. And when sin is tolerated, as stones that break the water's surface repeatedly, God's reflection is marred in the life of a Christian.

How often have you heard a comment like the following from a non-Christian? "All the Christians I know are hypocrites! They act pious on Sunday and they lie and cheat like anyone else the rest of the week." Or how about this one: "I visited a church last Sunday and not one person even spoke to me"? These observations reveal that a non-Christian has embedded expectations of the way a Christian should behave. They know that a Christian should be a reflector of God's image.

Note also that Genesis says God made two distinctly different humans—male and female—so that together they would mirror His image. In recent years we have seen a distortion of male and female. God made two distinct sexes, but there have been many efforts in recent decades to "homogenize" them.

What better strategy is there for Satan to use than to distort God's image on this planet by trying to get men to be unsure what a man is and to get women to be uncertain of what a woman is? But the Bible clearly outlines the responsibilities of the man and the woman. Together, as husband and wife, they mirror God's image.

Robert Lewis, author of the HomeBuilder's Couples Study, *Building Teamwork in Marriage,* notes: "Today we are being led to believe that men and women are interchangeable units with only a few apparent physical differences." Back in the 1970s, this point of view gained a real hearing, but in recent years even secular experts are now admitting how incorrect this idea is.[2] In Part Four we will look more closely at the different responsibilities God has given to men and women.

PURPOSE TWO: MULTIPLY A GODLY HERITAGE

One of the best ways to mirror God's image is through a line of godly descendants—our children—who will carry a reflection of His character to the next generation.

God's original plan called for the home to be a sort of greenhouse—a nurturing center where children grow up to learn character, values, and integrity. Psalm 78 instructs parents to teach their children to carry the message of who God is to the next generation, and through these lines of godly descendants, Satan's kingdom would be defeated.

Today, however, I observe one big problem with many Christian couples regarding childbearing and child rearing: They conform more to the world's standards than to God's. For example, many families comply with the popular slogan, "Two and no more." And many other couples opt for no children at all, even though they are perfectly capable of conceiving. There is a certain irony in this when you realize that one in seven couples struggle with infertility—"The inability to conceive a child or to carry a child to a live birth after one or more years of normal sexual relations."[3]

I'm not advocating that all families be large, nor is it wrong for a family to be small. But I do believe Christians are becoming unduly worried about "overpopulating the world." The world needs Christians to produce godly offspring. If Christians don't replicate a godly heritage and a legacy to carry biblical values and Scripture's truth to the next generation, others will.

Some people will say, "Well, we have to be careful. We might not be able to feed our children if we have too many." In some rare cases this may be true, but in most others it hides a different motivation. Having more children means having more responsibility and less time, money, and energy for self.

One thing our family has taught Barbara and me is that the more children you have, the less selfish you can be. I see a little bit more of my selfish side dying every day, and usually I don't like it. We have determined that we can't raise six children (and do it well) and be selfish simultaneously. We've tried!

As you plan your families, be very careful to get your orders from God and not from the world—the secular system in which we live.

Another problem I observe today in many couples is that they are not raising their children with a sense of mission and direction. They aren't imparting to them the importance of leaving a legacy of changed lives. They aren't evaluating their lives in light of the Great Commission of Matthew 28:18–20, where Christ commands us to preach the gospel to all nations.

Most parents do have some type of plan for their children; the problem is it doesn't go far enough. Usually parents plan what type of education they want their children to receive, what activities they would like to encourage, and what type of person they would like them to marry. But on the spiritual side, their plan usually doesn't go much further than making sure their children live a good life, go to church, and receive Christ.

Many Christians seldom think of encouraging their children to become missionaries or of showing them how to seek God to discover His plan for their lives. If our children do not gain a sense of "mission" as they grow up, they may slide into the pews as adults to live their entire lives without experiencing the privilege of God using them in a significant way.

PURPOSE THREE: MANAGE GOD'S CREATION

As He outlined the purposes for marriage in that first chapter of Genesis, God also commanded the man and the woman He created to "fill the earth and subdue it" (Genesis 1:28). Man is to rule over the animal kingdom as well as the plants he has been given for food and sustenance.

While ruling over his home isn't directly mentioned in the Genesis text, the implication is there. How can we rule over the fish of the sea, the birds of the air, and the beasts of the field if we can't control our own families? Again, we see oneness as a prime requisite for carrying out God's purpose of managing His realm. Husband and wife can't manage together unless they are unified in their marriage and cooperating in their responsibilities.

In our home, Barbara and I work hard at supporting one another. For example, on the practical front of discipline, we try to be careful that none of our children drives any wedges between us. When we do have disagreements about discipline, we try to resolve our differences in private, out of our kids' hearing.

And we spend lots of time interacting about the new phases the children go through. How do we prepare them for adolescence? Are we united in teaching values? We want to create character, not characters.

No, we don't do this perfectly. At times we struggle; but we always manage to agree on our main goals and purposes. The last thing we want is disagreement about where we are taking our kids. That would not only be deadly for a spirit of oneness between us, but it would be detrimental for our children. They wouldn't know who to follow—or which way to go.

No matter how many children God gives you, it's important to operate jointly in parenting. Again and again, I see families where the woman is expected to raise the kids. Contrary to male expectations, women are not made physically, emotionally, or spiritually to rear children by themselves.

At least once a year Barbara and I get away together for a "planning weekend" where we evaluate our parenting plans and directions. We talk about the character of each child, his or her unique gifts or problems, his or her direction in life, and each child's specific needs.

We talk about overall approaches to all the kids which we need to make together and a specific game plan for individual children in discipline, daily chores and routines, and interpersonal relationships. We've found that being united allows us to speak with one voice to them.

I truly believe that a man's greatest challenge is to come alongside his wife and run the three-legged race of marriage and parenting in perfect lock step, with a unified direction and oneness of mind and spirit.

There is a lot of discussion today about what it means for a man to be "head of the home" and "head of his wife." As we will see in Part Four, it doesn't mean that the man is to be lord and master of his manor, demanding his wife and children wait on him. I believe Scripture teaches the husband to be the servant-leader of his home, giving direction, support, and love.

PURPOSE FOUR: COMPLETE EACH OTHER

Scripture clearly outlines a fourth purpose for marriage: to mutually complete each other. That's why God said, "It is not good for the man to be alone. I will make a helper suitable for him" (Genesis 2:18).

Adam was in his own state of isolation in the Garden and so God created woman to eliminate his aloneness. Writing to the first-century church in Corinth, Paul echoes the teachings in Genesis 2 when he writes: "In the Lord, however, woman is not independent of man, nor is man independent of woman" (1 Corinthians 11:11). We really do need each other. As William Barclay's translation puts it: ". . . in the Lord, woman is nothing without man nor man without woman . . ."

Perhaps you saw the original *Rocky* film before Sylvester Stallone started spinning off sequels left and right. Do you remember the love relationship Rocky had with Adrian in *Rocky?* She was the little wallflower who worked in the pet shop; she was the sister of Pauly, an insensitive goon who worked at the meat house and wanted to become a collector of debts for a loan shark. Pauly couldn't understand why Rocky was attracted to Adrian. "I don't see it," he said. "What's the attraction?"

Do you remember Rocky's answer? I doubt that scriptwriter had any idea what they were saying, but they perfectly exemplified the principle for a suitable helper from Genesis 2. Rocky said, "I don't know—fills gaps, I guess."

"What's gaps?"

"She's got gaps, I got gaps. Together we fill gaps."

In his simple but profound way, Rocky hit upon a great truth. He was saying that without him, Adrian had empty places in her life and without her, he had empty places in his. But when the two of them got together they filled those blank spots in one another. And that's exactly what God did when He fashioned a helpmate suitable for Adam. She filled his empty places and he filled hers.

There's never been any doubt in my mind that I need Barbara, that she fills my "gaps." I need her because she tells me the truth about myself, the good, the bad, and the otherwise. I need Barbara to add a different perspective of life, relationships, and people. She also adds variety and spice to my life. She's encouraged me, for instance, to read more, and now I actually enjoy it.

PURPOSE FIVE: MODEL CHRIST'S MYSTERY OF LOVE

In his letter to the Ephesians, Paul draws a lovely picture that compares marriage to Christ's relationship to His bride, the Church. He writes:

> Husbands, love your wives, just as Christ loved the church and gave
> himself up for her to make her holy, cleansing her by the washing with
> water through the word, and to present her to himself as a radiant

church, without stain or wrinkle or any other blemish, but holy and blameless. In this same way, husbands ought to love their wives as their own bodies. He who loves his wife loves himself. After all, no one ever hated his own body, but he feeds and cares for it, just as Christ does the church—for we are members of his body. For this reason a man will leave his father and mother and be united to his wife, and the two will become one flesh. This is a profound mystery—but I am talking about Christ and the church. However, each one of you also must love his wife as he loves himself, and the wife must respect her husband. (Ephesians 5:25–33)

Marriage of a man and a woman is a picture or model of something that is far greater—the marriage of Christ and His bride, the church. As Barbara and I (and you and your spouse) are one, unified together, we are living out what Paul calls "a mystery."

When I was a young boy, I once saw a miniature replica of a Viking ship. It was intricately designed, displayed in a store window to show the finished model for sale in a boxed kit. That model showed me what a Viking ship looked like; otherwise I would have been left to my imagination to picture it.

The relationship of Christ to His church is, somehow, mysteriously modeled by a husband and his wife leading, loving, serving, and submitting to one another, as Paul described in Ephesians 5:25: "Husbands, love your wives, just as Christ loved the church and gave himself up for her." By loving and serving your spouse, you model the type of love Christ displayed in His life and death.

KNOW WHO THE ENEMY IS

Your marriage is far more important than you may have ever imagined. Did you realize that your marriage affects God's reputation on this planet? As someone said, "You cannot kill time without injuring eternity." In the same way, you can't have a mediocre marriage without poorly reflecting on God's character.

IF YOUR MATE IS UNRESPONSIVE TO GOD AND HIS PURPOSES

- Live a life that is "salty" before him or her (see Matthew 5:13). The salty life is so vibrant and alive with hope in Christ that it makes the unbelieving mate spiritually thirsty.

- Don't continue to nag or argue with your mate. Instead, prayerfully consider writing him or her a love letter, expressing your love and affirmation.

- Pray that God will bring your mate to repentance.

- In severe cases, when a mate is extremely adversarial or hostile, an "intervention" may be necessary (see Dr. James Dobson, *Love Must Be Tough*, Word Books, 1996).

- Find a "soul partner" of the same sex to meet some of the needs your mate may be incapable of meeting in his or her unresponsive state.

- Pray that God will use you, or bring significant others into your mate's life to give witness of His love and grace. All things are possible.

A lot of jokes picture marriage as a battlefield. I recall a quote from a magazine that advised: "Marriage is the only war where you sleep with the enemy."

I would rather picture the entire world as the true battlefield and your marriage as being God's smallest battle formation for winning the war. In truth, your marriage is taking place on a spiritual battlefield, not a romantic balcony.

Picture your marriage as two people joined together in a foxhole, cooperating in battle against a common enemy. Take a good look at your own foxhole. Are you fighting the enemy or each other? As a friend of ours told me, "I was so busy standing up in the foxhole duking it out with my husband that I had no time to be involved in fighting against the real enemy."

Keep in mind that opposition to your mate is actually opposition to the very purposes of God. Whenever you oppose your mate, ultimately you are opposing God Himself.

Why did you get married? And where will you go from here? Whose purposes will you fulfill? The purposes we have looked at in this chapter are God-designed, and because God created marriage, He has a plan to make it work. That plan is outlined in the next chapter.

HOMEBUILDERS PROJECTS

TO THINK ABOUT INDIVIDUALLY

1. How are you and your spouse doing in regard to fulfilling God's purposes for marriage? Go through all five purposes below and give your own ranking on a scale of 1 to 5.

   (1 = weak, 2 = fair, 3 = improving, 4 = strong, 5 = excellent.)

   God's Purposes for Marriage   How I Think We're Doing

   To mirror God's image

   To multiply a godly heritage

   To manage God's realm

   To mutually complete one another

   To model Christ's relationship to the Church

FOR INTERACTION TOGETHER

1. Talk together about God's five purposes for marriage and the rankings each of you made. Take a look at where you differ or have both ranked your marriage low. How can you strengthen your marriage in these areas during the coming year? Also look at areas where you both ranked yourselves high. Congratulate each other and talk about how you can keep these areas strong.

2. Decide on a plan of action to improve in the areas which are lacking. Write down the steps you plan to take. Make yourselves accountable to each other to carry it out.

HOMEBUILDERS
PRINCIPLES

When we yield to God and build together, from His blueprints, we begin the process of experiencing oneness.

The basis for my acceptance of my mate is faith in God's character and trustworthiness.

12

THE MASTER PLAN
FOR ONENESS

If God is your partner, make your plans large.
—Author Unknown

Last fall I divided my sixth-grade Sunday school class into three groups for an interesting contest. As my twelve-year-olds gathered in three circles on the floor, I explained that there was only one rule in our competition: Each group had to put together a thousand-piece jigsaw puzzle *without talking.*

I poured the contents of the puzzles on the floor in front of each group, warning them again that they could not talk. The first group went immediately to work, promptly setting up the top to the puzzle box, which gave everyone a clear view of the picture they were trying to put together.

The second group tried to do the same thing, but they didn't know that I had switched the top of their puzzle box with the top from *another puzzle.* I had deliberately given them the wrong lid. Not knowing that, they set up their box top to use as a guide to assemble their puzzle and went swiftly to work.

As the third group gathered around the pile of pieces I had poured on the floor, the kids were dismayed to discover that I had given them no box top whatsoever to use as a guide. They started to protest, but I reminded them there was to be *no talking!*

What followed was fascinating.

The members of Group One were somewhat frustrated by not being allowed to talk, but they still made steady progress because they had a correct picture or plan to work from. Everyone in that group got motivated as the outline of the picture started to emerge.

It didn't take the members of Group Two long to realize something was wrong. They kept trying to use the box top picture in front of them, but nothing seemed to work. And since they couldn't talk together, their frustration level soared.

One boy waved his hand in the air and acted as though he was about to burst. I relented and allowed him to whisper in my ear, "Mr. Rainey," he muttered, "you gave us the wrong picture. It's the wrong lid—it's just not there!"

I smiled, patted him on the shoulder, and said, "Shhh, no talking."

As I turned away, others in his group looked at me with pleading eyes, wondering what they could do. Their puzzle just wasn't coming together.

But Group Three really captured my attention. Because the group had no picture at all to go by, each kid was doing his own thing. There wasn't even an attempt at teamwork and, of course, there was no progress.

Some members just sat individually, randomly searching for two pieces that seemed to fit. Two of the boys were so bored they started launching puzzle pieces like miniature Frisbees across the room. Others just lay there with their eyes closed. Hopelessness hung in the air.

After letting them work a little longer, I called a halt to the competition and explained what was going on and then I made my point:

YOU CAN'T LIVE LIFE WITHOUT A PLAN

While I used my puzzle illustration with sixth graders, the same truth is even more applicable for couples who are building a home together. Whether it's life or marriage or a family—something is needed to help us bring order out of chaos. We need a plan if we are to fit our lives, marriages, and families together in a purposeful design.

IT TAKES MORE THAN BEING SINCERE

I often meet Christian couples who have problems because they make a common mistake: As sincere Christians they believe they are automatically living their lives according to the correct plan. The trouble with that naïve reasoning is that there are a lot of competing blueprints and pictures vying for their commitment.

Unfortunately, many Christian couples never stop to evaluate the picture of life they are trying to assemble. Many give in to the temptation just to increase the speed at which they jam the pieces of life together. They rush through life—getting married, rearing children, and assembling what they believe is a "picture of success," only to find at the end that the model they were building from was flawed. They had worked with a counterfeit instead of the real thing.

Other couples measure success in life by the size of their puzzle—that is, the number of pieces they can put together. They sacrifice order and quality for quantity, and the result is discord, disarray, loneliness—and isolation. Their picture never quite looks or feels right.

It's all too obvious that many marriages are being put together with no box top at all—or the wrong one. When this happens the result is always the same: the couple has used the world's plan for marriage—the 50/50 Plan—which always falls short. Statistics show over 91 percent of all single people get married, and every one of them is headed for one of two fates: isolation or oneness and real intimacy. Without a scriptural plan for marriage, they are surely destined for isolation.

God's blueprint includes two steps—reception and construction. You need both to build a marriage that is a godly stronghold of oneness. To find His plan we go to His blueprint—the Scriptures—particularly Genesis 2.

STEP ONE: RECEIVE YOUR MATE

As we revisit the Garden of Eden, we watch the drama unfold. God makes Adam, but then says, "It is not good for the man to be alone: I will make a helper suitable for him" (Genesis 2:18). To paraphrase this passage,

"I have chosen, according to My infinite wisdom, to make Adam incomplete, but now I will do something about that."

Adam may wonder what God means. After all, he has the perfect boss, a perfect job, even perfect retirement benefits. But he needs something—more precisely—some*one* else. Adam needs a helper, specifically made for him.

In the original text, the Hebrew word for *helper* means "wholeness." Here again is another picture of oneness. Adam needed someone who could make him complete, whole.

As the drama continues, God causes a deep sleep to fall upon Adam. He takes one of his ribs and fashions it into the woman. It's interesting to note that when God made Adam, the Genesis account tells us that he fashioned him from dust. But when He decided to make Eve, He used the same stuff of which the man was made. Man was flesh and blood and woman was taken from him. There is a picture of healing or completeness here, and I believe it's also a picture of oneness because man and woman are made from the same material.

How Did Eve Look to Adam? After making Eve, God presents her to Adam. He doesn't send her, tell Adam to come pick her up, or have Adam find her under a Christmas tree all wrapped up. Instead, God personally brings her to the man (Genesis 2:22).

Picture the scene. If Adam and Eve were getting married, the pastor would say, "Who gives this woman to this man?" And God would answer, "I do." The Lord God, Creator of heaven and earth and all that is in them, was intimately involved in the first wedding in history.

But now we have an all-important question: How would Adam receive Eve? He had been busy naming the animals, but had not found a helper suitable for himself. And he had never seen an "Eve" before. How would he respond? The way many read the familiar Genesis account, Adam's response was rather ho-hum: "This is now bone of my bones and flesh of my flesh; she shall be called 'woman,' for she was taken out of man" (Genesis 2:23).

But let's keep our little melodrama going and assume we are hearing the Genesis account for the first time. The *Living Bible* paraphrase comes closest to capturing the real spirit of Adam's response: "This is it!" Another way to interpret the Hebrew here is, "Wow! Where have you been all my life?" In other words, Adam was excited—he was beside himself!

Now, obviously, Eve looked pretty good to Adam. That's why he said, "This is bone of my bone and flesh of my flesh." She definitely looked better to him than all the animals he had just named, but there is something more here we don't want to miss. It is a cornerstone principle for marriage: *Adam had faith in God's integrity.*

Eve had done nothing to earn Adam's response. He simply accepted her because God made her for him and Adam trusted totally in Him.

Today marriages are insecure and crumbling because the woman hooked the man with her looks and he got her with his physique, charm, or ability to earn money. But what happens when the beauty fades? What happens when the husband falls ill, loses his job, or grows old?

I'm glad I do not fear the future with Barbara. I made a commitment to her, and it was based on more than how she looked and talked. I received her and accepted her on the basis that God brought her into my life—she fills my gaps.

To reject your mate is to reflect negatively on the character of God. It's like saying, "God, You slipped up. You didn't know what You were doing when You provided this person for me." Rejection of one's mate for weakness, or any other reason, is disobedience toward God and failure to fulfill His plan and purpose for your life.

STEP TWO: CONSTRUCT YOUR HOME

The second part of God's plan for marriage involves construction. You may be noticing a parallel to the Christian life in these blueprints for marriage. First, you receive (accept) Christ, then you build a lifetime of obedient discipleship. After receiving your mate as God's gift, you build a lifetime of obedience as husband and wife.

As the melodrama of God's presentation of Eve to Adam comes to a close, the script says, "For this reason a man will leave his father and mother and be united to his wife, and they will become one flesh" (Genesis 2:24).

This passage presents five guidelines for building a strong and godly marriage. This is not a multiple choice list; all five are required for success.

1. Leave. You must establish independence from the parents or any others who may have reared you. It's amazing how many people have failed to do this. They may look very adult and act very mature and sophisticated but, deep down inside, they've never really cut the apron strings.

The Hebrew word for *leave* literally means "forsake dependence on," and that's the problem. Many people get married, but they have not stopped depending on their parents. There are all kinds of symptoms: accepting money on a regular basis, going to parents for emotional support rather than to one's mate, running home if there is a problem. Dependence on parents undermines the interdependence you are to build as husband and wife.

There is also a hidden command in this passage to parents. We should let our children leave. A manipulative parent can undermine a marriage whether it's ten days or ten years old. We are to let go of our children and relinquish any "control" of their lives.

2. Cleave. Form a permanent bond. To cleave means making a commitment. Unfortunately, commitment is the missing ingredient in many marriages. My friend and FamilyLife Conference speaker, Mike Yoder, says, "Today, it's almost easier to get out of marriage than it is to get out of the Book of the Month Club."

Recently, in Dallas, ninety marriages were dissolved at one time as a judge cleared his congested calendar with one swift blow of his gavel. But in God's original plan, there were to be no escape hatches, no bail out clauses in the contract. When God joins two people together, it's for keeps.

3. Be physically intimate. That means to become one flesh in sexual intercourse. Notice the progression—leave, cleave, and then become one flesh. Physical intimacy comes *after* the walls of commitment have totally surrounded and secured the relationship.

Many people come to marriage thinking they know all about sex; but they know little or nothing about establishing meaningful physical intimacy that communicates love and caring. They may understand the plumbing, but they have no clue about building a real home bound together with true oneness.

4. *Become transparent.* Work at being emotionally intimate, totally open, and unashamed with your mate. The Genesis account says Adam and Eve were ". . . both naked, and they felt no shame" (Genesis 2:25). They felt no fear or rejection. Instead they felt totally accepted by each other. Being bathed in the warmth of knowing another person accepts you is what makes marriage a delight.

Barbara knows I accept and love her, just as she accepts and loves me. This enables both of us to be transparent, to be ourselves with one another. There is real freedom and fulfillment in knowing that it is okay to be just who you are and nothing else. No games, no masks, no veneer—only security, safety, and healing.

5. *Fulfill your responsibilities.* The final part of God's plan calls for fulfilling your responsibilities. The discussion of "roles" in marriage has produced a lot of heat and very little light. I believe we have been deceived into making some incorrect assumptions about what God intended.

The dictionary says a *role* is "the part played by an actor." That's where we are confused. In marriage, you don't have to become someone you are not by playing a role or part. According to the Bible, husbands and wives have clear responsibilities; and when they fulfill those responsibilities it allows the pieces of the puzzle to fall together.

Later in the book, in Part Four, we will take a much closer look at the responsibilities of husbands and wives and see how God's plan can result in the intimate partnership couples desire. God never forces a couple to be one in heart, mind, soul, and body, but He has spelled out the way to achieve it.

ARE YOU USING THE RIGHT TOP TO THE PUZZLE?

As my experiment with my Sunday school class proved, having the wrong box top for a jigsaw puzzle (or no box top at all) leads only to frustration. Teamwork is hardly possible when you are working against each other. The application to your marriage situation is simple: The reason so many marriages fail is that the husband is putting his part of the marriage puzzle together with his box top and his wife is doing her part of the puzzle with a different box top. You need to be certain that both of you are working from the right blueprint.

To bring it all down to a practical everyday level, work on a few pieces of your puzzle at a time. Trying to complete too much of the picture at once may cause you to be burned out, strung out, or wrung out. As a lot of puzzle fans do, start with the borders of your life, the parameters, the limits and priorities. Once you have those established, begin filling in the rest of the puzzle, a piece at a time. The more you start to see the picture emerge, the more hope and encouragement you have that you can get it done.

Never quit. God didn't give us His plan to discourage and defeat us. Working out any plan takes time. As Charles Haddon Spurgeon said, "By perseverance the snail reached the ark."

God also provides the power to put the puzzle together. This power is so important, so vital to building oneness in your marriage, that we will devote a separate chapter to what that power is and how you and your mate must use it to build your home.

HOMEBUILDERS PROJECTS

TO THINK ABOUT INDIVIDUALLY

1. Is there anything about your mate that you don't accept? Why? Are there areas in which you don't feel accepted by your mate? Why?

2. Are you building from God's five-step plan for marriage in Genesis 2:23? Rate yourself in each area, using the chart below.

GOD'S PLAN	MY RESPONSE	HOW THIS AFFECTS OUR MARRIAGE
	(Poor, Fair, or Excellent)	
Leave (become independent of parents)		
Cleave (make permanent commitment to mate)		
Be physically intimate		
Become transparent		
Play proper role		

FOR INTERACTION TOGETHER

1. Discuss your answers to questions 1 and 2 above. Question 1 can be sensitive, so pick a good time to talk, when you are both relaxed and not tired or irritable.

2. Compare your answers in question 2. Where have your responses to God been weak? How can you help each other improve?

3. To complete your interaction, work out together a statement of your acceptance of each other as God's perfect provision to meet your aloneness needs.

HOMEBUILDERS
PRINCIPLES

As two people *grow upward* in their relationship with God by walking in the Spirit, they grow together as one.

13

THE POWER FOR ONENESS

The Holy Spirit is God at work.
—DWIGHT L. MOODY

Why aren't more marriages successful? In the past few years there have been thousands of articles, books, films, videos, seminars, and workshops on marriage. Nonetheless, loneliness and isolation flourish while couples struggle to see intimacy and oneness maintained.

The problem is that believers who enter into marriage don't use all the resources and tools God makes available to build oneness in their homes. To describe this error, I often turn to an illustration used by Bill Bright, founder and president of Campus Crusade for Christ.

He tells of a man who saved his money carefully and faithfully and finally was able to travel overseas on a beautiful cruise ship. Because he was of modest means, it was all he could do to save just enough to buy his ticket. He decided to take along some cheese and crackers because he knew he didn't have enough money to eat in the fine dining rooms of the ship.

For several days he sat in his cabin watching the stewards go by, pushing carts full of luscious lobster dripping with butter, and plates full of prime rib with all the fresh vegetables, fruits, and other delicious foods one could ask for. Finally, he could stand it no longer.

As the steward went by, the man stepped out of his room, grabbed the steward's arm, and said, "Look, I'm hungry. I'll go to work as a steward. I'll do whatever I need to do, I'll scrub the deck, but I have to get some food. My cheese and crackers are getting stale and I've got to get something decent to eat."

The steward looked at him strangely and finally smiled and said, "But sir, don't you know? Your food comes with your ticket."

Many Christians live as this passenger on the cruise ship did. They are "cheese-and-cracker" believers. They eat hot dogs when they could be dining on steak with baked potatoes, sour cream, chives, and butter. Jesus clearly said that He came to give life more abundantly, and He meant it. If you and I are not experiencing that abundance, something is wrong—not with the Lord or His promises, but with us.

Whether you're single or married, there are three key ingredients for living a dynamic Christian life. However, these ingredients have even more significance when you apply them to the oneness you are trying to achieve as a married couple. I'll put these three key ingredients in the form of questions:

Are you and your spouse a part of the family of God?

Are both of you allowing Christ to control your entire lives?

Are both of you allowing the Holy Spirit to guide and empower your lives?

Read carefully, because what I'm about to say is the most important statement I make in this book: *Unless you can answer yes to all three questions, you will lack the power to build your home with the oneness God intends.* You'll find it impossible to follow all the practical advice I present, because you'll be attempting it in your own power. God provides the blueprint for marriage, and also gives us the power we need to follow that plan.

When I speak of your family, I essentially mean you and your spouse. God's ideal plan is that both partners in a marriage know Him personally, that they are first part of His family before they try to build a family of their own.

Back in the mid-1960s, Bill Bright developed a simple little way to understand what being in God's family means. He called these principles "The Four Spiritual Laws" and put them in tiny little booklets that have spread around the world to be used to lead literally thousands of people to a saving faith in Jesus Christ.

If you want to consider The Four Spiritual Laws in more detail, you can do so in the Appendix for this book. I am assuming, however, that most of you have already taken that first step of moving into God's family. This chapter is designed to speak to people who know Christ but who may not be experiencing Him to the fullest, especially within the bonds of marriage.

ARE YOU BOTH GIVING CHRIST CONTROL?

Perhaps the more basic question is why doesn't the average Christian allow Christ to be Lord? I know how cheese-and-cracker Christians feel, because I used to be one. For a long time, I treated Jesus Christ as a spare tire. When I had a "flat" (a crisis) I would pull Christ out of the trunk and run Him for a couple of days, maybe two or three hundred miles, whatever came first. But when the crisis was over, guess where Christ went? Back in the trunk.

Finally, I began to realize He was more than a spare tire, so I began treating Him as a hitchhiker. I let Him in the car with me, and I let Him ride part of the way. But I didn't expect Him to be a permanent passenger.

Then it dawned on me that if Jesus Christ is my Savior *and* Lord, He won't be satisfied with remaining a spare tire or a hitchhiker. He wants to drive the car!

I had no alternative but to give my total life to Him. At that point, Christianity changed from just being a fire insurance policy to the abundant life. I could not imagine trading what I now experience of Christ and Scripture for what I used to have.

But many Christian couples are treating Jesus Christ as a spare tire or hitchhiker, or even less. As Billy Graham has observed, most Christians today live in "self-imposed spiritual poverty."

Why? In essence, they just don't understand God. They think that if they give total control of their lives to God, He will punish them or send them into some kind of missionary service at the end of the earth.

Hampered by this basic misunderstanding of who God is and what He desires for His children, people fail to understand the Scriptures. They don't think the Bible has much for them today. After all, some might say it's an ancient book, full of thees and thous, but not much practical help.

DON'T LIVE WITH "INGROWN EYEBALLS"

Because many Christians fail to get into the Scriptures, they don't really experience God's forgiveness. They live with what I call "ingrown eyeballs," preoccupied with their own failures.

Others simply live in unbelief. They don't believe God's promises, one of which is that He gives you power to live the Christian life because you really can't do it yourself.

I had a good friend whose house burned down. As he and his family drove away from the smoldering ruins, he stopped for a moment to pray. He said, "Lord, as we drive to the Holiday Inn with nothing but the clothes on our backs and the car we are in, we remember You said You would give peace and joy in the midst of tribulation. So, right now, I'm going to claim that by faith. If there is anything to this Christian life, I need it to be true right now."

By the time they drove up to the Holiday Inn, they were all rejoicing and finding plenty of things to be thankful about. They chose to believe that God does care and is in control.

Here's an interesting question: If Jesus Christ walked out of your life right now, how would your life be different next week? If Jesus Christ is truly on the throne of your life, next week would be devastatingly different. You would be lonely, disoriented, confused, cut off from your Source of guidance, wisdom, and power. You would feel an incredible void or emptiness that Christ had filled before. But if you realize that your actions, thoughts, and words would be no different, you need to come to grips with the fact that Christ is not Lord of your life.

MAKING CHRIST THE LORD OF YOUR LIFE

Jesus Christ is already Lord of the universe, of course, but He waits patiently to have you make Him Lord of your own life through personal commitment. That means trusting Him in a way you may have never trusted Him before.

Years ago I went on a rock-climbing trip with several other Campus Crusade for Christ staff members. Our supervisor thought this mountain-climbing adventure would build leadership qualities and teamwork skills in all of us.

Because I hate heights, I was hoping I could learn leadership some other way! In fact, when I get anywhere above the fifth floor, I usually stand away from the window.

But no such luck. I wound up in the Sierras among the rock-domed peaks, along with several sadists called "trainers," and eleven other guys foolish enough to be "trainees." We spent the first day learning basic climbing techniques, and the next morning I was told we were going to rappel off the top of a cliff. I said, "Oh, really? Where is it?"

They said, "Right up there."

We were standing on the floor of a valley and I looked up fifteen hundred feet to a granite dome directly overhead.

"How are we getting up there?" I wanted to know.

"We're climbing," was the happy news. And so we started up. Some people scurried up like squirrels, but I resembled more of a sloth as I made my way skyward.

Finally, we all got to the top. I watched my eleven buddies go over the edge, hanging on to ropes to rappel 175 feet down to a granite ledge.

Rappelling is not that complicated, but there is one important principle. You back up to the edge of the cliff to the point where you can no longer stand on your feet; then you push off and *let the rope hold you.*

Several times I inspected where the rope was securely fastened to bolts sunk into the rock. There were four of those bolts, and I wanted to know: What were the bolts made of? How far did they go into the rock? How long had they been there and, above all, *would they hold me?*

My trainers assured me they had never "lost" anyone before. Besides, some guys a lot bigger and heavier than I had rappelled off this precipice with no problem. In fact, one guy had gone off in a wheelchair.

All these words of comfort did little to slow down the vibration of my knocking knees, but finally I began backing off the cliff. When I came to the point where I was totally horizontal, I looked back over my shoulder (something you're not supposed to do) and everything went kind of fuzzy. At that point the phrase "do or die" never seemed more relevant. I decided I had to go for it and I pushed off.

Somehow I made it to the ledge, 175 feet down. Did I become a confirmed rock climber and rappeller for life? No, I haven't done it since! But I did learn a lot about faith that day. I learned that you've got to believe the rope will hold you. *You have to trust yourself to the rope.*

Making Christ your Lord is exactly like rappelling down a cliff. You lean back and push off with a personal commitment to give Christ access to every area of your life. That means wanting 100 percent of God, not what one writer described as $3 worth:

> I would like to buy $3 worth of God, please. Not enough to explode
> my soul or disturb my sleep, but just enough to equal a cup of warm
> milk or a snooze in the sunshine . . . I want ecstasy, not transformation;
> I want the warmth of the womb, not a new birth. I want a pound of
> the Eternal in a paper sack. I would like to buy $3 worth of God,
> please.[1]

The Lord of heaven doesn't want to settle for being "$3 worth." He doesn't want to settle for being a spare tire or a hitchhiker. He finally chased me down and I'm glad He did. He loved me enough to make me realize He wanted to be my Lord, not just my Savior. I would not trade that commitment for anything. Once I had that settled, I could take the next important step: to allow God's Holy Spirit to guide and empower my life.

FILLED WITH THE SPIRIT

Most Christians agree that the Holy Spirit is the third Person of the Trinity. When I was a little boy growing up in a church that strictly used the King James Version, we referred to Him as the Holy Ghost. And for a long time I could only think of something that would be like Casper—floating through walls like a puff of smoke.

For years I referred to the Holy Ghost as an "It." But the Holy Ghost Jesus talks about is a Person. He was sent to glorify Christ as well as to be our counselor, advisor, advocate, defender, director, and guide. In short, if you are interested in living the abundant life Jesus promised, the Holy Spirit is vital.

Perhaps that's why being "filled with the Spirit" is not a suggestion; it is a clear command given by Paul in his letter to the Ephesians. He says, "Do not get drunk on wine, which leads to debauchey. Instead, be filled with the Spirit" (Ephesians 5:18).

Why would Paul put being drunk on wine in opposition to being filled with the Spirit? Because he wanted to help his readers understand what being filled means. When you are drunk on wine, you are controlled by alcohol. The same is true in a positive sense when you are filled with the Spirit. You are allowing the Spirit to control you.

The results of being filled with the Spirit are holiness and joy. Paul describes it as speaking ". . . to one another with psalms, hymns and spiritual songs. Sing and make music in your heart to the Lord, always giving thanks to God the Father for everything, in the name of our Lord Jesus Christ" (Ephesians 5:19–20).

We know the Holy Spirit works. What each of us needs in our own marriage is something to defeat our selfishness. On more than one occasion I can recall wanting to be angry at Barbara and yet at the same time facing the realization that my life is a temple of God, that the Holy Spirit lives in me with the same power that raised Christ from the dead. The Spirit helps me control my temper, impatience, and desire to say things I would later regret.

I still fail. But I have found as I inwardly yield my will to God, the fruit of the Spirit grows within me. Isn't it interesting that the deeds of the flesh listed in Galatians 5:19–21—immorality, impurity, strife, jealousy, drunkenness, etc.—produce isolation in marriage? But as we allow the Holy Spirit to control our lives, the fruits of the Spirit—love, joy, peace, patience, etc.—move us toward oneness.

The Holy Spirit fills marriages too. In Ephesians, Paul mentions one other result of being filled with the Spirit, and, as he does so, he moves into a discussion of family life—marriage and parenting. Immediately after telling us to be filled with the Spirit, to speak with psalms, to sing, and make music in our hearts, and to always give thanks in everything, he says, "Submit to one another out of reverence for Christ" (Ephesians 5:21). Obviously, a clear result of being "filled with the Spirit" is to have a submissive spirit. Men and women are to submit to each other and to serve each other's needs.

In marriage, there is to be a *mutual* submission where a man denies himself in order to love his wife as Christ loved the church. He is still the leader, but he submits his life to his mate. Any husband who is living out Paul's instructions here in Ephesians 5 could never treat his wife as a second-class citizen or with chauvinistic disregard for her feelings. That is the farthest thing from Paul's (and God's) mind.

"THE FAITHFUL COUPLE"

A few years ago I took my family on a vacation in Yosemite National Park. We camped near the Mariposa Grove of giant redwoods. All of us were fascinated and awed by those magnificent trees. As we walked among the forest giants, we came to what appeared to be a huge redwood tree about forty feet in diameter.

We were puzzled, however, by the sign at the base of the tree, which read, "The Faithful Couple." The ranger explained that some fifteen hundred years before, two trees had sprouted as seedlings on the forest floor about fifteen feet apart.

For the first seven or eight hundred years, the two trees had grown individually, but as they got larger, their trunks grew closer and closer together. Sometime around the age of eight hundred years, the trunks had touched and they began the process of fusing together as one tree. We all looked up and, sure enough, some forty or fifty feet above our heads we could see the two trees reappearing, each with its own separate identity. There they had stood throughout the centuries—"The Faithful Couple."

I thought to myself, *What a perfect symbol of godly marriage demonstrating oneness in Christ and spiritual vitality. As two people* grow upward *in their relationship with God by walking in the Spirit, they* grow together *as one—a faithful couple—but each with his and her own identity.*

As you and your mate ask God to empower you with the Holy Spirit, His fruit will become a growing, increasing part of your life together. And as the God of peace and harmony fills your hearts and takes up residency in your marriage, you will experience the oneness only He can provide. Loneliness and isolation flee in the presence of the Author of intimacy.

HOMEBUILDERS PROJECTS

To Think About Individually

1. What are your personal answers to the three crucial questions in this chapter?

   Am I part of God's family?

   _____

   _____

   _____

   _____

   _____

   Am I giving Christ control of my life?

   _____

   _____

   _____

   _____

   _____

   Am I being filled with His Spirit on a daily basis?

   _____

   _____

   _____

   _____

   _____

2. Have you ever lived like a "cheese-and-cracker" Christian? Are you living that way right now? What do you plan to do about it?

3. To be filled with the Spirit, you must walk in the Spirit (Galatians 5:25). You do this by faith—a process called spiritual breathing. When you slip, fail, or grow spiritually cold, "exhale" by confessing your sins (1 John 1:9). Then "inhale," and claim the filling of God's Spirit by faith.

1. Is the Holy Spirit directing us in our marriage? What signs of His fruit can we see?

	A LITTLE	SOME	A LOT
Love			
Joy			
Peace			
Patience			
Kindness			
Goodness			
Faithfulness			
Gentleness			
Self-control			

2. How can we help each other keep Jesus Christ on the throne of our lives?

PART
FOUR

Building a Solid Team

HOMEBUILDERS
PRINCIPLES

Understanding biblical responsibilities
not only results in freedom for the
husband and wife, but also helps you
work better as a team to combat
isolation.

Headship means leading, loving, and
serving, not demanding, dominating,
or demeaning.

14

THE MAKING OF A
SERVANT-LEADER

*He who thinketh he leadeth and turneth around to find no one following,
is merely taking a walk.*

—BENJAMIN HOOKS

There's a story of a man who died and arrived at heaven to find two signs above two different lines. At the end of one line the sign said: "*All Those Men Who Have Been Dominated by Their Wives, Stand Here.*" That line of men seemed to stretch off through the clouds into infinity.

Off to the side he saw a second sign that read: "*All Those Who Have Never Been Dominated by Their Wives, Stand Here.*" Underneath that sign stood only one man.

He went over to the man, grabbed his arm, and asked, "What's the secret? How did you do it? That other line has millions of men and you're the only one standing in this line."

The man looked around with a puzzled expression and said, "Why, I'm not sure I know. My wife just told me to stand here."

LEADERSHIP IS NO LAUGHING MATTER

We've all heard jokes about "who wears the pants in the family." But leadership in the home is no laughing matter. We are living in an era where our culture has spent the last two decades redefining the responsibilities of husband and wife—what the man and the woman ought to be and do in the home and out.

145

Male leadership in the home is under attack from all quarters in our culture, even from the government. I caught a sign of the times in a newspaper article headed, "STATE HOUSE REPEALS LAW APPOINTING HUSBANDS AS HEAD OF HOUSEHOLD." Describing the actions of lawmakers in Oklahoma, the story read, in part:

> After a debate punctuated with Scripture references, the House passed a bill Thursday refuting the law dating back to territorial days that recognized the husband as the head of the household. "I'm asking you to bring Oklahoma from the nineteenth century into the twentieth century before the twenty-first century gets here," said Representative Freddy E. Williams, Democrat from Oklahoma City who has pushed for the law's repeal for years.[1]

All these cultural pressures have taken their toll. James Dobson has pointed out that you can't redefine the role of women, who make up half the population, without drastically affecting men—the other half. Many men are confused and insecure about their leadership role for at least three reasons:

1. They don't know how to lead because they haven't been trained. They had no model at home and have no mental picture of what it means to lead a family. Consequently, they don't lead effectively or they don't even try.

2. They have quit trying to lead. After making attempts at leading, they have failed and given up. Because his wife may be difficult to lead, a husband will often simply quit trying.

3. They are lazy and passive. Some men have decided that the easiest thing to do is nothing. The simplest thing—with the smallest risk—is stay on the fence with both feet firmly planted in midair and let the wife do it. When a man is married to a strong wife who will take over, he often lets her do just that.

Fortunately, there is an answer. The Scriptures clearly give us the model for being a man, a husband, and father. I call that model the "servant-leader."

My hope is that the concepts I'm about to share will help you understand the biblical responsibility of a husband more clearly than you ever have before. When correctly interpreted and applied, these concepts will not only result in freedom for the husband and wife, but will also help you work better as a team to combat isolation.

GOD'S ORDER OF RESPONSIBILITY

According to the scriptural model, God's organizational structure for the family begins not with the husband, but with Christ. The apostle Paul spelled this out when he wrote that "the head of every man is Christ, and the head of the woman is man, and the head of Christ is God" (1 Corinthians 11:3).

In another well-known passage, Paul says, "the husband is the head of the wife as Christ is the head of the church, his body" (Ephesians 5:23).

There has been much debate, in and out of the church, on what the word *head* means. Some Christian feminists exegete away the man's leadership role completely and opt for "total equality" between husband and wife. At the other extreme are those who make strong emphasis on a man's authority over the woman and her need to submit to him without question, in absolute obedience.

In his commentary on Ephesians, William Hendriksen points out that God "placed ultimate responsibility with respect to the household on the shoulders of the husband." The Lord has assigned the wife the duty of obeying her husband, yet "this obedience must be a voluntary submission on her part, and that only to her own husband, not to every man."

But Hendriksen cautions against putting undue stress on a husband's authority over his wife. The apostle Paul compares the husband as head of his wife to Christ, who is head of the Church, "his body, of which he is the Savior" (Ephesians 5:23). This comparison of the husband with Christ, who is the head of the Church, reveals in what sense a man should be his wife's "head." William Hendriksen writes, "He is her head as being vitally interested in her welfare. He is her protector. His pattern is Christ, Who, as head of the Church, is its Savior!"[2]

God has given the husband a position of authority and "headship," but instead of emphasizing how his wife should submit, the husband *should concern himself with how he should lead.* "Head" does not mean male dominance, where the man lords it over the woman and demands her total obedience to his every wish and command. God has never seen women as second-class citizens. His Word clearly states that we are all equally His children: "There is neither Jew nor Greek, slave nor free, male nor female, for you are all one in Christ Jesus" (Galatians 3:28).

When Paul penned those words to the church at Galatia, they came as good news, indeed, especially for women. According to historian Will Durant, in the first century the plight of women was pitiful. The Greeks and Romans viewed their women as second-class citizens, necessary only for personal pleasure or bearing children. Women, said the Greeks, should see little, hear little, and speak as little as possible.

Even though the Jews had God's laws and teachings about the sanctity of marriage, they didn't do any better. In fact, the Pharisees, the spiritual elite of Israel, had a prayer that said, "Thank You, God, that You did not make me a Gentile, a slave, or a woman."

In short, women just weren't held in a very high regard until Jesus Christ stepped into time. And, ironically enough, Paul, who had been a Pharisee of the Pharisees, was His chief spokesman. Paul's writings helped pave the way for an entirely different approach to women that had never been seen before. The teaching of the New Testament clearly shows that women are to be respected, revered, and treated as equals with men.

Unfortunately, many husbands haven't heard the message. They degrade their wives by neglect or with insensitive and abusive treatment. I believe the women's movement occurred in part because men did not give their wives the value and significance God assigned to them when He created Eve and presented her to Adam in the Garden.

HUSBAND AND WIFE ARE INTERDEPENDENT

When husbands—particularly Christian husbands—don't uplift their wives, they create a hunger within them that demands that they search for a way to find significance and value as persons. One of the supposed "benefits" of the women's movement is that it has made women more independent of men, fully capable of supporting themselves and not really needing men at all. I'm convinced, however, that, more often that not, an unbalanced view of what independence really is results in a world full of lonely wives (and husbands). But the biblical view of men and women, particularly married couples, is that husband and wife are to be interdependent—that is, they need each other.

The concept of women being independent of men and men being independent of women only suggests more isolation, not oneness. God made men to need women and women to need men. As Paul wrote, "In the Lord . . . woman is not independent of man, nor is man independent of woman" (1 Corinthians 11:11). I believe this is another way of saying that God made us for oneness, not isolation. He made us to be interdependent within the family unit, not to do our own thing, but to lean on one another.

WHAT IS A REAL LEADER?

As a husband seeks to fulfill his God-given title of "head of his family," he faces three key responsibilities that outline his job description: *to lead, to love,* and *to serve.*

A husband's first responsibility to his family is to lead. The dictionary defines a leader as "someone who commands authority or influence, who shows the way, who guides or conducts, who directs and governs." John Mott said, "Leaders are persons who know the road, can keep ahead, and pull others alongside of them."

Are you a leader? Men who are "natural" leaders have no trouble answering, yes. They know how to take over, control, guide, and get things done.

What about the man who is not naturally gifted in these areas? What about the man who has a passive personality but is married to a very assertive, take-charge sort of woman? What do Paul's words about the husband being the head of the wife say to him?

Paul says the same to everyone. God has placed the husband in a position of responsibility. God designed this position of responsibility and the mantle of leadership comes along with it, whether the husband feels capable of wearing that mantle or not. Your wife may be resisting you, fighting you, and spurning your attempts to lead, but it makes no difference. I believe she subconsciously wants you and needs you to lead. You are not demanding this position; on the contrary, God placed you there. You will not be perfect, but you have to be persistent enough to pick yourself up and keep on going anyway.

What keeps you going is the fact that you're accountable to God for the leadership you give to your family. Every person will someday stand before God and give account of his life. And I think part of that account for husbands is the love, care, and servant leadership he gave to his family. What I am saying is that the tone, direction, and environment the husband sets as leader should have a great influence on the spiritual maturity of his family's household.

GOOD LEADERSHIP IS UPLIFTING

There is a story about a kite that was soaring high in the sky and saw a beautiful green field of flowers some distance away. The little kite thought to itself, *You know, it would be fun to fly over there and get a closer look at all those beautiful flowers—they are much prettier than all those rocks I'm flying over right now.*

But there was one problem. The string holding the kite didn't seem long enough to let it fly where it wanted to, so it pulled and tugged and finally broke loose. Happily, the kite soared for a few moments toward the field of flowers, but then came crashing down. What had seemed to be holding the kite down was actually holding it up.

The wife is the kite and the string is composed of two cords: the scriptural principle of a man's responsibility to lead, and the woman's responsibility to submit to his headship. The husband's love is the wind that enables the kite to soar into the sky. Without this wind—the secure, encouraging environment the husband creates through his leadership—the wife will feel tied down, but not uplifted. The string was not intended to be a hindrance. Along with the wind, it is actually what is holding the kite up.

If a husband leads properly, he doesn't have to ask or demand his wife to submit. She is willing to follow his lead because he is creating an environment that allows her to operate happily and effectively. The husband who orders his wife, "Just submit to me for once!" is probably not the type of leader to whom a woman would wish to submit.

As I attempt to create an environment of good leadership for Barbara, I don't demand absolute subservience and total obedience. Nor do I discourage dissenting opinions. She is free to speak the truth to me and to differ with me. She is free to question my decisions because that may well be God's way of sharpening my thinking, changing my behavior, or reversing a decision.

If there is one person whose opinion I want and need, it is Barbara's. I want to know what she thinks because she is my most valued friend and counselor. I need her perspective. I trust her and she has confidence in my leadership.

A good way to build trust is to pray together. The couple who prays together cannot become isolated. Talking to God together is essential in experiencing intimacy.

Recently I was on a trip and, as I always do, I called Barbara at home to see how things were going. She was experiencing problems with sibling rivalry between two of our children, and she said, "You know, I think we just need to start praying more about this problem." I agreed and we had prayer right there over the phone. Prayer together eliminates barriers and fuses our hearts as we face problems together.

A GOOD LEADER IS A GOOD LOVER

Flowing out of the responsibility to lead is the responsibility *to love your wife unconditionally.* Ephesians 5:25 says, "Husbands, love your wives, just as Christ loved the church and gave himself up for her."

This is the kind of love that casts out all fear. Even when Mom and Dad argue, the kids know that neither Barbara nor I is going to leave. If the kids sense there's some tension between Dad and Mom, we occasionally remind them, "Hey, remember, we've told you we're in this for keeps. We're committed, you don't need to *ever* worry about that."

I can still remember an argument my parents had when I was five. There wasn't anything physical, but some heavy verbal blows were thrown. Divorce was not in vogue then, but their disagreement made such an impression on me that I can remember wondering, *Will Mom and Dad get a divorce?* My mother and father had a great marriage, but that one disagreement shook me to my toes.

I can't help but wonder what must go through kids' minds today. As a dad and the leader of your family, perhaps you need to affirm your children more often by letting them know that you and your wife are totally committed.

DON'T LET HER RUN ON EMPTY

Your unconditional acceptance of your wife is not based upon her performance, but on her worth as God's gift to you. If you want to love your wife unconditionally, always be sure her emotional tank is full. One of the best ways to do that is to affirm her constantly. Let her know verbally that you value her, respect her, and love her. I've discovered that I simply can't do enough of that.

Some evenings I come home and I'm absolutely amazed at how busy Barbara's been for me and the children, running errands, settling squabbles, fixing meals—it's endless. Occasionally, I'll miss my cue to encourage her and she'll say, "You know what I would like you to do? Just tell me you appreciate what I'm doing for you!"

When Barbara says something like that I realize that I have failed to notice that her emotional gas gauge has begun to bang on E—for Empty. I can try to refill it with generalizations like, "Sweetheart, you're terrific!" or "You're the greatest!" But it's even better to get much more specific:

"Thanks for being consistent—you're a fabulous example of a real Christian woman."

"I appreciate your doing all my laundry . . . thanks for even ironing the napkins—you're incredible!"

"Thanks for looking so nice when I come home . . ."

"Thanks for being there . . . for always putting the kids and me ahead of yourself."

"I appreciate always being able to count on you to follow through, no matter what."

"Thank you for being faithful to me."

LOVE TAKES ACTION

There is no question that words communicate love, but so do actions. We need both. As the apostle John wrote in one of his letters, ". . . let us not love with words or tongue, but with actions and in truth" (1 John 3:18).

One of the missing ingredients in male leadership in many homes is sacrificial *action*. When is the last time you gave up something for your wife—something you genuinely value, like your golf game? Your hunting or fishing trip? Your hobby? Sometimes you need to give up something you love so your wife can have a break and *see* your love for her.

A few years ago I was invited to a leadership meeting in Dallas. As I packed I noticed that Barbara seemed in low spirits. She had that I've-been-cooped-up-here-too-long-with-this-menagerie look, and it occurred to me it really didn't make a lot of difference if I attended that Dallas meeting or not. Oh, there would be plenty of kindred spirit fellowship with some "leaders," good food, and lots of ego strokes. But what about my wife? She obviously needed a break far more than I did.

Suddenly I started unpacking my suitcase, and Barbara asked, "What are you doing?"

"I'm not going anywhere," I said. "It's *you* who is going somewhere."

I called a local hotel and arranged to have Barbara stay there for two nights that weekend by herself. That's something she loves to do—think, plan, pray, study, and read, all by her lonesome. It refreshes her.

A Loving Leader Is a Servant

Rounding out your responsibilities as a loving leader is caring enough for your wife to be willing to serve her. According to the New Testament, being head of your wife doesn't mean being her master, but her servant. If any term is misunderstood by husbands today, it is "servant-leader." Many men think it sounds like a contradiction in terms. They believe that a leader is served by others. But consider these three quotations:

Arnold Glasgow: "A true measure of a man is not the number of servants he has, but the number of people he serves."

Oswald Chambers: "True greatness, true leadership, is achieved not by reducing men to one's service, but by giving up oneself in selfless service to them."

Jesus Christ: ". . . the Son of Man did not come to be served, but to serve, and to give His life a ransom for many" (Matthew 20:28).

Jesus didn't just talk about serving; He demonstrated it when He washed His disciples' feet (John 13:1–17). Christ, the Head of the Church, took on the very nature of a servant when He was made in human likeness (Philippians 2:7).

When Jesus talks about serving, does that include the way husbands should treat their wives? Obviously it does, and there is no better way to serve your wife than to understand her needs and try to meet them.

Do you know what your wife's top three needs are right now? If she's a young mother, she's got a certain set of basic needs. If your children are grown and gone and you're in the empty nest, your wife has a different set of needs that you should try to meet.

In his book *His Needs, Her Needs* Willard Harley lists the five top needs of men and women he has gleaned from the thousands of couples whom he has counseled over the years. Not surprisingly, the top need for men is sexual fulfillment, but the two top needs for women are affection and conversation.[3] If your wife is like the majority of women in Harley's survey, her basic needs are to be held and to be talked with and listened to.

Along with knowing your wife's needs, you ought to be aware of her concerns. What worries her? Troubles her? Pressures her? What drains her emotional gas tank?

I often ask men at our conferences, "When was the last time you stuck your face in the toilet bowl and cleaned it for your wife?" Without doubt, one of the most despicable duties in all the world is cleaning toilet bowls. I recall the time some green things began to grow up out of our toilet because Barbara simply hadn't had time to get to it. So I armed myself, face mask, wet suit, and all, and went in there and cleaned it.

It is not hard to find ways to be a servant to your wife. There are plenty of common courtesies such as opening the door for her, stepping back and letting her on the elevator first, pulling out the chair and helping her get seated.

Some men tell me, "Well, that's okay when you're dating, but now we're married." And I reply, "You may be married, but you're still competing for your wife." There is a whole world out there that wants to take your place. If you don't lift your wife up and say, "Honey, my great claim to fame is that I'm your husband," then you may be setting her up for *something* or *someone* to take your place.

To care for and serve your wife means making her your number-one priority on this earth. How can you tell if she's number one? It will be reflected in your schedule and how much time you have for her. Not your children, not your job, not the church, but your wife should come first, just behind Jesus Christ.

What about your wife's hopes and dreams? I'll bet she has plenty—do you know what they are? Are you cultivating her gifts? If she has a knack for decorating, do you help her develop that?

In today's economy, the working wife is practically a given. Many families believe they need two incomes just to keep all the bills paid. This is a sensitive area, and only you and your spouse can answer this issue for yourselves. But what I try to help husbands and wives think about is, "What is the source of all our bills?" Is it needs or is it wants? Perhaps it would be possible for your family to get by on a little less, especially during those first formative years of your children's lives.

It's the husband's responsibility to take a long, hard look at why his wife is working outside the home—and the results of that job. Is she exhausted and are the kids lonely and isolated? Does this job put her at the edge of her limits? Is there really any time to talk and play and live together? Is your wife working to help provide real needs, or is her check going for material toys and the pursuit of that elusive myth called "The American Dream"? If so, then you need to consider where you as a couple want to succeed.

I repeat, that's a hard question, but it must be asked, especially by the family's servant-leader—the one who is responsible and accountable for the welfare of his wife and children.

To be a servant-leader takes strength, courage, patience, and the willingness to adapt and modify your own preferences in order to love your wife. In *Straight Talk to Men and Their Wives,* James Dobson includes a description of servant-leadership by a surgeon who saw it with his own eyes:

I stand by the bed where a young woman lies, her face postoperative, her mouth twisted in palsy, clownish. A tiny twig of the facial nerve, the one to the muscles of her mouth, has been severed. She will be thus from now on. The surgeon had followed with religious fervor the curve of the flesh; I promise you that. Nevertheless, to remove the tumor in her cheek, I had cut the little nerve.

Her young husband is in the room. He stands on the opposite side of the bed, and together they seem to dwell in the evening lamplight, isolated from me, private. Who are they, I ask myself, he and this wry-mouth I have made, who gaze at and touch each other so generously, greedily? The young woman speaks.

"Will my mouth always be like this?" she asks.

"Yes," I say, "it will. It is because the nerve was cut."

She nods and is silent. But the young man smiles.

"I like it," he says. "It is kind of cute."

All at once I *know* who he is. I understand, and I lower my gaze.

One is not bold in an encounter with a god. Unmindful, he bends to kiss her crooked mouth, and I so close I can see how he twists his own lips to accommodate to hers, to show her that their kiss still works. I remember that the gods appeared in ancient Greece as mortals, and I hold my breath and let the wonder in.[4]

TO THINK ABOUT INDIVIDUALLY

1. Use the following statements to rate yourself as "head of your family." Mark each statement from 1 (strongly disagree) to 5 (strongly agree).

_____ My leadership style makes submission easy for my wife.

_____ My leadership style is a reflection of high integrity.

_____ My leadership style is characterized by a servant attitude.

_____ My leadership style causes our home to be well managed.

_____ I convey acceptance to my wife.

_____ I show love for my wife with sacrificial acts.

_____ I demonstrate love even when I don't "feel" it.

_____ I know my wife's needs.

_____ My wife knows that I am aware of her needs.

_____ My wife knows she is my top priority.

_____ My wife knows she is a big part of my life.

If you scored less than a 4 in any of these areas, analyze why and what you can change.

2. List your wife's five greatest needs. What are you doing to meet those needs? How could you do more?

3. List some specific ways you can improve in each of these areas of responsibility:

I can become a better leader by:

_____

I can become a better lover by:

_____

I can become a better servant by:

_____

FOR INTERACTION TOGETHER

1. Get together with your wife and discuss your answers to
   the above questions. If leadership and submission are
   sensitive areas for you, be sure to do this when there are
   no major tensions or distractions. Go slowly and listen
   carefully to what your wife says, especially about her
   needs and your leadership style.

HOMEBUILDERS
PRINCIPLES

For oneness to become a reality, a
wife must also fulfill her God-given
responsibilities toward her husband.

15

HOW TO LOVE
YOUR HUSBAND

BY BARBARA RAINEY

A woman must be a genius to create a good husband.

—BALZAC

*B*ecause *I think women would enjoy hearing about being a wife and mother from someone who has experienced what they go through, I asked my wife, Barbara, to write the next two chapters. I think you'll enjoy them!*

Not long ago I had one of those no-good, horrible, very bad days that come along occasionally. It was just before Thanksgiving and Dennis and I were getting ready to take all six of our children along on an eight-day trip that would combine conference speaking with some vacation time.

Some workmen were installing an alarm system on our house and were supposed to finish on Monday, but they didn't. They were still working on Wednesday, with their questions, their drills, their hammers, and their mess, while I was packing, washing, cleaning the house, and getting everything ready to leave very early the next morning.

But they were only part of my problems, which multiplied very quickly. At 9 A.M. my washing machine sprung a massive leak and emptied its entire load of soapy water all over my kitchen floor. I called several repair places, but they all had the same story: "There's no way we can get anyone out there for at least a day or two."

So that left me trying to figure out where the nearest Laundromat was. Actually, that worked in quite well with other plans because our youngest child, Laura, was sick and I was getting ready to take her to the doctor. In addition, Ashley, our oldest, had a piano lesson.

Leaving the other children with a friend who had come over to help, I loaded Ashley and Laura into the car and we took off.

It turned out Laura had an ear infection. I got her prescription, put several loads of wash through the Laundromat machines, picked up Ashley, and tore back out to the house, not arriving until well after 2 P.M. I was wearing down, but I had to keep cleaning and packing.

I didn't get much done. The phone kept ringing, and the workmen kept asking questions. And, through it all, Laura kept fussing and banging on her ear.

Suddenly it was 5 P.M. and I had nothing planned for dinner. Worse, I hadn't packed any suitcases and the four older kids had youth group meetings to attend that night at church. I called Dennis and we decided the simplest thing would be to buy hamburgers in town. I loaded up all the kids and we met Dennis, gulped something down, and dashed to the church where we dropped off the four older children. I rushed back home with the two little ones and put them to bed, while Dennis stayed in town to do some last-minute work at the office and bring the other children home later.

They arrived home at 10 P.M. and I still hadn't finished packing for the trip. Totally exhausted, I continued gathering enough bulky winter clothes—coats, hat, gloves, boots—for all eight of us.

"YOU KNOW, HONEY, IF YOU'D JUST . . ."

Dennis had to make some phone calls. Later, about midnight, he came upstairs and started helping me pack. He was tired and I was out—but still on my feet. As he pulled one of his suits out of the closet, he made one of those classic male observations about organization. "You know, honey, you could avoid all of this last-minute stuff if you'd just do a little planning ahead."

He didn't say it cuttingly or even with any irritation in his voice. He actually meant to be helpful. Nonetheless, I felt the anger rise to the very top of my scalp. I bit my lip, saying nothing, but thinking, *Here I've been working hard all day, handling all kinds of interruptions, and he talks about organization!*

We both finally fell into bed around 2 A.M., and it seemed that I had slept maybe five minutes when the alarm went off at 5:30. Somehow we got ourselves and the children dressed, dragged everything to the car, and headed for the airport. I was so tired I could barely function, and as we zoomed down the freeway, Dennis again tried to give me some helpful pointers on getting ready to go away on trips:

"You know, honey, you try to accomplish too much before we leave on these trips. If you'd just learn to prioritize and do the really essential things, this could be a lot easier on everybody, particularly you."

That did it. The steam I had managed to keep inside the night before came shooting out, and I fumed, "Priorities! Priorities! How do you prioritize a busted washer and having to drag six loads of clothes to the Laundromat, not to mention a sick child? How am I supposed to prioritize workmen who keep the house in a state of total disaster all day just before I'm leaving? Here I try to get everything right so we don't have to come home to chaos, and you talk about getting organized and setting priorities!"

Dennis was stunned. His dependable, loving wife (who was normally unflappable) had flipped. I was kind of shocked myself. I seldom "lose it" with Dennis, but this time it was all just too much. The rest of the ride to the airport was quiet, and so was the plane flight. Everything he had pointed out was done with good intentions, and he actually had been trying to help me, but all it did was hurt, and I responded badly.

Believe me, it is sometimes difficult to maintain oneness and intimacy in marriage. I know what the Bible teaches: We are to give thanks in all things, the good, the bad, and the otherwise. But at this particular moment I didn't want to give thanks for *anything*.

And so, in addition to all my other frustrations, I had guilt to carry around with all the other bags I'd packed. I was tempted to ignore our problem and let it slowly fade away. But that would hardly have been any help to Dennis, who would speak on "relationships" throughout the week. And what about our times as a family together?

So, after we had arrived, unpacked and settled in, I told Dennis I was sorry for getting angry, not because I was concerned about the speaking he had to do, but because I was tired of being miserable. He hugged me and said, "Honey, I'm sorry I said what I said. I wasn't being very sensitive to you. You do a great job of keeping everything straight and getting all of us ready—I hate it when we're at odds with each other."

I tell this story here, not to gain sympathy, but simply to say it's not easy to be a wife. There are times, as I try to follow Dennis's leadership, when I experience stress, have to take risks, or make sacrifices because he doesn't always do things as I would.

For you, the risk, the sacrifice, or the stress may be holding a part-time or full-time job, hosting social functions, participating in sports, or any number of other things that push you out of your comfort zone. I can identify with what one wife plaintively said: "I've sweltered at baseball games, I've shivered through football, I've been sunburned and mosquito-bitten on fishing trips. Why can't you be like other husbands and not take me anyplace?"

Wives have always found it difficult to live with what they want most—a husband. What we as women need today, perhaps more than at any time in modern history, is a clear mental picture of our responsibility as wives. The social changes brought about by the women's movement have been significant; but they have created a wake of grass-roots confusion. In the midst of our twentieth-century experience, God's design for husbands and wives still stands.

YOUR UNIQUE PURPOSE AS A WIFE

Scripture delineates distinct reasons for our existence as human beings that are common to men and women, but wives have the privilege of being created for what I believe is an additional higher purpose—*completing man where he was lacking*. Genesis tells us that God realized it wasn't good for man to be alone and so he decided to make a "helper suitable for him" (Genesis 2:18).

To be a helper or helpmate was God's special intent and purpose for a wife. I love the story told about Pete Flaherty, a county commissioner in Pittsburgh, and his wife, Nancy. They were standing on the sidewalk, surveying a city construction project, when one of the laborers at the site called out to them. "Nancy, remember me?" he asked. "We used to date in high school."

Later, Pete teased her. "Aren't you glad you married me? Just think, if you had married him, you would have been the wife of a construction worker."

Nancy looked at him and said, "No, if I'd married him, he would have been a county commissioner!"

That story makes a good point: God has designed women to help their husbands become all that God intends them to be. As I fulfill my God-given purpose as helpmate to my husband, I see three specific commands in Scripture that make up the basis of my responsibility to him. They include *submission to his leadership, showing him respect,* and *loving him.* When I meet those responsibilities, it helps build oneness between my husband and me. If I don't, it means tension, troubles, and eventually isolation.

DISTORTED VIEWS OF SUBMISSION

Just mention the word *submission,* and many women immediately become angry and even hostile. This controversial subject of submission has been highly debated and misunderstood.

The dictionary defines *submission* in a negative way. As a noun, it means subservience and abasement. As an adjective it means nonresisting, unassertive, docile, timid, passive, and subdued. As a verb, it means to yield, to surrender, to give in or succumb to, to bite the dust or lay down arms, to raise the white flag, cry, or say "uncle," to resign oneself, acquiesce, throw in the towel, give up the ship, or grin and bear it.

Who wants to be submissive like that? I certainly don't. These negative definitions of submission often lead to abuses of the concept—and, may I say, abuses of wives by husbands who fail to understand its biblical meaning and the man's role in a marriage.

Some husbands and wives actually believe submission indicates that women are somehow inferior to men. I've known women who think that if they submit they will lose their identity and become "nonpersons." Others fear (some with good reason) that submission leads to being used.

Another misconception is that submission means blind obedience on the part of the woman. She can make no suggestions to her husband, question nothing, and only stay obediently barefoot and pregnant in the kitchen.

A few years ago during a FamilyLife Conference, I received a letter from a wife in attendance, which illustrates how confusing submission can be to some women. She had been married a little over ten years and told me:

> As you pray for miracles as a result from this conference, please pray for one in my corner. For the first time last night, we actually shared and communicated a little bit, but my husband still has no clue how crushed and defeated I feel when it comes to our relationship.
>
> I always thought God's idea of submission was pretty much to do whatever, whenever and however I was told. Basically, a master-slave relationship. In the last year I have been discovering that that is not at all what God had in mind.

This wife misunderstood what her husband needed. She mistakenly equated submission with slavery. She incorrectly assumed that she had no voice, but husbands need the input of their wives to lead them and the family wisely. Our good friend and pastor, Robert Lewis, says, "Man needs a 'helper,' and without his wife's special attention, he is prone to imbalances and blind spots."[1]

SUBMISSION IS VOLUNTARY

We've looked at the world's definitions of submission, but what does God have to say? God has emphasized submission by restating the commands to wives several times in Scripture (Colossians 3:10, 19; Ephesians 5:21; 1 Peter 3:1–2; Titus 2:4–5). Scholars give different opinions for this emphasis. Some say it was because He knew it was so hard for wives to do. Another view says that it was because the husband needs the wife's cooperation and help so much. I believe both views are true.

The Greek word used in the New Testament for submission is *hupotasso*, which means "to voluntarily complete, arrange, adapt, or blend so as to make a complete whole or complete pattern." Donald Grey Barnhouse has said, "Both the Greek and Latin carry the idea of throwing oneself under, as a foundation, as an assistant, or to use the biblical phrase, 'a helper *fit for him.*'"Therefore, as I voluntarily submit to my husband, I am completing him. I am helping him fulfill his responsibilities, and I am helping him become the man, the husband, the leader God intended him to be.

The chart on the following page compares the world's concept of submission with the concept in Scripture. Remember that, according to Scripture, you submit voluntarily. Building oneness in marriage can only work when both partners choose to fulfill their responsibilities with no pressure or coercion. To become the servant-leader God has commanded him to be, Dennis needs my voluntary respect and submission. I choose to let him lead. And when Dennis loves me the way *he* is commanded to, it is easier for me to submit to that leadership.

I do this with an attitude of entrusting myself to God. In one of his letters, Peter tells us that even though Jesus suffered terrible pain and insults, He did not retaliate. "Instead, he entrusted himself to him who judges justly" (Peter 2:23). This kind of trusting is something a wife does every day of her life. When you entrust your life to the Father, it's a lot easier to be the wife of an imperfect man, particularly when you may have disagreements.

WORLD'S VIEW OF SUBMISSION	SCRIPTURE
Non-resistant	Loyalty
Unassertive	Completing
Bowing	Allegiance
Cowering	Faithful
Subservient	Obliging
Second-class	Willing
Lower/inferior	Flexible
Sweet-talking	Adaptable
No initiative	Blending
No backbone	Consent to
	Agree to
	Defer to

DECISION MAKING IN MARRIAGE

When Dennis and I have a decision to make, usually we do it by unanimous agreement. Generally, even if we begin talking about a decision from opposite perspectives, we typically work through the process of sharing our thoughts, come to an agreement, and make the decision as one. It is rare that we continue to disagree, but it has happened.

When our oldest daughter, Ashley, was four and a half, we found ourselves facing our first schooling decision. Ashley's birthday is in late August, meaning she would be the youngest child in her class.

I had enrolled her in an excellent preschool program to help prepare her for kindergarten. The director of the nursery school, as well as Ashley's teacher, said she had done beautifully in preschool and would do just as well in kindergarten the next year. I agreed.

Back home I reported all these facts to Dennis. I laid it all out carefully and, I thought, convincingly, but to my surprise, he didn't agree. I couldn't believe that he wasn't buying my persuasive logic. He simply said, "I think we should hold her out for a year."

I pursued with my arguments: "She makes friends easily. The teachers all think she should be in school next year. Why can't you agree with me?"

Dennis couldn't really give me a reason. He just felt that Ashley shouldn't go to school—even kindergarten—as a young five-year-old.

I backed off and waited a couple of weeks, prayed about it, and tried again. I presented all my facts, trying to beef up every point to make my position more convincing, but Dennis didn't budge.

We went on like this for several weeks, and I realized I wasn't making any progress. I was becoming more entrenched in my position, and he was likewise immovable in his. In a word, we had reached an impasse.

I decided I had to do something, so I prayed and said, "Okay, Lord, You know that I'm right and he's wrong. And I pray that You will change his mind . . . but Lord, if I'm wrong and he's right, I want You to change my attitude. I'm willing to do whatever You want me to do, but You know I think he's wrong."

What changed was my attitude and perspective. In the days that followed, God gave me peace. And as my stance softened, I began to see Ashley more objectively, as a little girl who needed another year to be a child without the pressures of school. It turned out that starting Ashley in kindergarten as a young six-year-old was one of the smartest things we ever did for her. We discovered several years later that Ashley is dyslexic (an inherited difficulty with reading) and the extra year at home gave her a much better chance to deal with learning to read.

I'm glad the Lord broke our impasse by reminding me that I need to have the right attitude. I needed to trust God with Dennis's decision and submit my will to His.

Is God Big Enough?

To wives who may find themselves in situations with their husbands similar to the one we had over Ashley's schooling, I have three questions:

1. Have you clearly—and as unemotionally as possible—communicated the facts to your husband (perhaps putting your thoughts in writing)? Have you both really taken the time to hear each other on the issue?

2. Are you believing God in your circumstances, or are you allowing the circumstances to overwhelm you?

3. Is God big enough to take care of your husband without your help?

That's often the hard part—wanting to be too much of a helpmate, especially when you "know" your husband is wrong and you are right. But it's good to ask yourself when you can't agree, "Is God big enough to take care of my husband without my help in this situation?" "Will I follow Jesus' example and entrust myself to the Father?"

There have been many times, too, when Dennis has followed my advice and instincts in the decision-making process. As we anticipate sending our children to college, we discuss how we'll come up with the money. Over the years Dennis has been presented with opportunities to make financial investments. Because we have committed ourselves to make all important decisions together, he asks my advice.

In particular, I have consistently advised Dennis not to invest in stocks. It's not because of my knowledge of financial matters, but purely intuitive feeling. I don't insist that he take my advice in these matters, because it's not worth the potential disagreement.

But Dennis has heeded my input in every case that I can remember. In most of them it was wise that he did. In one instance the tip would have proved financially profitable, but both of us trust God's sovereignty. I feel that had we invested in that venture it would have been a distraction for Dennis.

Decision making for the Christian couple should not be reduced to an issue of who is right and who is wrong, or who is in charge and who is following. Instead, a husband and wife should seek to discover God's will on a daily basis by talking things out together with an attitude that trusts God, committed to doing what He leads them to do.

There is a profound promise that appears in Scripture repeatedly: "For with God nothing will be impossible" (Luke 1:37). Think about that for a minute. Nothing is too hard for God. Your husband, your marriage, your ability to make decisions together may seem impossible to *you* at the moment, but nothing is impossible for God. Nothing.

THOUGHTS FOR THE WIFE WHOSE HUSBAND WON'T LEAD

- Analyze the situation objectively. Has your husband really abdicated total leadership? See if you can find some areas where he is leading and begin to appreciate and thank him for those.

- Be sure you are a good follower. Some women are stronger leaders than their husbands, and he may never have had a chance to truly lead. Do a study from the Scriptures of what a good follower does.

- Don't expect your husband to be the perfect leader immediately. It may take him years to develop leadership in certain areas. Give him room to grow.

- Learn to appreciate the differences between you and your husband and accept them. It may be that God has made you different in your leadership abilities and styles so that you really do need one another.

- Read *The New Building Your Mate's Self-Esteem* (Thomas Nelson, 1995), in which Dennis and I share from our own experience how a man needs a wife who will believe in him, accept him, and build him up. Go through this book together and discuss how you can encourage and build esteem in each other.

- Pray. One of the fiercest battlegrounds today is for male leadership in the family. Your prayers could become the catalyst that ignites your mate's heart to become God's man, husband, and father.

In our marriage, submission has not been a major problem for me, but that does not mean following my husband has always been easy. I like what Jeanne Hendricks says: "His human nature challenges my own pride. Yet as I submit to God, so must I submit to, respect, and love my husband. The two relationships go together."[2]

A WARNING

Some of you reading this book live in situations where you are subjected to things that are excessively unhealthy, inappropriate, and destructive. If you are in a situation like this, you need to listen with extra discernment to someone wise who is trained regarding your particular problem. At times it may be inappropriate or even life threatening for you to apply the principles of submission unquestioningly. For example, if you are being physically abused, you need wisdom on how to be wise, strong, and straightforward. You may have to say, "I love you, but enough is enough."

Loving, forgiving, and submitting does not mean that you indefinitely tolerate significantly destructive behavior. For constructive and practical help on this subject, see *Love Must Be Tough* by James Dobson.[3]

ONENESS INCLUDES GIVING RESPECT

As he finished his description of male and female responsibilities in Ephesians, Paul made an interesting summary statement which included the second responsibility for wives: He commanded the men to love their wives as themselves and added ". . . the wife must respect her husband" (5:33). Respecting your husband is the perfect complement to submitting to him. Respect and submission go together, as the old song says, "like a horse and carriage." You can't have one without the other.

Respecting your husband means reverencing him, noticing him, regarding him, honoring him, preferring him, and esteeming him. In addition, the wife is to defer to him, praise him, love and admire him exceedingly (Ephesians 5:33). Practically speaking, to respect him means to value his opinion, to admire his strength, intellect, wisdom, or character, to appreciate his commitment to and involvement with you, to consider as valid his needs and values. From a negative view it means to be inconsiderate, insulting, critical, and nonsupportive.

One way to respect your husband is to consider and understand the weight of his responsibilities (be sure you read Chapter 14). It is easy to look at your husband and see what is wrong instead of what is right. As someone once said, "Faults are like the headlights of your car; those of others seem more glaring."

One of the negative results of the women's movement, in my opinion, is that much of the "consciousness raising" has led to heavy introspection on the part of women regarding their own needs, wants, and desires—in short, their own fulfillment. The biblical approach for wives is not a focus on self, but giving attention to their husbands and what they need as they try to fulfill all their God-given responsibilities.

And our husbands have many needs. The macho man who is self-contained, independent, and invulnerable is a myth. One day Dennis gave me a list of what he considered to be the needs most men have. He listed number one as self-confidence in his personhood as a man. (His sexuality comes in here, too, and I will comment on that later.) Most men need more self-confidence. They need to believe in themselves more.

The second major need, according to Dennis's list, is to be listened to, and number three was companionship. Number four was that men need to be needed, and number five, they need to be accepted.

To bolster Dennis's confidence, I try to encourage him by being his number-one fan. Every husband wants his wife to be on his team, to coach him when necessary, but most of all to be his cheerleader. A husband needs a wife who is behind him, believing in him, appreciating him, and cheering him on as he goes out into the world every day.

The word *appreciate* means "to raise in value." When I give Dennis words of praise and encouragement, I raise his value, not only in my eyes, but in his eyes as well. And that gives him more self-esteem and a better self-image as a man.

Psychologist William James said, "The deepest principle of human nature is the craving to be appreciated." And Charles Swindoll added this: "We live by encouragement, and die without it. Slowly, sadly, and angrily."

ONENESS DEPENDS ON LOVE

Third in God's trinity of responsibilities for wives is "to love their husbands" (Titus 2:4). A good description of the kind of love your husband needs is "unconditional acceptance." In other words, accept your husband just as he is—an imperfect person. As the Kenny Rogers song puts it, "She believes in me."

Perhaps most important of all from a man's point of view, love means being committed to a mutually fulfilling sexual relationship. I realize there's a whole lot more to love than sex, but we're looking at how to fulfill God's command to love our husbands. Therefore, we must look at love from their perspective, not just our own.

Surveys show that sex is one of a man's most important needs—if not the most important. When a wife resists, is uninterested, or is only passively interested, her husband may feel rejection. It will cut at his self-image, tear at him to the very center of his being, and create separation. A "lonely" husband can be created quicker by sexual isolation than any other way.

A friend shared something with me that I believe is profound. She said, to put the sexual dimension of a man in perspective, think of his needs this way. He can send his clothes to the laundry, eat all of his meals out, find companionship with friends, be accepted and respected at work, and be listened to by a counselor, and in all those things not go against the will of God. But if he meets his sexual needs with someone other than his wife, it is sin.

My husband's sexual needs should be more important and higher on my priority list than menus, housework, projects, activities—even the children. It doesn't mean that I should think about sex all day and every day, but it does mean that I find ways to remember my husband and his needs. It means I save some of my energy for him. It keeps me from being selfish and living only for my own needs and wants. Maintaining that focus helps me defeat isolation in our marriage.

I believe that one reason there are so many affairs, even among

Christians, is that too many Christian wives are not valuing their husbands' sexuality, their genuine, God-given physical need. By rejecting them at that point, they severely undermine their self-esteem. I must accept and *respect* this important part of my husband's masculinity. If I don't love and accept him in this area, my other demonstrations of love will be hollow.

Another way to love your husband is to accept the lifestyle that comes with his schedule. Learn to be content with your schedule and avoid comparing it to your friends who don't have to wait for their husbands to get home for dinner.

For most of our marriage, I have learned to be content with a schedule that didn't allow me to spend summers gardening. For years, I bought seeds every spring and planted beds of flowers and a few vegetables. Then, about June 1, we packed up and left for most of the summer for Dennis's teaching assignments, conferences, and meetings. We also had to learn how to live out of a suitcase (and even out of the car!) a great deal of the time.

During those years I had to leave my house empty or attended by someone else. All my beautiful flowers and other plants died by the time I got home. Recently, I have had a couple of summers mostly at home and have been able to garden on a limited basis. But I'm aware that our schedule could easily change again, and I would have to readapt.

Although I haven't always enjoyed the consequences of our schedule (the stress of traveling with our brood, packing and unpacking repeatedly, finding someone to watch and care for our home, etc.). I've never criticized Dennis about it. Unanimously we made the decision to travel in the summer. When it gets to be too much, I tell him and we make adjustments.

My husband's schedule is important to me. I choose to go with him to be a part of what he does, to watch and help and be available to him. I know he needs me and I want to be there.

How It All Fits Together

If you've ever sewn a dress, or attempted to sew one, you know how a pattern works. The pattern is made of many pieces, some large and some small, none of which accurately resemble the finished product.

WHAT TO DO IF YOU HAVE AN UNRESPONSIVE HUSBAND

- Find a godly woman who can become your friend, mentor, and sounding board. If you are married to a husband who doesn't lead, love, and care for you, then you need a woman who can give you wise advice, help you entrust yourself to God, and keep a balanced perspective while not becoming bitter.

- Take a life inventory to see if there is anything you need to do, give up, or deny that would help ensure the success of your marriage. Is anything competing with the attention God wants you to give your husband? What action do you need to take?

- Ask five other friends to pray for your husband and for his spiritual responsiveness to God. Pray that God would bring "significant others" into his life who would model a whole-hearted love for Christ.

- Know your own limits. Always take time to take your needs to God.

- Schedule a spiritual retreat by yourself, or with a best friend, one or two times a year. Also be sure you have a daily quiet time when you can reflect, pray, and allow God to minister to you.

- *Caution:* Beware of criticizing your husband to your parents. Most in-laws have a low tolerance for imperfections in the man who married their daughter. Be careful of "running home" to their listening ear.

When you lay out the pattern and cut the cloth, you don't have a garment—but only some scraps of cloth. But when it's properly fitted together according to the pattern directions and made usable with buttons, a zipper, or snaps, these incomplete pieces make a whole dress.

Every pattern has two pieces for every part: two sleeves, two bodice pieces, a front and back skirt; even the collar and facing pieces are usually in twos. That's how it is in marriage too. God has designed a master pattern for husbands and wives that, when followed, will create a whole, usable, beautiful marriage.

Just as the same dress pattern can be made in a wide variety of sizes and colors with numerous differences in detail, so my marriage may look different from yours. But both of us, if we acknowledge Christ as Lord of our lives, must work out our marriages according to God's pattern. The key is for each wife to follow the divine pattern, to know her part and how to fit it in with her husband's.

I have experienced many frustrations in trying to fit my part of the marriage pattern with my husband's. At times I have felt it was too hard. I heard a verse used in a sermon once, unrelated to marriage, that clearly answers this "it's too hard" feeling. God says, "What I am commanding you today is not too difficult for you or beyond your reach" (Deuteronomy 30:11).

I know by faith and am convinced by experience that God's "pattern" for me as a wife is not meant to restrict my creativity in expressing who I am. If I trust the pattern, the finished product is a life that reflects the full beauty that its Creator intended for it. When this becomes a reality in my life as a wife, I experience oneness with God, oneness with my husband, and a real freedom to be all that God made me to be.

Some of you may be in a difficult marriage with a very imperfect man. The rewards have been few. But for you and all other wives, the choice remains the same. Will we listen to the world or the Word of God? He has promised to reward those who obey Him, who follow His pattern. Let that be your hope. "Therefore, we do not lose heart . . . For our light and momentary troubles are achieving for us an eternal glory that far outweighs them all" (2 Corinthians 4:16–17). Let us resolve as Christian wives with a great God who blesses our obedience to help our husbands by submitting to them, respecting them, and loving them. The joy of true intimacy and oneness will be our mutual blessing.

H O M E B U I L D E R S   P R O J E C T S

TO THINK ABOUT INDIVIDUALLY

1. Rate yourself on a scale of 1 (strongly agree) to 5 (strongly disagree) with the following statements:

_____ My attitude toward being a helpmate reflects trust in God.

_____ My attitude toward submission and respect reflects trust in God.

_____ My attitude toward my husband is filled with love and a desire for oneness.

MY HUSBAND WOULD SAY:

_____ I am growing spiritually.

_____ I understand his responsibilities.

_____ I devote adequate time to him.

_____ I concentrate on his needs enough.

_____ I am a positive encouragement to him.

_____ I am his good friend.

_____ I am very fulfilled.

_____ I accept him regardless of his performance.

_____ I respect him.

_____ I consider him my top priority.

_____ I always back him up and support him.

_____ I express much love in our sexual life.

_____ I sacrifice myself for him.

2. List your husband's five greatest needs. What are you doing to meet those needs? Where could you improve? (Why not ask him to list what he considers his top five needs and then compare?)

3. In what specific ways could you improve in the following areas of responsibility?

Loving my husband is _____

_____

In the area of submission, I _____

_____

As far as respecting my husband goes, I _____

_____

FOR INTERACTION TOGETHER

1. Get together and discuss with your husband your answers to the questions above. If his leadership and your submission is a sensitive area, be sure you pick a time that is not rushed or tense. Listen carefully to what your husband tells you, especially about his needs and his perception of your attitude.

HOMEBUILDERS
PRINCIPLES

Mothers literally shape the future by
influencing the next generation.

16

A MOTHER'S INFLUENCE

BY BARBARA RAINEY

Maternal Love:
A miraculous substance which God multiplies as He divides it.
—VICTOR HUGO

I'm not sure about you, but for me being "Mom" is an incredible experience. Mothering is my greatest joy and fulfillment, but at times it's also my area of greatest challenge and worry. It can be a very lonely responsibility.

As a mother, I have my days when everything is relatively easy and I wonder why I ever struggle. The children are loving to one another and circumstances seem to flow smoothly. But there are other days when I wonder if it will ever be fun again. Will it ever be smooth and easy again? Am I ruining my kids for life?

I try to keep a journal, and, while I am not very faithful at it, I do sit down and write out my feelings on occasion. A couple of summers ago we were attending important Campus Crusade for Christ meetings and one morning I was not able to attend a session because I had to stay home with a sick child. I was feeling sorry for myself, so I wrote:

> I really wanted to go to the meetings this morning. Today is the day of
> praise and worship. And I love worshipping in song and prayer like we
> do at these meetings, but here I am in the apartment being a mother.

Mothering doesn't stop. The children's needs don't stop, so once again I am isolated and my husband is not. My identity. It's a problem. Because of my humanity, my identity is subject to attack by my emotions, by other people's perceptions and expectations, and by my abilities and by my failures. Learning the truth about myself and standing on that truth is a lifelong process.

Two emotions that I sometimes feel as a mother are guilt and discouragement. And it's my guess that's probably true for a lot of moms. I have high standards for myself and my children as well. When I fail to respond to my kids as I should, or when they disobey or act irresponsibly, as children do, I experience disappointment. In the midst of the stress of daily life, I often find myself on a teeter-totter of emotion, one moment feeling down and discouraged and the next rewarded as only a mother can be.

"I LOVE YOU ANYWAY"

I remember a day when Ashley and I went shopping, and as we came in carrying all the bags, a big bottle of cream rinse fell out of Ashley's arms, hit the garage floor, and splattered everywhere. Because our family is so large, we often buy industrial quantities, and this was the good stuff that cost a small fortune. All I could say was, "Oh, *Ashley.*" Though I didn't form the words, my voice implied, "How could you be so careless?"

I could see Ashley felt terrible, and I let her go on into the house with the rest of the groceries while I cleaned up the mess. Then I went inside to unload groceries and suggested that the kids help pick up the house a bit. Uncharacteristically, Ashley made a comment about the house being so messy it wouldn't make much difference anyway. My pride was offended at the truth of her statement, but I realized she was still smarting from the embarrassment of dropping that big bottle of rinse and so I said nothing.

That night I found a note from Ashley: "Dear Mommy, I am sorry I called your house a messy place. Will you forgive me? And the rinse breaking. It was dumb. I hope you and I can go shopping again. Love you more than you can imagine. Love in Christ. Ashley."

One Christmas I received a similar note that also took me from the depths to the heights. I had bawled out Benjamin for messing up his bedroom. Afterward I said, "Benjamin, all you are going to remember about me is that I griped at you and that I yelled at you about picking up your room, and you're going to grow up just having all these horrible memories of me."

That night he wrote me a note and gave it to me. It said, "Thank you for being a great Mom. That's what I will remember the most. I love you. Benjamin."

Yes, being a mother can be challenging, hard, frustrating, and lonely, but there are those priceless moments that come every day in the form of notes, a quick hug and a kiss, or something said as only a child can say it. And I believe God gives mothers those moments to spur us on, to help us hang in there and not give up hope. One of my favorite verses is, "Let us not become weary in doing good, for at the proper time we will reap a harvest if we do not give up" (Galatians 6:9).

I believe that if I persevere God will give me a ministry of influence to the next generation. By modeling a "Oneness Marriage" with Dennis, we are teaching our children how to avoid isolation when they're married. And by concentrating most of my efforts on raising children who will not only know the Lord but follow His will for their lives, I'm helping shape the future.

President Teddy Roosevelt once said:

> When all is said, it is the mother, and the mother only, who is a better citizen than the soldier who fights for his country. The successful mother, the mother who does her part in rearing and training aright the boys and girls who are to be the men and women of the next generation, is of greater use to the community, and occupies, if she only would realize it, a more honorable as well as more important position than any man in it. The mother is the one supreme asset of the national life. She is more

important, by far, than the successful statesman, or businessman, or artist, or scientist.

To have that influence on the future through my children demands that I objectively evaluate my life as a mother in light of that goal.

A MOTHER OF INFLUENCE IS A CRITICAL THINKER

"Knowing how to think" may not sound like something to trouble you. Oh, there may be times it's so noisy you can't think, but thinking critically probably isn't one of your top-felt needs as you consider rearing your children. Nonetheless, I believe critical thinking is foundational to being a mother of influence.

Our society is sending the wrong signals to mothers. It tells mothers they are dispensable. Today there are trained caretakers, trained nannies, trained day-care workers in fully equipped day-care centers. It tells us that all mothers need to do is provide maid and shuttle service, and offer purchasing advice. I even sense a subtle implication that mothering is no longer very important—that someone better trained can raise them just as well, or even better.

I doubt that many Christian mothers consciously choose the world's perspective of parenting; what I do fear is that far too many Christian mothers aren't fully committed to the biblical view of mothering. One of my favorite verses is Paul's advice to "not conform any longer to the pattern of this world, but be transformed by the renewing of your mind" (Romans 12:2). That's what I want as a mother—to constantly let God transform me through the renewing of my mind, so I never unconsciously adopt the "worldly wisdom" of the generation in which I live.

IT'S TIME TO CHALLENGE OUR CULTURE

There are four questions that I often use to challenge what our culture is telling me. The first is: *Why am I doing what I am doing?* For example, you may want to ask, "Why am I sending my child to preschool?" Or perhaps, "Why am I involved in Junior League, PTA, or the midweek women's Bible study?" And you may want to ask, "Just why am I working full-time at the bank?" Or, "Why are my children taking these particular lessons?"

Do these things contribute to my being a mother of influence? Are they distracting me from my primary role? I think mothers should ask, "Why?" about everything they do.

I didn't do much critical thinking about my role as mother until several years ago, when we were faced with another schooling decision. Our choice to homeschool taught me that God's creativity is not all used up. There are options and alternatives. Also, it was very freeing to realize that I could think critically and creatively about our children and our values and make decisions based upon what I felt was right. I didn't have to do what everybody else was doing.

MOTHERING AS YOUR CAREER

To be a mother of influence, a mother needs to give the majority of her attention and focus to her children and their needs. We must rise above the mentality of merely providing for their physical needs and wants to the higher calling of preparing them for life. "A true mother," said Ruth Graham, wife of Billy Graham, "is not merely a provider, housekeeper, comforter, or companion. A true mother is primarily and essentially a trainer."

The problem is, a majority of mothers are now working outside the home either part-time or full-time, which severely limits the amount of time they are able to devote their children. I realize there are many and varied reasons for this outside-the-home employment—from sheer survival to lifestyle needs to personal fulfillment. I want to help you think objectively for a few minutes about the reasons for your situation, if you're working outside the home.

To begin with, let's look at a verse in the Bible that summarizes what wives who are mothers of dependent children are to do, "to love their husbands and children, to be self-controlled and pure, to be busy at home, to be kind, and to be subject to their husbands, so that no one will malign the word of God" (Titus 2:4–5).

Notice the priority of commitment to her husband first and her children second. Her character is described as self-controlled, pure, and kind. And, then there is that little phrase, "busy at home." God wants the focus of her busyness, her activity, her schedule, to be *at home*.

WORKING MOTHERS

My challenge is not to wives without children or mothers of grown children; nor is it to mothers who have to work for the family's survival, as the young mother I know who has three young children. She has creatively arranged her work schedule to the weekend night shift at a local hospital to earn the maximum wage in the minimum amounts of time.

But for those mothers whose children are still home, and who work for a "fulfillment" need, or to maintain a higher standard of living, or who work out of fear—a fear that a possible divorce would leave them unable to provide for themselves—I want to encourage you to think about your choices.

Contemplate the implications of the word *career*. A career speaks of a lifelong occupation, a process that is not temporary. That defines well the title of *mother*. Working mothers are not a new phenomenon. What *is* new is the shift in career focus from full-time mother with a job on the side, to a full-time employment career focus with an attempt to mother in whatever time is left.

Many women are finding through experience that the expectation of achieving both goals with excellence is impossible. Based upon the Bible's priority for wives and mothers (husband, children, and home), the questions must be asked, *Is this job, this career, the best use of my time? Will I have more influence for the future through my employment or through my children?*

I'd also like to challenge you to think critically about the common belief that, "Women *must* work today in order to survive." Look honestly at your finances with your husband and determine whether the extra money you bring in meets *needs* or *wants*. I know some women who honestly believe that they need their income to survive, when in reality they could get by just fine on their husband's income if they gave up some things they *think* they need.

A FEW GUIDELINES

If, in fact, you must work or feel you cannot quit anytime soon, here are some guidelines and suggestions to help you continue to think critically.

First, *I believe a mother should have a job only if her husband is in total agreement.* A lack of oneness at this point can be critical. The two-career marriage may solve some financial difficulties, but it creates others.

You might disagree over the dispersion of two incomes. Perhaps you have different hours, different positions, different responsibilities. All of this can put you at odds with your husband, because in a sense you are competing with, not just completing, him. The working woman may feel independent from her husband.

A second factor a mother should consider as she thinks critically about work are *her capabilities, time, energy, and creativity.* Dr. James Dobson said, "There is only so much energy within the human body for expenditure during each 24 hours, and when it is invested in one place, it is not available for use in another . . . I have observed that exhausted wives and mothers become irritable, grouchy and frustrated, setting the stage for conflict within the home."[1]

If a woman must work, I think a job with flexible hours that can be pursued at home is the best option. I know of a woman in my church who found it necessary to earn extra income for her family. She had a small child and didn't want to put him into a day-care or baby-sitting situation. She began to pray and ask the Lord to provide a creative alternative for extra income.

Because she was an avid photographer, she soon discovered this might be an area she could go into, and she developed her own small photography business, working out of her home. She became quite good at it, but nonetheless kept her business limited. She was always sure that whenever she had appointments she could leave her little boy with her husband or with a friend.

This woman found a creative solution to the problem of needing extra income and not neglecting her number-one responsibilities of being a wife and mother. And that's the key—keep your priorities straight. Once you bring children into the world, your responsibilities as a mother come right behind your responsibilities to God and your husband.

Third, *a mother must consider her children's needs.* In his book *The Hurried Child,* David Elkind says, "When we have to hurry young children, when they have to be at a day-care center or with a baby-sitter, we need to appreciate their feelings about the matter. Giving children a rational explanation helps, but it isn't enough to deal with the child's implicit thought— 'If they really love me, they wouldn't go off and leave me.'"[2]

He goes on to talk about responding to the feelings of children. Communicate to your children how you feel about leaving them and how you look forward to being with them again. We cannot assume they don't feel the loss of your presence just because they have become accustomed to it. He concludes by saying, "Children are very sensitive to signs of parental caring."

In 1981, Burton White said, "For more that 20 years I've specialized in the study of successful child-raising . . . I firmly believe that most children will get off to a better start in life when they spend the majority of their waking hours being cared for by their parents."[3]

In conclusion, the issue of working mothers needs to be faced first of all as a career focus issue. To what will you give your life? Your children or your paid vocation?

Jesus said, "No one can serve two masters" (Matthew 6:24). Clearly, the home and a profession are not to be masters, but they are both full-time jobs in the same sense of a servant's work for his master. Mothering is not just a full-time job, it's a twenty-four-hour, till-death-do-us-part career. I don't believe mothers can serve both—a husband and children, and a job—without one or both suffering some neglect. Think critically about it.

WHAT ARE YOU REALLY SAYING?

The second question I ask myself to think critically about is, *What am I communicating to my children by what I do and by what I say?* What are they perceiving? What are they learning? What values am I modeling?

When I heard the tinkling sound of porcelain shattering, my mind first raced back to my grandmother. She had purchased the Hummel figurine "Little Apple Girl" back in the early 1930s when she was in Germany. I had received it after her death; it was special *and* valuable.

I'll never forget the day I saw it advertised in the newspaper: "Come see the Little Apple Girl Hummel exhibit," the advertisement read. I didn't get excited until I read that Little Apple Girl was on display and she was worth $15,000. I called Dennis and he immediately started talking about selling it and buying a bass boat. No way. I put it up high in our bedroom—supposedly in a safe spot. (Later we found out that our figure was just a "bit" smaller—the one on display was three feet tall and mine was four inches high—and worth only $150!)

And so as I heard it break that day, I knew that Little Apple Girl had developed a split personality! Before I even knew who caused the figurine to break, I was angry—I had *just* reminded the boys they couldn't play ball in the house.

When I arrived at the scene of the crime I found the guilty party, Samuel (then four years old), sheepishly awaiting his sentencing. I told him to go sit on his bed because he was going to get a spanking. I picked up the pieces of my apple girl and discovered she was not beyond repair.

Holding the pieces in my hand, I went to Samuel's room, took his precious blue-eyed face in my other hand, and said, "Samuel, do you see this?" His eyes became little blue saucers, probably wondering whether his fate would be electrocution or hanging.

He nodded. His eyes met mine and I made my point: "I want you to know, Samuel Rainey, that I love you more than this." Glancing down at the remnants I cradled in my hand, I went on: "And I love you enough to spank you for disobeying me."

Dennis, who witnessed the whole event, said he was really proud of me for the values that scene represented. I don't know if Samuel will remember that day or not, but I will! It reminds me that I am trying to model values that are worth imitating by my children. I had made a rule—no playing ball in the house—and Samuel had broken that rule, with difficult consequences for both of us.

Another concern I have for my own children is the pressure to be busy. There is a strong current in our country to involve our children in a myriad of activities at younger and younger ages. Parents feel it. They want to produce the brightest, best-dressed, and most-talented children. They fear that if they don't provide Tommy with music lessons at age three, gymnastics at four, art and nature studies two afternoons a week in the summer, and T-ball by the time he is five, he will grow up handicapped, deprived of the opportunity to discover greatness.

And what do the children feel? Do they really want all this activity? Are they interested because their friends at nursery school are involved, or because their parents have persuaded them to want it? It is my opinion that children who grow up with an abundance of activity and busyness become adults who can't live without it—sort of "activity junkies." They don't know how to contemplate, to rest, to think, to "be still and know that I am God."

I also believe that when parents indulge their children in this way, they foster selfishness. Children grow up being catered to and soon learn to expect it and even demand it.

CAN YOU GIVE UP SOMETHING?

My third question is, *Am I willing to deny myself?* Now, if God had asked me, "Are you willing to deny yourself in order to be a mother?" before my first child was born in 1974, I would have quickly answered yes. But if God had said to me, "Barbara, are you willing to deny yourself your watercolor painting, your sewing, quilting and handiwork, your time with your friends—in fact, nearly all of your personal interests and talents in order to be a better mother?" my response would have been more hesitant, more deliberate. I probably would have still said yes—because I would have thought: *Well, I can do it all!*

I'm thankful that God didn't ask me to give up all those things at once, because they were very important to me at the time. Gently, over the years, however, He has guided me in setting aside most of these talents and interests in order to be more focused as a mother.

And it's been hard, because I don't like denying myself any more than you do. It's painful to give up things I like to do—things that I enjoy, things that make me feel creative and comfortable. I have fought it all the way, always looking for some compromise to have time for my kids as well as for some of my hobbies and personal goals. But compromising never works.

Even today God continues to show me that I cannot have it all or do it all. And I'm one who'd like to. I would like to rear my children and be an artist on the side, have lunch with my friends, or work in our office a couple days a week. I hope that someday God will give some of those things back, but that's His choice. Right now I've made my choice for influencing six lively, lovely kids, and I wouldn't trade them for any number of paintings, quilts, or leisurely lunches.

Do You Make Your Children Feel Needed? An area of self-denial that's been particularly hard for me is helping my children feel needed by giving them jobs to do in our home. If you want to train your children to do the dishes or clean the kitchen, you've got to lower your expectations of what a clean kitchen is really like, gradually raising it as they get older. If you want to teach your child to help with the laundry, you've got to expect clumsy folding jobs. And if you dare to help your children learn how to cook, you had better be ready to put up with spills, splatters, and splashes!

All our kids have weaknesses when it comes to household responsibilities. Ashley, our oldest, is a pack rat. She saves it all and wants a souvenir from every exciting moment of her life. They're all too precious to throw away.

Benjamin is the champion of expediency. He wants to put off his cleaning chores, because, "If I vacuum now, it'll be dirty again by tonight." He's right. The floor doesn't seem to stay clean more than five minutes.

Samuel, however, is motivated by play, so as a rule he'll do his work quickly but only partially. Completion takes too long. And the basketball competition is too much fun.

And then there are our youngest three: Rebecca, who is eight, is quite responsible but she won't touch the mess if it's not hers, because that "wouldn't be fair." Deborah is our Little Miss Distracted. She starts picking up the playroom, but before long she's decorating the room—or herself. As a four-year-old, Laura devotes herself this year to washing the silverware, which she has had to learn to do without complaining, a disease to which all our children seem to be susceptible.

Because I'm a perfectionist and *none* of our children are "neat-freaks," I feel at times that I'm not just lowering my standards but giving them up entirely. I dream of living in a one-room house with a concrete floor and a drain in the middle of it—sort of an industrial strength, kitchen/living room!

I find I'm learning a couple of things. One is that if I want to communicate that Dennis and I really do need our children and are depending on them, then I have to let them fail and make mistakes. I've also learned that you can't count on them unless you *really do* count on them. If you give children responsibility and then take it away, they don't feel needed, they feel rejected.

This is so important today. I believe that teenagers are peer dependent because they aren't needed and valued at home. If they are isolated from you, they are fair game to be needed by someone else! In his bestseller, *The Third Wave*, Alvin Toffler wrote that much of teenage rebellion today occurs because teenagers no longer feel needed by the family unit nor economically productive during the turbulent prolonged adolescent years. The Lord is showing me I have to settle for less for a while in order to teach my children and help them feel needed.

MOTHERHOOD IS RISKY BUSINESS

The last question I ask myself to think about critically is, *Am I willing to take risks to be a mother of influence?* The Old Testament tells the story of how Jochebed, the mother of Moses, hid her baby son for the first three months of his life because Pharaoh had decreed that all Hebrew baby boys were to die. When she could hide him no longer, she made a little boat out of a basket and set baby Moses floating down the river.

Pharaoh's childless daughter found Moses and adopted him. In this way, God rescued Moses from certain death and honored his mother's faith. Jochebed was willing to take a risk for the sake of her child because she feared God more than she feared Pharaoh.

What are you willing to risk for your child? Would you risk the ridicule of family and friends to stay home full-time when they don't think it's really necessary? Or maybe you need to move to a smaller town where it's healthier and safer for your children to grow up, even if that means a cut in income.

As I mentioned in the last chapter, I am not much of a risk taker by nature, but as a mother I find myself having to take risks anyway. It seems to come with the territory.

As a mother in today's culture, I urge you to hang on tight and not let the world drag your kids to destruction. I'm not advocating "smother love," but I am saying being a mother today calls for courage, determination, and a tenacity that will never quit, no matter how confused things can seem at the moment. Howard Hendricks has said, "The more like the culture we are, the less impact you will have." Mothers of influence need to be more countercultural.

In this lonely, frenzied, hostile world, children desperately need a stable biblical model, or they will become isolated, unstable, and what Dr. Ken Magid called "high-risk children without a conscience."

A Mother and an Alligator. A story that has remained riveted in my mind ever since I read it concerns a couple who built a home on the banks of a small pond at the headwaters of a creek in Florida, not far from the Gulf of Mexico. Their twelve-year-old son, Michael, loved to snorkel in the two-acre pond, and one evening as twilight fell, he and two cousins, Kelly and Jill, went for a swim just after dinner. Kelly decided to come ashore but the other two youngsters remained behind, continuing to enjoy the wonders of snorkeling in the clear waters of the pond.

Oblivious to any danger, they were unaware that a huge alligator was bearing down on them. Neighbors spotted the beast and tried to distract it with shouting and clapping, which alerted Jill, who managed to make it to shore. But Michael, head under water, could hear nothing as he floated peacefully, peering at the rocks below.

The alligator lunged for Michael's head. As its jaws snapped shut, its teeth slashed a six-inch wound in his scalp and ripped the snorkel mask from his face. Miraculously, the boy's head came free, and he began swimming for shore as fast as the huge flippers on his feet could move him. Only momentarily diverted, the alligator spotted the boy and was after him again. By this time his mother had heard all the screaming and came running to the water's edge where she saw her son only twenty feet away in a race against death. He was swimming as fast as he could, but the alligator was gaining on him every second.

The mother reached out to grasp her son's hand just as the beast opened its huge jaws and snapped them shut on the boy's left leg. What followed was a grim tug of war between the one-hundred-pound mother and the four-hundred-pound, eleven-foot alligator. Clutching her boy's hand in a death grip, she pulled with superhuman strength and suddenly, unaccountably, the beast let go! Perhaps the eighteen-inch rubber flipper on the boy's foot was the cause—no one is sure—but the frantic mother dragged her son out of the water and up the bank to safety as the alligator sank back into the pond with what witnesses called a "disappointed look" on its face.

Three months later, Michael, his wounds completely healed, showed a visitor the spot where the attack took place. There were few outward signs of his brush with death. The scar on his scalp was now covered by his hair, and his left leg, broken by the force of the 'gator's jaws, had mended. Scars on his calf and ankle were covered by his socks. Proudly, however, he showed the visitor the three small scars on the back of his right hand, inflicted not by the alligator, but by his mother's fingernails. She had literally drawn blood when she pulled him from the jaws of certain death.[4]

There is no doubt in my mind that this mother would have been dragged to destruction herself before she would have let go of her son. And her courage gives me new resolve to face my everyday tasks. The world in which we live is every bit as great a threat to our children as a hungry alligator. The fate of our children hangs in the balance every day. A godless culture is hungrily pulling at our children and will devour them unless we hang on with a strength that will never let go.

By God's grace, I'm committed—are you?

FIVE STEPS TO CRITICAL THINKING

1. *Get away.* The key is not to spend all your time doing errands or shopping. Instead, take some time for a personal retreat—just you and the Lord. Take an hour or two, a morning, or a whole day. I love what Anne Morrow Lindberg wrote about this:

   > The world does not understand, in either man or woman, the need to be alone . . . Anything else will be accepted as a better excuse. If one sets aside time for a business appointment, a trip to the hairdresser, a social engagement, or a shopping expedition, that time is accepted as inviolable. But if one says: I cannot come because that is my hour to be alone, one is considered rude, egotistical, or strange. What a commentary on our civilization, when being alone is considered suspect; when one has to apologize for it, make excuses, hide the fact that one practices it—like a secret vice![5]

2. *Read books that challenge your thinking.* Don't be intimidated into following the crowd because you haven't thought things through. Reading helps you do that.

3. *Pray.* E. M. Bounds wrote, "Stronger than all other laws, and more inflexible than any other decree, is the decree,

'Call upon me and I will answer you.'"[6] Yielding our children to God frees us from being controlled by worry and fear, and enables us to trust Him with their lives. It also frees us to pray for God's will for their lives.

4. *Use the four questions to evaluate your life and the influence you are having on your children.*

5. *Plan and set goals.* Think through what you want to teach your children. What values do you want to instill? How will you accomplish those? As Henry Kissinger said, "If you do not know where you are going, every road will get you nowhere."

HOMEBUILDERS PROJECTS

TO THINK ABOUT INDIVIDUALLY

1. Get alone and stop to ask yourself these questions:

   Why am I doing what I'm doing? (What is necessary? What could be dropped? What could I change?)

   What am I denying myself in order to be a mother? (What would I rather be doing? Am I resentful?)

   What messages do I send my children with my lifestyle? (Do my actions match the values I say I believe in? Am I communicating love by what I do and say?)

2. Rate yourself between 1 (strongly disagree) and 5 (strongly agree) with the following statements:

   _____ My children know I love my husband.

   _____ My children know I love them.

   _____ My children know I sacrifice myself for them.

   _____ My children know they are a top priority.

   _____ My children know my home is a top priority.

   On which questions did you score below a 4? Think about how you can change or improve and why.

3. What are the two greatest needs of each of your children? How can you be more effective in meeting those needs?

FOR INTERACTION TOGETHER

1. Sit down with your husband and discuss your answers to the questions above. Get his input to see where he believes you are being too hard on yourself and where he may have suggestions on how you can improve or change.

2. What does your husband believe are the two greatest needs of each of your children? Compare your answers, then talk together about how both of you can meet those needs more effectively.

HOMEBUILDERS
PRINCIPLES

The basis for leading your family is
your humble dependence upon God
to give you guidance.

God calls the father to be a manager,
a minister, and a role model.

17

A WORD TO DADS

There is little less trouble in governing a private family
than a whole kingdom.

—MONTAIGNE

When an eleven-year-old boy was asked to write an essay on what he liked best about his home, he came up with this:

> My mother keeps a cookie jar in the kitchen, and we can help ourselves except we can't if it's too close to mealtime. Only my dad can anytime. When he comes home from the office, he helps himself, no matter if it is just before we eat. He always slaps my mother on the behind and brags about how great she is and how good she can cook. Then she turns around and they hug. The way they do it, you'd think they just got married or something. It makes me feel good. This is what I like best about my home.[1]

That little boy's essay says something that all fathers should never forget: Little eyes are watching. Little radar units are focusing in on that man called "Dad," desperately wanting his love and approval, yearning for the warmth and security that only he can provide.

As I do my best to be Dad to our brood, I become more and more aware of those eyes every day. They want me to notice, to be aware. And I want them to know I care.

THE FIRST GAME DAD EVER SAW HIM PLAY

In his book *A Father . . . A Son . . . and a Three-Mile Run*, Keith Leenhouts tells a moving story about a father who got to watch his son play the game of his life. The son was an Ivy League football player who was short on talent but long on dedication. He rarely played, but never missed a practice. The player's coach also was impressed with his devotion to his father; often he saw them walking arm in arm through the campus.

Just before the biggest game of the year, the player's father died. So the coach was surprised when the player asked if he could start the next game. The coach hesitated, knowing the player could make a crucial mistake that could destroy the team's chances to win, but he finally consented. Here I'll pick up the story:

Oh no! The coach groaned as the opening kickoff floated end over end right into Jerry's arms. But instead of fumbling, as the coach expected, Jerry hugged the ball tightly, dodged three onrushing defenders, and raced to midfield before he was finally tackled.

The coach had never seen Jerry run with such agility and power, and perhaps sensing something, he had the quarterback call Jerry's signal. The quarterback handed off, and Jerry responded by breaking tackles for a twenty-yard gain. A few plays later he carried the ball over the goal line.

The favored opponents were stunned. Who was this kid? He wasn't even in the scouting reports, for he had up to then played a total of three minutes all year.

The coach left Jerry in, and he played the entire first half on both offense and defense, tackling, intercepting, and knocking down passes, blocking, running—he did it all.

During the second half Jerry continued to inspire the team. When the final gun sounded, his team had won.

In the locker-room bedlam reserved only for teams that have fought the impossible fight and triumphed, the coach sought out Jerry and found him sitting quietly, head in hands, in a far corner.

"Son, what happened out there?" the coach asked as he put his arm around him. "You can't play as well as you did. You're just not that fast, not that strong, or that skilled. What happened?"

Jerry looked up at the coach and said softly, "You see, coach, my father was blind. This is the first game he ever saw me play."[2]

As I tell this story at FamilyLife Conferences, I see many a man in the audience cry as he remembers the influence his father had on his life. I often become teary eyed myself, because my dad was my hero—a model man in many ways.

I Remember "Hook" Rainey

I often ask in FamilyLife Conferences: "What do you remember most about your father?" And while men are thinking about their dads, I tell them about my dad—about his integrity and my memories.

I can recall how my dad would slam the door when he came home at 5:30 in the evening. It rattled the entire house. He wore Old Spice aftershave, which was mixed with the smell of propane or gasoline that he pumped for nearly forty-five years.

I remember often walking in to find him reading his newspaper. I would pull it down and say, "Hey, Dad, let's play catch." More often than not, he would lift his tired body out of the easy chair that wore his imprint, put on his mitt, and out we'd go.

Everyone in town called him "Hook" Rainey, a nickname he had picked up during his days as a pitcher in semipro ball. He was a lefty and had a "wicked" curve ball that would come up to the plate and then just "fall off the table." He loved to tell me about the time he pitched a game against Dizzy Dean. Right up until his death in 1976, I would ask him, "Who won that game?" Somehow he never could remember the score.

I remember going with my dad at Christmastime to deliver presents to the poor. It was something he loved to do every year. And I remember his funeral, which brought out five hundred people—about one-third of the population of Ozark, Missouri. My father's integrity was the highest you could ask for. He would let people cheat him before he would take any kind of advantage. His character was strong and his influence was powerful.

He taught a little Sunday school class of sixth-grade boys and I remember the year my buddies and I came into his class. Back in fifth grade, "the rowdies" bounced off the walls, shooting spit wads, flying paper airplanes, and, in general, driving the teacher crazy. But when we entered Dad's class, radical personality transformations occurred. The spit wads dried up and the paper airplanes crash-landed after the first lesson.

Hook Rainey demanded our respect and, although he is gone, he lives in the memories of those who watched him. Today I draw on Hook Rainey's integrity and model my life after his.

And I miss him.[3]

YOU CAN'T MANAGE ON THE DEFENSIVE

The apostle Paul, while writing to his protégé, Timothy, says a father must be someone who manages his own household well and keeps his children under control (1 Timothy 3:4). Paul is describing the qualifications of an elder, but I think these words apply to any Christian father as well.

I think of three phrases that describe my father accurately: family manager, family minister, and family role model. I doubt if my dad ever thought of himself in those terms, but he did them all and he did them well.

My father managed our home with quiet authority, and he definitely had me and my brother under control. He didn't spank us much, because he didn't have to. The aura of power and authority surrounding him usually kept us in line, and when we strayed he moved in to discipline us appropriately.

DAD NEEDS TO BE THERE

If you're a dad reading these pages, let me ask you some questions. What kind of memories will your children have of you? Will they remember a father who spent time with them, played with them, laughed with them? Or will they think of you as someone who was preoccupied with work, unfinished projects, or a hobby in which you were embroiled?

And now let's really get personal: What would happen if you switched the energy you gave to your job with the energy you give to your home and family? What would happen to your work? *What would happen to your home?*

I realize that may be an unfair question, because by necessity many men work long hours away from home. But what I'm getting at is that too many fathers give almost *all* their energy to their jobs and leave none for the family. I have a friend who has a three-by-five card on his desk that reads: *Leave Some for Home.*

He realized that without that reminder shouting at him daily, he'd go home on "empty," with no energy, over 95 percent of the time. His job was that draining.

We need to balance things out if the next generation is to get the kind of leadership it needs. Today we need fathers who are determined to guard the doorway of their homes and protect their families against sin. We need dads who are determined to succeed at home, regardless of the cost.

Good management in a business means being close to the people you manage. This takes time and physical proximity. A principle of marksmanship applies here very well. The farther away you place the target, the more likely you are to miss the bull's-eye, because error increases with distance. As leaders and managers of our homes, we fathers must reduce the distance between us and the people we lead. The bottom line is that you and I can't lead from afar. *We've got to be there.*

Is There a Minister at Your House?

When I suggest to fathers that they are to be ministers to their families, they tend to shy away, thinking I mean they have to be accomplished theologians and do a lot of eloquent praying before meals. But that's not what being a family minister is all about.

My dad never preached to us (although he did give me a few stiff lectures on the proper speed to drive a car). And his prayers weren't filled with flowery phrases or big words. But Hook Rainey was our family's minister, nonetheless, because he cared for his flock. Every Christian dad is an "elder" in his own home and is charged to "shepherd the flock of God that is among you" (1 Peter 5:2 NKJV).

In simple everyday ways, my father pointed us to God by living a life that did not compromise. He was a man of his word, and when he promised us he'd do something, he did it. Now that I've become a father, I have tried to follow in my dad's footsteps as I care for the needs of our children.

TAKE TIME FOR THE TEACHABLE MOMENTS

By making your family a priority and by being there, you'll find plenty of opportunities to tell your children about what's really important in life. I'm learning to take advantage of the "teachable moments"—when my kids are open to spiritual truth.

Years ago I was cuddled up next to our daughter Ashley on the lower bunk at bedtime. Somehow we found ourselves discussing the second coming of Christ. I told her, "Yes, Jesus is coming back, and He's going to take all those with Jesus in their hearts with Him, and it's going to be fantastic."

"I've got Him in my heart," said Ashley, "and when He comes, I'm going with Him, right?"

"That's exactly right," I told her. "You'll go up there and we'll all be together."

Then she asked, "What about Benjamin?"

"When it comes time for him to invite Jesus into his heart, he'll do that," I assured her.

About that time Benjamin's head popped up over the edge of the top bunk. Looking down, he said, "Dad, tomorrow would you tell me how to invite Jesus into my heart?"

"Sure, buddy, sure."

Then Benjamin slid back under the covers and went to sleep.

The next morning I asked him, "Remember what we were going to talk about?" He did, and we walked back into the kids' room, where I explained the gospel to him. He had heard it many times, but this time he said he was ready to invite Christ into his life.

"Are you sure you know what you're doing?" I said.

"Yeah. I want to invite Him in, right now." So he prayed and asked Jesus into his heart to be forgiven of his sins.

Do you know what his next words were?

"Daddy, could we play ball?"

I couldn't know at that time whether Benjamin had made a true, life-changing commitment to Christ. But the fact was that when he was interested, *I was there.*

Those rare teachable moments do exist, especially at bedtime. I find that my kids will let me talk about anything to keep from going to bed. I have some of my greatest times with them then, and occasionally I can even pull out some "heavy" theology.

A date with Ashley. Another favorite way I minister to my kids is to take them out on dates. And I'll never forget the first date I had with Ashley. She was a little over three years old, with chubby cheeks and wisps of hair fringing her face. I called her on the phone from the office and said, "Hi, this is Dad. I would really like to have a special date with you tonight, Princess."

I heard a little giggle and then her tiny voice saying, "Mommy, Daddy wants to take me out on a date!"

Barbara already knew my plan and so they went back to the bedroom and had Ashley all dressed up by the time I pulled up in front of the house. I went to the door and knocked and Barbara opened it. "Hello, Ma'am, is your daughter home?" I asked.

Ashley was just around the corner giggling and having a great time getting all that attention. She came out and we held hands as we walked down the steps of the front porch out to the car. I walked around to her door and opened it and she got in.

We had an old Rambler station wagon at the time with a bench seat and as we started out, Ashley very properly sat way over on her side. I said, "Ashley, you know when Daddy and Mommy go on a date, she sits right here," and I patted the seat right next to me.

"Okay," she said, and she slipped over, stood up, and put her little arm around my neck. There we were, driving down the road, laughing and talking about what we would do.

I said, "Let's go to one of those places where you can just eat what you want to eat. We can just pick and choose." And so we went to a restaurant and got chocolate pie, chocolate milk, and chocolate ice cream. We laughed about what Mom would say if she knew we were having all that sugar, and then we went to a movie. Ashley had a great time crawling all over the seats and occasionally watching *Bambi*. We ate popcorn. We spilled popcorn. We bought Cokes. We spilled Cokes. We did it all, and we did it right.

After the movie we drove home with the faint green light from the Rambler dashboard shining in our faces. I turned and asked, "Ashley, what was your favorite thing about tonight?" Before she answered, the thoughts raced through my mind. Would she say she liked all that chocolate? Maybe it would be the popcorn, the Cokes, or *Bambi*. Her little hand came over to pat me on the arm and she said, "Just being with you, Dad, just being with you."

It's too bad we didn't have a little more popcorn. I became a pool of melted butter right there.

Ashley perfectly articulated what all children want—to *be with their dad*. They don't want money or stuff. They just want a relationship with their dad. On the other hand, this past month I had a date with Rebecca, my eight-year-old, and when I asked her the same question she said, "Why, Dad, it was going shopping with you and the matching shorts and shirt outfit you *bought* me." Take heart—you don't win every time!

To be a minister to your family doesn't take deep spirituality or a seminary degree. All it takes is time and some shepherding, never moving faster than your little sheep can follow. And always remember: Your goal is to give them a heritage, not just an inheritance.

Think about what you are accumulating. Is it money? Titles? Adulation? Honors at work? What are you accumulating with your kids? You can't give them memories if you are isolated from them and not with them. The effects of isolation on children should never be underestimated.

Recently I had a conversation with our two teenagers. Wanting to warn them about what could happen if they become isolated from their mother and me, I said, "There will be a lot of things that you, your mom, and I will go through as you grow up. But one of the most important issues in our relationship is that you and I don't become isolated from one another, or that you don't become isolated from your mom."

Like a pair of typical teens, they had other things that they wanted to be doing. But they listened patiently as I went on:

"That's what the enemy wants—he wants you to become isolated from us and think that we are your enemies, that we don't have your best interests in mind. But if isolation creeps into our relationship and you start hiding from us, then not only is our relationship in trouble, but you are, as well. An isolated teenager can be convinced of anything." And then I added with emphasis, "*Anything.* I hope you understand."

Maybe after we've had conflict someday they'll remember those words. And, possibly, they'll seek to reestablish our relationship, because it makes sense to them, and because it's dangerous to do otherwise.

A ROLE MODEL OF GOD'S TRUTH

Albert Einstein was with a group of aspiring young scientists in his laboratory one day and he decided to give them a lesson, not in physics, but in being real men. He pushed his glasses up on his nose, pointed his bony finger, and said, "Gentlemen, try not to become men of success. Rather, become men of value."

That's a great piece of wisdom for every dad to impart to his kids. Instead of pushing your child to become a success, let him or her know that you prefer that they become men or women of value.

And the best way to do that is to show them, not simply tell them. Every dad is the family role model, whether he wants the job or not. My father played that role as well as he played any. He modeled integrity and honesty for me every day of his life.

At his funeral, a man came up to my mother and me and said, "I knew your husband all his life—from the time he grew up, all the way through his days of playing baseball. I watched him start a business. In all the years he did business in this town, I never heard a negative word about Hook Rainey. He never cheated or took advantage of anyone."

THE CHAIN SAW INCIDENT

God said of David that he shepherded his people "according to the integrity of his heart" (Psalm 78:72 NKJV).

When I think of that verse, my humanity comes back to haunt me. Several years ago, Benjamin and I were out on our property, which is located on a ridge overlooking a lake. One of our property lines borders a forest owned by the city.

Our view of the lake from the house was being obstructed by several trees and Benjamin and I were doing a little lumberjacking to improve the view.

We came upon a big oak that stood just across my property line on the city side. This particular tree was one of the major obstructions to our view and I started up my chain saw.

"Isn't that tree on city property, Dad?" Benjamin asked.

"No," I shouted over the buzz of the saw. "Not necessarily. Property lines are never that exact. Besides, there are millions of trees out here—they'll never miss it."

The chain saw sliced through the oak in a second and down it crashed, its little orange markers to delineate the property line still showing and the eighteen-inch stump clearly visible on the city's side of the line.

The next morning I was out on my back porch reading my Bible and I looked down the hill. There was the oak, still lying there. After a couple more days, I didn't even want to go out on our back porch to look at the view.

And then the Lord began to make noises like a chain saw in the back of my mind. Every time I read the Bible I saw trees. Finally, I looked down at that tree and said, "Oh, man, you've got to be kidding me. Have I got to go to the city and confess my sins?"

And the Lord said, "Yep."

I put off that phone call for two months, but finally I dialed City Hall to find someone to whom I could confess. I was hoping for some engineer I didn't know, but do you think the Lord would let me off that easily? Never!

Instead, I was directed to a city employee who lived nearby—practically one of our neighbors. With Benjamin standing next to me, I made the call, told him who I was, and said, "I cut down a tree on city property—just across from my own. I'm wrong and I want to make restitution."

I fully expected threats of prosecution, but the man was very gracious. He thanked me for my call and appreciated my promise not to do it again. Then he said, "The property lines out there aren't that exact anyway." I thanked him. As I hung up I turned to Benjamin who had heard the whole thing. "What did he say?" Benjamin asked.

I put my arm around him and said, "The man from the city was glad I called and told him what happened. He says it's okay as long as I don't do it again. You know, Benjamin, your dad may not be perfect, but he really wants to do what's right."

Benjamin didn't say much—he just nodded—but I could tell he was soaking it all in. I wasn't trying to be profound, just transparent. I had to hope he understood his dad's willingness to do what is right.

You Can Build out of Marble—or Manure

There is a saying, "What a man is determines what a man does." That is a weighty statement, but I like a quote from one of Eugene O'Neill's plays even better: "You do not build a marble tower out of a mixture of mud and manure."

I'm comforted by the fact that a man's character is shaped by his relationship with God. That's where my hope really lies. God hasn't given up on me. He is still squeezing the mud and manure out of my life—and building the marble tower instead.

Have you ever run on a track team or participated in some kind of relay race at a picnic? I used to run on our high-school relay team and we found all kinds of ways to lose—slow starts, sloppy hand-offs, running out of the lane.

Scripture speaks of running a different kind of relay, the kind in which you don't want to be disqualified. The psalmist speaks of telling generations to come about the Lord and His wonderful works, and then he says:

> For He established a testimony in Jacob, and appointed a law in Israel, which He commanded our fathers that they should make them known to their children; that the generation to come might know them, the children who would be born, that they may arise and declare them to their children, that they may set their hope in God, and not forget the works of God but keep His commandments . . . (Psalm 78:5–7 NKJV)

Now that I'm a father, I want to run the father-son/daughter relay as best I can. It's not just the guy who finishes first who will make the impact—it's the dad who finishes with his torch still burning brightly. And I want to run and give that torch of my love for Christ to my children, instructing them to carry it on to the next generation.

I can't think of a better time to be alive—and to be a dad.

HOMEBUILDERS PROJECTS

To Think About Individually

1. Think about how you have fulfilled the roles of family manager, family minister, and family role model. On a scale of 1 to 10 (10 being excellent), how do you see yourself?

As a family manager, I am a _____

I can improve in this area by _____

_____

As a family minister, I am a _____

I can improve in this area by _____

_____

As a family role model, I am a _____

I can improve in this area by _____

_____

2. List the two greatest needs of each of your children. How can you be more effective in meeting those needs?

For Interaction Together

1. Sit down with your wife and discuss your answers to the questions above. How does she rate you as a family manager, minister, and role model? How does she believe you can improve in each area?

2. What does your wife believe are the two greatest needs of each of your children? Compare your answers, then talk together about how both of you can meet those needs more effectively.

PART
FIVE

....

Building Oneness
Through Communication

....

HOMEBUILDERS
PRINCIPLES

Transparency is the path to oneness.

Transparency begins by creating an atmosphere
where it is safe to be totally open.

18

COMMUNICATION OR ISOLATION?

The primary speech organ,
the birthplace of our words,
is the human heart.

—KEN DURHAM[1]

"Tap-tap . . . tap-tap-tap . . . tap-tap-tap-tap . . . tap-tap-tap . . ."
Captain Red McDaniel rapped carefully on the walls of his cell in the Hanoi Hilton, practicing the special camp code prisoners used to communicate with each other. He knew he had to be careful. One of the strictest rules in this celebrated Vietnamese POW camp was "No communication with other prisoners."

His communist captors wanted to keep all of their American "guests" isolated and vulnerable. Anyone trying to communicate would be tortured and McDaniel had already been through that.

Shot out of the sky during a Vietnam War bombing mission, McDaniel had been captured by the Vietcong and brought to the notorious compound known as the "Hanoi Hilton." In terrible pain from injuries and utterly exhausted, McDaniel was put into a small room with no windows.

Immediately a prison officer entered and read him a long list of camp regulations. Rule number one was no communicating with anyone except his captors. For the next three days, he was interrogated and tortured as the North Vietnamese tried to break his will and get him to give them information on his unit and future targets of American planes.

THE REAL ENEMY

Finally, McDaniel's tormentors let him sleep for six hours. Then, instead of resuming his torture, they introduced him to solitary confinement. McDaniel was shoved into a dark cell, totally separated from other prisoners. Here, as the long hours and days passed, McDaniel met his real enemy—isolation. He was without human contact, without conversation. All he knew was the dulling, silent darkness of isolation.

As the interminable hours went by, McDaniel came to fear isolation far more than the threats of torture by his Vietcong captors. The highlight of each day was being taken to the washroom where he managed to whisper briefly with two other Americans who were brought in at the same time. They told him about the camp code, an acrostic system that involved using a certain number of taps (or other signals) to spell out letters of the alphabet. McDaniel came to recognize the code as his lifeline, his only link with sanity.

For McDaniel, it was communicate or die. He was a POW for six years and would often be left in solitary confinement for as long as eighteen months, having no way to communicate with other Americans except through tapping out messages with the camp code or passing notes through the camp's "pony express" system. He wrote the notes on toilet paper, using a bamboo stick for a pen and "ink" made of water and brick dust.

How McDaniel survived his long years of imprisonment is vividly described in his book, *Scars and Stripes*.[2] McDaniel watched other POWs brought in to be tortured and then placed in solitary confinement. He saw almost fifty of America's finest trained men go into isolation never to be heard from again.

If the new prisoner couldn't learn the code and communicate with fellow Americans within thirty days of his arrival, he would gradually start to draw inward and deteriorate. As the days went by in the dark cell, the prisoner would slowly lose the will to live. He would stop eating, and as his stomach became bloated, he would actually start to feel "fat." Little by little, the prisoner would deteriorate as the strange predator, isolation, sucked his very life out of him.

THE MOST COMMON PROBLEM IN MARRIAGE

At first glance, the horrors of the Hanoi Hilton seem unrelated to a marriage relationship. But in a very real way, we all face the same problem Red McDonald had—communicate or your marriage will die. A four-year study of several hundred couples by the Family Service Association of America found that poor communication is the most common problem in a marriage, occurring about twice as often as any other problem. And *lonely?* What better word describes those husbands and wives trapped in the stony silence of a marriage void of meaningful interaction?

True, good communication is a longed-for luxury in all kinds of relationships. Nothing is as easy as talking; and nothing is as difficult as communicating. Just ask the public welfare departments of our nation. Some of the letters they receive make you realize how difficult it is to understand what people mean by what they say:

> I cannot get sick pay. I have six children. Can you tell me why?
> I am glad to report that my husband who was reported missing is dead.
> Mrs. Jones has not had any clothes for a year and has been visited regularly by the clergy.

Or you can go to the car insurance companies and read some of the accident reports they have to decipher:

> Coming home I drove into the wrong house and collided with a tree I don't have.
> The guy was all over the road. I had to swerve a number of times before I hit him.
> I had been driving for forty years when I fell asleep at the wheel and had an accident.

217

I was on my way to the doctor with rear end trouble when my universal joint gave way, causing me to have an accident.

I pulled away from the side of the road, glanced at my mother-in-law, and headed over the embankment.

All these people knew what they were trying to say, but their use of words left a little to be desired. Using words correctly and skillfully is an important part of communication, but more important is something even more basic—developing the kind of attitude that makes you willing to communicate.

The Great Cover-Up

Communicating effectively begins with discovering the meaning and correct use of transparency. By transparency, I don't mean detecting a phony as in "I always could see right through him." The transparency I'm talking about is the kind described in Genesis before the Fall: "Now although the man and his wife were both naked, neither of them was embarrassed or ashamed" (Genesis 2:25 TLB).

Adam and Eve were "without disguise or covering, without any mask." Not only were they uncovered physically, they did not cover up emotionally. Before the Fall, Adam and Eve are a picture of true transparency—being real, open to each other, and unafraid of rejection.

But after the Fall we read, "Suddenly they became aware of their nakedness, and were embarrassed. So they strung fig leaves together to cover themselves around the hips" (Genesis 3:7 TLB).

Those famous fig leaf aprons were only part of their cover-up. Sin introduced a lot more than modesty. It also brought deceit, lying, trickery, half-truths, manipulation, misrepresentation, distortion, hatred, jealousy, and many other vices—all causing us to wear masks.

Many people spend a lot of time and energy acquiring facades and veneers to hide their insecurities. They are afraid that if someone finds out what they are really like, they would be rejected. It's no wonder so many wives and husbands are afraid to tell each other who they really are.

For men, in particular, transparency can be very threatening. Most men still believe weeping openly is a sign of weakness. They shy away from tears because it means being vulnerable, and they have been taught that men are to be strong, self-contained, and invincible. Fortunately, this pattern has been changing in recent years.

The Scriptures, however, emphasize being transparent and vulnerable. Paul modeled transparency when he wrote to the Corinthians, many of whom were not exactly his admirers, and said, "For I wrote you out of great distress and anguish of heart and with many tears, not to grieve you but to let you know the depth of my love for you" (2 Corinthians 2:4). Paul was not afraid to weep or say, "I love you." Jesus wept over the death of Lazarus (John 11:35) and lamented His rejection by hardhearted Jerusalem (Luke 13:34).

TRANSPARENCY IS NOT IMPULSIVE

At the same time, Scripture warns about being *too* open and honest. Solomon wrote, "When words are many, sin is not absent, but he who holds his tongue is wise" (Proverbs 10:19). The Living Bible paraphrase of this proverb is even clearer: "Don't talk too much. You keep putting your foot in your mouth. Be sensible and turn off the flow!"

The old saying claims, "Sticks and stones can break my bones, but words can never hurt me." But words *can* hurt. They can cut, rip, and wound. As Solomon said, "Reckless words pierce like a sword, but the tongue of the wise brings healing" (Proverbs 12:18). If you're a spouse who uses words recklessly, then you would do well to "hold your tongue."

Many couples would improve their relationships if one or both partners would start to use words that are gentle, full of encouragement and praise. If we need anything in marriage, it is partners who do more affirming of one another.

GREAT WORDS BUILD SELF-ESTEEM

Thoughtless words chip away at your mate's self-esteem. As we grow up, our self-esteem can be whittled by parents, brothers and sisters, teachers, coaches, employers, and friends who don't know any better, or who speak in moments of anger or irritation. I clearly recall the day my high-school typing teacher leaned over her desk after I had disrupted class again and said, "Dennis Rainey, you'll never amount to anything!"

Those words hurt. I've never forgotten them. Fortunately I had a pair of parents who believed in me and a good number of other teachers who were an encouragement.

I remember the words of another teacher who planted positive thoughts in my mind. I've forgotten the name of our sixth-grade basketball coach, but I'll never forget how he started every practice. It was 1960 and we were all twelve years old. Our coach would walk in and shout, "What's the good word, guys?"

And we would all stop warming up and roar back in unison, "STATE CHAMPS, 1966!"

You see, our coach had us looking forward to six years down the road when we'd be seniors in high school and trying to win a state basketball championship. He started every practice with that question, and he often used it when we'd stop for a breather between drills:

"What's the good word, guys?"

"STATE CHAMPS, 1966!"

I wish I could report that we won the state title in 1966. Unfortunately, we lost in the first round. But all of us did become better players than anyone thought we would because a coach with vision planted a goal in the minds of fledgling basketball hopefuls who hardly knew how to dribble.

The words you speak can affect your mate's self-esteem. Your tongue can either be a verbal ice pick that chips it away, or a paintbrush that adds splashes of vibrant color by affirming and encouraging your mate.

HOW DO WE LEARN TO BE TRANSPARENT?

If the Bible encourages proper transparency but cautions against using the tongue recklessly, how can we tell the difference between what is appropriate and inappropriate? How can we learn to encourage and build each other up rather than discourage and tear each other down? How can we learn to be open with each other, but not too open?

Like most skills, you have to start at the bottom and work up. In his excellent book *Why Am I Afraid to Tell You Who I Am?* John Powell described five stages or levels of communication: cliché, fact, opinion, emotion, transparency. As the progression suggests, you work up to transparency slowly and gently.

The fifth, or lowest, level is cliché conversation—"elevator talk" in which you speak but share nothing with another person: "Hello, how are you doing? Hot, isn't it? Have a nice day." As Powell observed, if someone asked, "How are you?" and you really started to tell him in detail, the other person would be flabbergasted. Instead, you usually just say, "Just fine; thank you."

Moving up the scale a notch, level four conversation involves reporting the facts. You share what you know but little more than that. You expose nothing of yourself and are content to report what so-and-so said, or what so-and-so did. When marriages slip into advanced stages of isolation, couples will often revert to fact sharing, giving nothing of themselves to each other and inviting nothing in return.[3]

At level three, you share your opinions—your ideas and judgments about things. At this level you finally start to come out of your shell and reveal a little bit of who you are. You begin to take some risks as you reveal what and how you think.

But as Powell pointed out, you are very careful about doing this. You watch the other person carefully and, if you sense even the slightest question or rejection, you retreat.

At level two, you start sharing your emotions, what you feel. Powell called this "gut level communication," because now you are definitely out of the closet and letting the other person know what you are feeling.

It is here that you must be careful to avoid hurting your mate. But so many marriages are in such need of sharing feelings, the risk must be taken.

If you can't share feelings with your spouse, you marriage is on superficial ground. You won't grow, and neither will your partner.

Level one communication is transparency—being completely open with the other person. Transparency means sharing the real you, from the heart. Level one communication requires a deep degree of trust, communication, and friendship.

The transparency level is reserved for your spouse and perhaps a few others who are very close. It is doubtful that you will become transparent with very many people and, in fact, it can be dangerous as I pointed out in Chapter 7. Sharing too much of who you are with someone of the opposite sex can lead to an affair.

When a couple reaches the transparency level, they are operating with oneness. One can bear witness to the other and say, "You know, I think you're angry."

And the other can say, "Well, you know, I really haven't understood that, but I guess you are right. I am really upset about that."

Barbara and I often communicate at this level. I may get going on something that really has me worked up, and I'll ask her, "What do you think I'm saying here?"

"Well," she says, "it sounds to me as if your real problem is that you are ticked over being behind in your work."

"You're right," I reply, "I am." And then I have to figure out what I can do to diffuse that anger and turn it into something constructive. To remain angry only gives the devil a foothold and ensures isolation (Ephesians 4:27).

TRANSPARENCY SAYS, "I NEED YOU"

One of the greatest benefits of transparency is that it brings peace of mind. As husband and wife open up to each other, they take risks—tiny ones at first. Then, if they succeed, they take bigger steps of self-revelation. And when this happens, what they are really doing is saying to each other, "I need you."

At FamilyLife Conferences, one of the projects involves a husband taking his wife's hands in his, looking her in the eye, and saying three crucial words: "I need you." Even though most wives respond by literally beaming with appreciation, many men still find this a very difficult thing to do. In fact, some tell me that saying, "I need you," is far more difficult than saying, "I love you."

I understand that, because those words express vulnerability, an admission that a man isn't complete in and of himself. To say, "I need you," means you are not self-sufficient. It's ironic that when couples are dating, they don't have much problem expressing their need for each other. After getting married, however, the words stick somewhere south of the man's Adam's apple.

Early in our marriage I had that problem, but now I often tell Barbara I need her. Those words affirm her and let her know that she is a woman of value, a woman I trust, a woman who is my life partner in the truest sense.

For some husbands the struggle to become transparent is long and arduous. A couple married thirty-one years came to a FamilyLife Conference, sent by relatives who insisted that they attend. The husband was almost totally closed as a communicator, and because I knew of their problems, I monitored them carefully throughout the weekend. At the close of the conference, I drew them aside and asked, "What did you get out of the conference?"

The husband stood facing me while his wife sat on the stage, chin in hand, staring at the floor. I could tell he was struggling even then to express himself, but he finally said, "Well . . . I guess the most significant thing is that we've been married thirty-one years and I haven't told my wife I love her until this weekend."

He reached down to tenderly squeeze his wife's arm and went on to admit, "This is the first weekend in twenty-four years we've been away from the children."

I looked over at his wife, who had begun sobbing quietly. While they had made progress toward intimacy, it obviously had been a painful weekend. Her tears were mixed—the pain of isolation blended with the joy of a breakthrough to transparency and oneness they had never known before. She had been a very lonely wife, but they had taken one small yet significant step toward a better marriage.

LOVE CREATES AN ATMOSPHERE FOR OPENNESS

Transparency begins with a firm commitment to creating an atmosphere where it is safe to be totally open. Inside Barbara's wedding band is the inscription "1 John 4:18." That verse of Scripture says, "There is no fear in love. But perfect love drives out fear." We both know we are totally committed to our love for each other, and we can be open to each other without fear.

Because I'm the more open one in our marriage, I work at making the message engraved in Barbara's wedding ring words of assurance. A problem that has often plagued us is my behavior when we go out to dinner with another couple or couples. Because I'm the gregarious, life-of-the-party type, I'll pick up a lagging conversation by asking a good question. All I'm trying to do is get to know the other people and keep the evening alive and interesting. But I frequently err by not allowing time for Barbara, who is not as aggressive, to enter into the conversation.

Early in our marriage, we would drive home after a dinner party and I would say, "Goodness, sweetheart, we were with those people for several hours and you didn't say two or three words all evening."

And Barbara would say, "Well, you didn't give me a chance."

We would usually drive a few blocks in silence, and I would apologize for not including her.

Later I would ask her what she thought of one of the people at the party. Whereupon Barbara would begin to make profound observations about what had taken place that evening and what had been said. She has keen insights and perceptions about people. I've learned to rely on her insights.

Instead of getting irritated or impatient when Barbara is sometimes reluctant to share her feelings, I see my own tendency toward openness for what it is—a gift from God to be used wisely, and never as a condescending put-down. I've also sought ways to gently encourage Barbara to open up—and she's learning to risk a little more as well.

Although we've been married since 1972, we are still learning how to communicate. In particular, I am still learning how to listen, an important skill for building intimacy in marriage. In the next two chapters we will see why.

HOMEBUILDERS PROJECTS

TO THINK ABOUT INDIVIDUALLY

1. If you are the open, transparent type, analyze how you are relating to your mate, particularly if he or she is more closed and less transparent. Do you overwhelm your mate or do you try to draw him or her out gently and lovingly?

2. If you are the more closed and less transparent partner of your marriage, what are you doing to try to open up? Do you make an honest effort to respond to questions your mate may ask to get communication going? Make a commitment to explain and describe your feelings to your mate. Be determined to talk them out, even if you find it difficult.

3. At what level do you communicate most, especially with the people in your family?

    _____ Clichés _____ Facts _____Opinions

    _____Emotions _____ Transparency

4. At what level does your mate communicate most, especially with the people in your family?

    _____ Clichés _____ Facts _____ Opinions

    _____ Emotions _____ Transparency

5. As part of your commitment to more transparency and freedom to communicate in your marriage, memorize any of the following Scriptures:

    "Don't talk so much. You keep putting your foot in your mouth. Be sensible and turn off the flow!" (Proverbs 10:19 TLB).

"Reckless words pierce like a sword, but the tongue of the wise brings healing" (Proverbs 2:18).

"Wise men store up knowledge, but the mouth of a fool invites ruin" (Proverbs 10:14).

FOR INTERACTION TOGETHER

1. Talk together about how easy or difficult it is to share feelings and be transparent with one another. (NOTE: If one mate is extremely closed, go very slowly here. Don't pressure him or her.)

2. Try facing each other, holding hands, looking each other in the eye and saying, "I love you." Then continue by saying, "I need you." Talk together about why you love and need one another.

HOMEBUILDERS
PRINCIPLES

**Resolving conflict begins with a commitment
to listen and understand.**

19

TO TURN CONFLICT INTO ONENESS, BEGIN TO LISTEN!

It is best to listen much, speak little, and not become angry.
—The Apostle James
(JAMES 1:19 TLB)

Quibbles.
Quarrels.
Squabbles.

What do you argue about at your house? At our place, the answer is "just about everything." At our home conflicts are as normal as breathing. One university statistician told me that, with eight people in our family, we have at least sixty-four different interpersonal relationships. It's no wonder that some days Barbara and I feel we've been ringside and, possibly, *in* the ring with our gloves on.

Our girls collide over their dolls. Our boys bicker over who has to take out the garbage. At dinner, it's who gets to sit by whom, and in the car the prized seat (middle front between Mom and Dad) is the cause of minor warfare nearly every time we head out of the driveway.

Yet, with all the juvenile wrangling that goes on, the most surprising conflicts have not occurred among the children, but between Barbara and me. Our arguments and disagreements are over pressures, schedules, deadlines, and, more often than not, missed communication. Somebody was right when he said communication is not what is *said*, but what is *heard*.

One area where we continue to struggle is fixing up the house. Barbara's Ethan Allen ambitions to have things just right are often frustrated by her husband's inept mechanical ability.

At present we need a trellis to hide all the junk under our deck at the rear of the house. I got a bid from a carpenter that sounded like he thought we wanted to add a spare room. The price was well out of our reach, but Barbara had her usual practical solution: "Well, sure, sweetheart, you can build it."

After seventeen years of marriage, Barbara still hopes my 2-percent hands will magically gain mechanical skill. But going out to buy lumber, measuring, sawing, and hammering are just not my idea of relaxation. And so Barbara prays for me to get out there and put up a trellis, while I ask God to help me find a carpenter I can afford.

ALL COUPLES HAVE THEIR CONFLICTS

Few couples like to admit it, but conflict is common to all marriages. The man who wrote the following letter to Ann Landers undoubtedly had no idea of the conflicts in store for him when he began a marriage that has lasted over three decades:

> Dear Ann: Right hand to God, this is no joke. I am both mystified and burned up. Please give me your opinion. I can't go to anyone else.
>
> I am 58 years old, married to a good woman for 34 years. Our marriage is no better or worse than most others. She's not perfect, but then neither am I. The problem: I'm a heavy sleeper and I snore. My wife says my snoring has gotten really bad this past year, and it interferes with her rest.
>
> Last night she gave me a head band with a bicycle horn attached to it. The horn is in the back. When the snorer turns to sleep on his back the horn blows and wakes him up. I tried the blame thing on and it was

very uncomfortable. Also, the horn is loud and it would scare me out of my wits if it blew during the night. I refused to wear it.

Do you feel I am justified?

Embattled in Elmhurst

Dear Em: You're darned tootin'.[1]

CONFLICT CAN LEAD TO VIOLENCE

Of course, conflicts can get a lot more serious than arguments over remodeling or snoring. Sometimes they can spawn strange stories.

Tony and Frances Toto made *People* magazine with their story of the bitter fruits of conflict in their marriage. In 1984, Toto, an Allentown, Pennsylvania, pizza parlor owner, survived several attempts on his life by assailants who did everything from hitting him on the head with a baseball bat to shooting him on two different occasions while he slept.

The person behind all this was his wife, Frances, who had hired the hit men to do the job. The first time Tony was shot, he was hit in the head, but lived. The second time they shot him in the chest, but somehow he survived that too.

What was the Totos' source of conflict? Apparently, Tony was a ladies' man and his wife decided to do a little straying herself. Amazingly, when Tony discovered that Frances and her lover were behind the attempts on his life, he forgave his wife, paid her attorney's fees, and even visited her regularly in prison after she was convicted of soliciting for murder.

Four years later, Frances was released from prison and welcomed back home by Tony and their four children. According to Tony, they are more in love than ever. "I'm in one piece and still laughing." Tony said, "I think if you find the right person, you have to stick with it. I don't understand why people break up over silly things."[2]

THE POSITIVE SIDE OF CONFLICT

So far it sounds as though conflict is an evil to be avoided at all costs, especially in a marriage, but that's impossible. Every marriage has its tensions, and it isn't a question of avoiding them, it's a question of how *you* deal with them. Conflict can lead to a process that develops intimacy or isolation. You and your partner must choose how you will act when conflict occurs.

Conflict often starts with something small, even inconsequential. As someone said, people who claim that small things don't bother them never slept in a room with a mosquito. It's the little things that rob a marriage of its romance—and its oneness. The little things, left unresolved, lead to bitterness, anger, and loneliness.

Another reason we have conflict in marriage is that opposites attract. It's strange, but that's part of the reason why you married who you did. Your mate added a variety, spice, and difference to your life that it didn't have before. But after being married for a while (sometimes a short while), the attractions become repellents.

The Peacemaker vs. the Prizefighter

A typical pairing is the peacemaker and the prizefighter. The peacemaker would rather hide than fight. The peacemaker says, "It's okay, let's forget it, it isn't worth the hassle."

The prizefighter lives life in the ring and "seems" to love hearing the bell. He says, "Let's put on the gloves and duke it out. There's nothing as enjoyable as a good, hearty, spirited conversation."

I counseled one couple caught in this struggle. The husband came from a long line of prizefighters and grew up watching his whole family having "spirited discussions" with rolled-up sleeves and loud, angry voices. The beauty of it—for their family—was that they could discuss issues, argue vehemently, even attack one another, and then hang up their gloves, hug, and make up.

But his wife came from a long line of peacemakers who swept everything under the rug. Her family avoided discussions and disagreements as though it was a transmittable disease. And so what kind of a marriage did these two have? He was chasing her around the house, trying to get her to "put on the gloves," and she was dashing about trying to find a place to hide.

You might be able to guess who landed between them—their daughter. I talked with this girl when she was in her early thirties, and she told me that when she was six or seven, she began wedging herself between her mom and dad.

"I desperately wanted Dad to understand how Mom felt," she said. "I'd tell him Mom didn't like to fight. Why couldn't he understand that? And then I'd go to Mom and say, 'Mom, why don't you talk about these things with Dad? You need to understand that he gets frustrated if he can't talk it out.'"

But it seemed the harder she tried to pull her parents together, the more they seemed to move apart. She became so deeply disturbed by the unresolved conflict isolation she saw between her mother and father that she told me, "Hardly a day passed that I didn't think about committing suicide." It took years of long-term counseling to help her come to terms with the problem.

There is a lot at stake in the way you and your mate handle your conflicts. It's not just the intimacy in your marriage that's on the line, but the lives of impressionable sons and daughters as well. The warning of the African proverb is a chilling one: "When the elephants fight, it's the grass that suffers."

THE VALUE OF A LISTENING EAR

Saint Francis of Assisi was never married, but he gave all married couples golden advice when he prayed, "Lord, may I seek to understand more than to be understood." Most conflict in marriage arises because one or both partners refuse to hear the other or they don't take time to listen.

I ran across an ad in a Kansas newspaper that said, "I will listen to you talk without comment for thirty minutes for $5.00." Phone calls poured in from all over the country in answer to that ad. Ten to twenty people called every day—just wanting someone to listen.

Paul Tournier, the Swiss psychiatrist, advises husbands and wives to "be preoccupied with listening in your marriage." The Scriptures tell us the same thing: "Everyone should be quick to listen, slow to speak and slow to become angry" (James 1:19). Unfortunately, usually we are slow to listen, quick to speak, and even quicker to become angry. Most of us don't need hearing aids—we just need aids in hearing.

Perhaps you took a speech course in high school or college. That course most likely taught you the basics of speaking. The problem is most of us have had little training in *how to listen*. We know how to argue and win our point—but we are neophytes when it comes to listening. As a result, poor listening habits show up in several different forms:

1. *Pseudo-listening*. Husbands are often guilty here. Dad comes home and drops into the easy chair trying to relax with TV before dinner. Little Johnny comes in and says, "Hey, Dad, can Jimmy and I sleep out down by the railroad tracks tonight?"

Lost in a nonlistening fog, Dad mumbles, "Uh, guess so—sounds okay to me . . ." But after little Johnny leaves, the words finally penetrate and reach Dad's brain. He bolts upright and bellows, "The railroad tracks! Come back here!"

2. *Selective listening*. One problem with learning to listen well is that all of us can listen at least five times faster than anyone can talk. While your spouse is trying to express something really important, you may be thinking of things you want to get done around the house and phone calls you have to make. Or you may drift off into that well-known territory "a million miles away."

Another form of selective listening can happen when you're having an argument. You listen only for what you want to hear, thinking, *Aha! Weak reasoning there. I'll nail her to the wall on that one. What's her next point? Aha! Got her again.*

With this kind of selective listening, you're not trying to *hear* what your mate is saying; you're simply building your case.

3. *Protective listening*. The protective listener doesn't want to hear much at all, especially something threatening. His mate may have been trying to tell him things for centuries, but he has insulated his heart from hearing—he *refuses* to listen.

Sometimes I come home and Barbara wants to talk, but I don't *want* to listen. She gets into the problems of her day and goes on describing them in great detail. I want to say, "Sweetheart, what is the bottom line? What is *the* issue here?"

But Barbara isn't really interested in any bottom line. I'm finally beginning to understand that many times she doesn't want my brilliant solutions. She just wants to be heard. Why? Because she's been in Romper Room all day and needs to relate to another adult.

4. *Surface listening.* This is another form of selective listening that concentrates on hearing just enough to keep the conversation going but not enough to really understand your mate. Good listeners, though, don't spend their time in the shallows; they go deep and really zero in on what others are saying.

If conflicts are to be resolved we must learn to put away our poor listening habits and give our mates our undivided attention.

THE NEED FOR FOCUSED ATTENTION

Recently I received a letter from a wife who shared how her husband's poor listening habits affected her. She wrote,

Dear Dennis:

I have one small request. Next seminar you give please reiterate several times throughout the conference the importance of being alone with your spouse. A "no-no" is to go out to eat with other couples because you don't put into practice what you've just learned and invariably the guys will talk "boy talk" and the girls will gab about kids or clothes, etc.

My husband is finishing up his surgical residency, so as you can imagine our entire eleven years of marriage have been spent with pressures of studying and outrageous work loads. He's a great guy, one in a million, neat Christian and adored by everyone who knows him. My one complaint is that when we attend a party or go out with another couple, he talks about work, cars, etc., and ignores me.

At the conference, we ate all our meals with another couple. By the last day it occurred to me that we hadn't gotten to know each other better.

Instead, my husband began telling me that he and Dan were "kindred spirits," and what a great guy he was. So for all the time and money invested in the weekend, he came away getting to know his buddy better. Get my drift?

Needless to say, my self-esteem has lagged quite a bit as a result of his interest in his friends. It would be different if we saw each other and communicated regularly.

P.S. I threatened to not go to his big medical meeting this past week because he leaves me to go talk "shop." Almost had him on one knee begging me to go (so he wouldn't have to explain where I was!).

I definitely got this lady's drift! Her husband has neglected to see his wife's need to be listened to—to have his undivided, focused attention.

Focused attention couldn't be better illustrated than in the following story about some workmen who were storing huge blocks of ice in deep beds of sawdust in a dark ice house. One of the workmen dropped his watch into the thick sawdust and searched for it in vain for several days. Finally, a young boy offered to help him find it. Asking everyone else to remain outside, he went into the ice house and came out in just a few minutes holding the watch. "What happened?" said the incredulous workman. "How'd you find it so fast?"

"Simple," said the boy. "I went to the middle of the room, put my ear down next to the sawdust, and *listened.*"

In your marriage is your focused attention detecting the ticking of your mate? In some marriages that ticking may suggest a time bomb ready to go off because someone isn't being heard.

EYEBALL TO EYEBALL

The first step toward focused attention is to *look right at the person you are listening to.* When I face members of my family eyeball to eyeball, they can generally be sure they have my attention.

Frequently, I come home and my kids are waiting to tell me about their dead bunny, how Mom unfairly disciplined them, or how they got a good test score that day at school. They want me to understand their feelings and hear their stories, but at times I don't want to understand, because I'm dead tired and just want to relax.

My kids, however, don't let it go. I trained them too well. With rising volume they insist: "Dad . . . Daddy . . . DADDY!!!" until I turn my face and look right at them. Then I'll go through the motions and say, "Yes, what do you want?"

About that time Barbara will say, "Children, it would be better to talk to your dad in a few minutes, but not right now. Your father is not home yet."

"Yes, he is, Mom," they exclaim. "He's right here."

Barbara says, "Yes, we know he's right there, but he doesn't know it yet. Be a little patient with him."

And sure enough, she's right. After I have a few minutes to relax, I can usually give real focused attention. The tip-off is that the glaze is gone from my eyes and I am really looking at the people who are trying to talk to me.

ACTIVE LISTENING ACCEPTS AND UNDERSTANDS

Another term for focused attention is *active listening*, which means that you are interested in what your spouse is feeling, not just in hearing some information. You listen with the desire to understand and accept how your spouse feels. You never tell your spouse, "That's dumb, you shouldn't feel that way. That's stupid."

Perhaps the way your spouse feels is not based on facts or reality, but that's beside the point. *This is how your spouse feels*, and facts don't really matter. To tell your spouse that her feelings are stupid and invalid doesn't promote oneness and understanding.

To practice active listening, try sending back messages of empathy that let your spouse know that you are trying to put yourself in his or her shoes. Don't try to evaluate or offer a lot of advice. Just reflect the feelings that you hear being communicated.

For example, I may come home and Barbara will greet me with, "I'm about ready to ground that child. She's impossible!" (I'm being purposely vague here to protect the guilty!)

My first inclination is to move in and play Mighty Leader and ask, "What did she do now? Where is she? I want to talk to that kid!"

But if I want to actively listen to Barbara, my first comment might be, "It sounds as if you and 'that child' might have had a long day."

Then Barbara will give me the details on the problem if she wishes or talk about her tough day, which really may be what is on her mind.

Once you establish communication with your mate through focused attention and active listening, you can seek clarification by *asking questions*. Questions are like crowbars that dislodge thoughts and emotions from another person's heart. But you have to use those "crowbars" deftly and gently.

Asking the right questions is particularly valuable if you're married to a person who is reserved and has a hard time opening up. And when you're disagreeing at even the mildest level, use questions to focus on clarifying valid points rather than defending yourself against what you feel are incorrect accusations. Focus on discovering the truth rather than gaining indictments. Ask questions to gain understanding, not to make judgments.

FROM THE MOUTH OF A MISTRESS

Years ago I found some profound observations about listening—comments made by a mistress. Look at these words from Melissa Sands, founder of "Mistresses Anonymous":

> Ask any mistress. Her man doesn't do anything but talk endlessly. Mistresses are experts in the art of listening. People think a mistress has a sexual manual that keeps them bewitched, but actually what she really has is the capacity to listen.
>
> Men have mistresses because they have needs that they are unable to fill in their other lives. By needs, I mean needs to communicate—sexually, verbally, tactilely.
>
> They don't get these needs filled at home because they see their wives

when they are tired or worried about money, or early in the morning when both are at their worst, at all the wrong times.

Mistresses, however, see their men when they are at the peak of their day in energy and motivation. A married woman makes time for her job, her kids, the PTA, even her mother-in-law, but she does not make a special time for her husband. The mistress does.[3]

From the mouth of a mistress comes a bit of real wisdom on how to make your marriage affair-proof: Gain all of the skills you can to become a better listener. Then, genuinely listen to your mate—so you can avoid conflicts.

HOMEBUILDERS PROJECTS

TO THINK ABOUT INDIVIDUALLY

1. What leads to conflict between you and your spouse? List at least four or five things—even "inconsequential" ones.

2. Of which of the following "bad listening habits" are you guilty? Which ones is your mate guilty of?

MY MATE	MYSELF	
_____	_____	Pseudo-listening that fakes interest.
_____	_____	Selective listening that tunes in only now and then.
_____	_____	Protective listening—"Don't bother me."
_____	_____	Service listening—not really with each other.

3. What can you do to break any bad listening habits? When do you plan to start?

FOR INTERACTION TOGETHER

Sit down together and share your answers to the questions above. Use the following ground rules:

1. Listen carefully to what the other person is saying.

2. If you start to get irritated and find yourself headed for conflict, call time out and read the next chapter!

HOMEBUILDERS PRINCIPLES

The goal of confrontation is not winning or losing, but gaining peace, oneness, and intimacy.

20

THE SECRET OF LOVING CONFRONTATION

Rare is the person who can weigh the faults of others
without putting his hands on the scales.

—AUTHOR UNKNOWN

Over the years I've made a list of the different things couples fight about. Here's part of my list:

- sleeping in the dark or with a night-light on
- the number of blankets on the bed
- leaving windows open or closed
- where to keep the temperature—at 43 degrees or 96 degrees
- how to blow your nose
- how to chew gum
- how to eat food
- what kind of music to play on the radio
- how loud the music is played
- where clothing is thrown after it's taken off
- the proper way to hang toilet paper
- what time to go to bed or get up
- the way she or he drives

That list could go on for pages.

And, of course, there is that matter of "being on time." In college I learned to operate on Vince Lombardi time. Lombardi, the legendary coach of the Green Bay Packers, never tolerated any player being late for practice or to a team meeting. And if someone were late, he was sent out to run a few dozen laps just to remember Lombardi wasn't fooling.

In college my watch was always set five minutes fast. I still do the same today, because I want to arrive at my appointments ahead of time, not "fashionably late."

Unfortunately, however, Barbara runs by a different kind of watch. Over the years she's tried to get herself on Vince Lombardi time, but she still struggles. And, of course, when she's late it turns her husband into a mini version of Vince, not something that particularly encourages intimacy in our marriage. I don't ask Barbara to run laps, but on occasion I do make some untimely remarks on her tardiness.

ONLY ON SUNDAY

For some reason Sunday—the "day of rest"—seems to be our sternest challenge. If you have no trouble getting to church on time, the following story may not seem relevant, but it's my hunch that many people, especially those with small children, can identify.

Our church service starts at 8:30 A.M., so out of necessity we *try* to get up early on Sunday because we have a lot of people who must get showered, dressed, and fed, with hair combed, bows in place, and ties on straight. It's amazing how many people can populate our bathroom—and I can never find *my* hairbrush.

But no matter how early we arise and try to get it all together, invariably I get out to the car, ready to go, and there is *no one* there with me. Where is everyone? I honk the horn, glancing at my Vince Lombardi watch. Then I begin to mutter and murmur—an attitude hardly conducive to preparing one's heart for worship.

Finally, Barbara comes out with all the kids. They fly into the van like a covey of quail, yakking at each other. But Dad isn't in the mood: "Be quiet, kids!"

Finally, we get the doors closed and I peel out of the driveway and up the hill. Barbara glances at the speedometer and calls out, "Fasten your seat belts, children, we're going to church!" When they start arguing about the piece of toast one of them bootlegged into the car, I've had enough. "One more word and you're in big trouble!" I bark at them, " *We're going to church to learn about Jesus.* "

There we are, zooming down the road. It's white-knuckle time and I'm breaking every law in the land to get to church. And, of course, I'm talking to Barbara with a verbal Gatling gun: "Why were you so late? Do you know how many times we've been late to church? I was out there waiting for all of you for ten minutes."

She gives me a look that would freeze water at the equator and says, "Do you know how many people *I got ready* this morning?"

"Well, I certainly tried to help. I got out the cereal boxes and found my own socks."

We whip into the parking lot of the church and I try to stop without screeching the brakes. Barbara is still ticked at me and I'm red under the collar. By the time we get to the church door, I try to regain composure: "Good morning, Pastor! God bless you, it's really great to be here. Wonderful day the Lord made."

We sit through a stirring church service, featuring an excellent sermon on patience. Then we round up the kids, pile them back in the van, and head for home. I decide to spring for Sunday lunch out as a peace offering and later that afternoon, when all the kids have scattered to their various activities, Barbara and I sit down to talk.

Barbara will say, "You know, Sweetheart, this morning I didn't feel as if you really helped me get everyone ready. You went downstairs and read the newspaper while I was trying to get six kids presentable enough to go to church."

I know she's right and I have to say, "I'm sorry, I was wrong. How can I be more help next time?"

And then Barbara will explain (for what must seem to her the fiftieth time) some things that I can do. Fortunately, Sundays like the one I've just described don't happen as often as they used to. I have learned how to be a better help and not let selfishness win the day. And, I'm still working on Barbara to get on Vince Lombardi time!

CONFRONTING ONE ANOTHER WITH LOVE

Over the years I've learned to listen to Barbara because she learned the art of *loving confrontation*. Wordsworth said, "He who has a good friend needs no mirror." Blessed is the marriage where both spouses feel the other is a good friend, who will listen, reflect back, understand, and work through whatever needs to be dealt with. To do this well takes loving confrontation.

Loving confrontation means "making the most of the best and the least of the worst." First Corinthians 13 reminds us that love never expects the worst of others. Love believes the best about the other person.

I know of a man whose wife repeatedly asks him to slow down because he just goes too hard. From sunup to sundown he's going, doing, hustling, constantly on the move. He never seems to listen to his wife, who is really the anchor and source of stability in their marriage, and who often feels like a lonely voice, crying in the wilderness.

Others have also attempted to share their concern with him about the Type-A pace he maintains, but he is indifferent to them as well. Only time will tell if he ever hears the warnings being issued by his wife and friends. Sad to say, this kind of man often doesn't hear warnings until he gets very sharp pains in the chest and finds himself on the way to the hospital.

BELIEVING THE BEST

If you want to practice loving confrontation, you can't believe your mate is out to get you and you can't be out to get your mate. Be willing to hear what God may be saying through your mate. It could be that He is trying to send an important message to you through him or her.

Some of us don't want to hear because we would rather be comfortable than Christlike. Many of Barbara's best statements to me are the ones that hurt a bit, but I need to hear them because it keeps me on the right track.

As I give her focused attention, I try to be concerned about the total content of the message rather than the method of delivery. In other words, I want to hear what she is trying to say but I avoid defending myself.

Some spouses have rabbit ears that catch every word and twist it into things that were never meant. It's no surprise that people who are defensive seldom feel their mate wants to communicate very much. When your words get fed back to you in a way that causes tension and embarrassment, you soon learn to avoid taking risks. It's easier to say little—or nothing.

To be open to your mate's observations and criticisms takes an attitude that sees your mate as your friend, not your enemy. If you picture your mate as an enemy, his or her attempts to communicate will sound like nagging. Then, because you don't listen, he or she has to say it again and again and you both wind up playing the nagging game.

To avoid nagging at our house, we have developed some useful techniques. For example, when Barbara finds herself telling me something repeatedly, she writes that message on a three-by-five card and puts it on the refrigerator. Or she will make a "Honey Do" list on a sheet of paper and tape it to the side of the refrigerator where it quietly reminds me of my responsibilities. Either way, it's the three-by-five card or the list that nags me; she doesn't.

Women are stereotyped as the most likely to commit the sin of nagging, but men can do it too. Being nagged at is not much fun. Someone has said nagging is like being nibbled to death by a duck. It is essential for husbands to listen when their wives do send a message.

THE KEYS TO GENTLE CONFRONTATION

The book of Nehemiah seems like an unlikely source for advice to married couples, but in the first chapter are five principles for approaching confrontation wisely. Nehemiah had a problem. He was in exile back in Babylon and he heard the wall of Jerusalem had been broken down and the city was wide open to being overrun by enemies, vandals, and animals.

Nehemiah wanted to take a group of people back and rebuild the wall, but he would have to confront King Artaxerxes to gain permission. Because the king could have seen this request as rebellion or insubordination, Nehemiah had to move carefully. What he did contains some excellent principles for handling confrontation in any relationship.

First, before Nehemiah went to the king, *he took time to pray.* Most problems in marriage could be solved if husband and wife first took them to the Lord and let Him simmer them down a bit before they actually begin to talk. This doesn't have to be a long, formal exercise. Sometimes it could be as quick as "Lord, help me try to understand her point of view and be gentle."

Second, Nehemiah opened his conversation with the king by saying, "May the king live forever!" In other words, *he expressed loyalty, encouragement, and support.* He let the king know that he was on his team, that he wasn't a traitor with a hidden agenda. To apply this concept to your own marriage, affirm you mate and create a climate of trust so he or she can hear what you are trying to say.

Third, *Nehemiah was truthful.* He came out with the problem and told the king the walls of Jerusalem were in rubble and the few Israelites who had survived were in great danger.

The principle here is to state enough of the truth to let your mate understand the situation. Don't blow him or her away, with a full-length feature film on the problem. Simply lay out the facts.

Fourth, *Nehemiah had an attitude of submission.* He let the king know he was not only pursuing his own interests, but those of the king as well. As we have already seen in Chapter 14, this is a great point for husbands to remember. Scripture teaches the husband is head of the wife, but it also teaches that Christians are to submit to one another.

Finally, *Nehemiah is specific in his request.* He asked the king for supplies, protection, and letters to take him safely through various countries in order to get to Jerusalem.

The best way to be specific in requests with your mate is with the "I" message. Never use the "you" message, which accuses and condemns your mate ("You never listen to me . . . you're always late . . ."). The "I" message says, "I feel insignificant and ignored when you don't seem to listen." Or the "I" message says, "I get very nervous when we're late for church; it's important for me to be on time."

To use a "you" message almost always guarantees being judgmental, which never helps either of you communicate.

The result? Nehemiah received his requests. Is there a possibility that the way you have been "approaching" your mate has lacked grace and tactfulness? Why not try it Nehemiah's way next time?

KEEP JUDGMENT OUT OF IT

Perhaps the greatest roadblock to loving confrontation is the well-known "log" that seems lodged in the eyes of many husbands and wives. Jesus taught us to judge not lest we also be judged. You should not criticize the splinter in your mate's eye when you have a log in your own (see Matthew 7:1–3). Here are five tips Barbara and I found useful in keeping judgment out of confrontation.

1. Check your motivation. Will what you say help or hurt? Will bringing this up cause healing, wholeness, and oneness—or further isolation? Prayer is the best barometer of our motivation. When we take our situation to God and He shines His light on us and the problem, then we usually see our motivation for what it is.

2. Check your attitude. Loving confrontation says, "I care about you. I respect you and I want you to respect me. I want to know how you feel." Don't hop on your bulldozer and run your partner down. Don't pull up with your dump truck and start unloading all the garbage you've been saving. Approach your partner lovingly.

3. Check the circumstances. This includes timing, location, and setting. Perhaps the most important is timing. The time for Barbara to confront me is not just as I walk in from a hard day's work. And the same is true for her. To bring up something that bothers me while she's in the middle of settling a squabble between the children is unwise.

For us, the time to have a tough talk is after the kids are all in bed, or we find it useful to get up early in the morning and have a conversation then.

As for location, the time to have confrontations is not over the dinner table with all those little eyes watching. Some spouses seem to enjoy confronting each other indirectly at dinner parties, or perhaps in a restaurant with friends. They make sarcastic remarks or let everyone know they have a problem by making a "joke" out of it. Somebody has said it's wise to "never say never," but in this case I believe we need to make an exception. *Never* criticize, make fun of, or argue with your mate in public.

4. *Check to see what other pressures may be present.* Be sensitive to where your mate is coming from. What's the context of your mate's life right now?

Just before Barbara and I leave for a conference, we can feel the pressure build. We can almost count on some conflict. Knowing this helps us give a little more grace to each other.

5. *Be sure you are ready to take it as well as dish it out.* Sometimes confronting your mate can turn into a boomerang. He or she may have some stuff saved on the other side of the fence that will suddenly come right back over on you. Beware of "projecting"—the word psychologists use to describe seeing your own faults in others. You may start to give your spouse some "friendly advice" and soon learn that what you are saying is not really his or her problem, but yours!

How to Keep the Discussion in Focus

First, *stick to one issue.* Don't bring up several. Don't save up a series of complaints and let your mate have them all at once. Deal with one thing at a time and focus on the problem, rather than the person. For example, you need a budget and your mate is something of a spendthrift. Work through the plans for finances and make the lack of budget the enemy, not your mate.

It would be tempting to say, "If you'd just stop spending so much, we could get along fine." This only makes the mate who is more inclined to spend feel like the enemy and the bad guy.

Another good practice is to *focus on behavior rather than character.* This is the "you" message versus the "I" message again. You can assassinate your mate's character and stab your mate right to the heart with "you" messages such as, "You're always late—you don't care about me at all, you don't care about anyone but yourself." The "I" message would say, "I feel frustrated when you don't let me know you'll be late. I would appreciate it if you would call so we can make other plans."

Focus on the facts rather than judging motives. If your partner forgets to make an important call, deal with the consequences of what you both have to do next rather than say, "You're so careless, you just do things to irritate me."

Above all, *focus on understanding your mate rather than on who is winning or losing.* When your mate confronts you, listen carefully to what is said and what isn't said. It may be that your spouse is upset about something that happened at work and you're getting nothing more than the brunt of that pressure. In other words, you are not the problem and all your mate is trying to do is vent some pent-up frustrations and feelings.

It's true that your mate shouldn't vent a problem from work on you, but that's part of being a loving partner who is willing to listen and to help. The goal is to share with your mate out of love, and diffuse the conflict that leads to isolation.

To repeat, the issue is not whether you win or lose, but how you play the conflict game. If you play with respect and consideration for your mate's feelings, both of you will win every time. And if somebody makes an error, there is one more skill that covers over other sins. We'll look at that next.

HOMEBUILDERS PROJECTS

To Think About Individually

1. Go through the following statements. On a scale of 1 to 5 (1 meaning strongly disagree, and 5 meaning strongly agree), rate how you and your spouse are doing in each area. Any answers below a 4 suggest some kind of unresolved conflict.

a. _____ We spend the right amount of time together.

b. _____ We spend the right amount of time with friends.

c. _____ We spend the right amount of time with in-laws.

d. _____ We spend the right amount of time in Christian service.

e. _____ We spend the right amount of time in family recreation.

f. _____ We spend the right amount of time in making decisions.

g. _____ We share the same child-rearing philosophy.

h. _____ We divide the household responsibilities fairly.

i. _____ We are very satisfied with our sexual relationship.

j. _____ We share a common philosophy on finances and budgets.

k. _____ We are satisfied with our problem solving procedures.

l. _____ We are satisfied with our manner of discussing serious issues.

m. _____ We are satisfied with our commitment to Jesus Christ.

n. _____ We have the freedom to properly express strong feelings in our home.

o. _____ We have the freedom to properly demonstrate affection in our home.

2. Check yourself on how well you use Nehemiah's approach to handling confrontation:

a. I pray at least briefly before we deal with a problem.

_____ Always _____ Sometimes _____ Seldom

b. When dealing with any problem, I always express loyalty, encouragement, and support to my mate.

_____ Always _____ Sometimes _____ Seldom

c. I tell my mate the truth, but never try to blow him or her away.

_____ Always _____ Sometimes _____ Seldom

d. I am willing to submit to my mate and hear what he or she is trying to say.

_____ Always _____ Sometimes _____ Seldom

e. I try to make specific requests with an "I" message and avoid "you" messages.

_____ Always _____ Sometimes _____ Seldom

FOR INTERACTION TOGETHER

1. Choose a time when you are able to be alone and relaxed enough to talk freely. Your goal is to uncover problem areas or deal with ongoing problems and move toward solutions. Pray together, then share your answers to questions 1 and 2 above. Several problems may surface, or you may have one or two on which you can focus. If you have more than one or two, save them for another session. Zero in on one or two basic problems and try to use principles discussed in this chapter to solve the problems and plan for steps of action. Close in prayer, asking God to help you deal with any conflicts in your marriage.

HOMEBUILDERS
PRINCIPLES

**Forgiveness means giving up
your rights to punish another.**

21

RETURNING A BLESSING
FOR AN INSULT

Love means to love that which is unlovable, or it is no virtue at all:
forgiving means to pardon that which is unpardonable,
or it is no virtue at all.

—G. K. CHESTERTON

The year our son Benjamin was five, he and I went down to pick out our Christmas tree. I decided to put it in its stand out on the front porch and, flexing my "gifted" hands, I went to work.

The trunk of the tree was enormous, while our Christmas tree stand, which I think was made by a subversive nation trying to overthrow America, was much smaller. So, I got out my power saw and began slicing away at the trunk of the tree to carve it down to a diameter that would fit the stand. Amazingly, I did a pretty good job and didn't cut off any of my own arms or legs or any important lower branches of the tree!

But when I slipped the tree into the collar of the stand and tried to tighten up the three bolts that hold it in place, I discovered that the base of the tree would not reach the little prongs on the bottom of the stand that help hold the tree up and in place.

I was getting a little frustrated, but then I got a brilliant idea. I headed for the garage, with Benjamin and Barbara in tow. She had joined us on the porch because from my past experience she knows anytime I start doing something with my hands she needs to protect me from myself.

I found a round piece of wood (the same size of the tree) and sawed off a small piece. Then I said proudly, "I'm taking these five nails and I'll tack this wood to the bottom of the tree trunk. That will make it long enough to reach the prongs in the stand and then it should work okay. If that doesn't work, I'm canceling Christmas."

Benjamin followed me back to the porch and watched carefully as I put the piece of wood in place and tried to sink the first nail. At first blow, it bounced away, off the porch, into the leaves, and was lost forever. Undaunted, I tried a second nail, which I did get started but it soon suffered a 90 degree convulsion. The third and fourth nails experienced a similar fate.

By this time I was well beyond frustrated and into angry. When I picked up the fifth nail, I doubt that I could have driven it into butter. After two blows, it bent also and with that I threw the hammer across the porch and it hit the wrought-iron railing with a horrendous "CLANG!" I'm not sure how many neighbors had been peering out their windows to see what all the racket was about, but now all of them were.

Stomping off the porch, with pine needles flying everywhere, I dragged the tree out to the car, threw it in the trunk, slammed the car in reverse and backed into the street. As I was about to slam the transmission into "drive," I looked over my shoulder. There was little Benjamin, standing on the edge of the porch, holding on to the wrought-iron railing, his eyes as big as Christmas tree ornaments. He must have thought I was canceling Christmas for sure!

Well, I peeled out anyway and drove to the tree lot. I threw the tree on the ground, explained my problem, and asked the attendant, "Can you fix it?" The attendant gave me a patient shrug, took a piece of spare tree trunk lying on the ground, sawed off a small section, took one nail and tacked it on the bottom of my tree. I didn't time him, but I would estimate it took him less than a minute to complete the task.

I gritted out a "Thanks," then loaded the tree back in the trunk and headed for home. Then God got my attention. I could distinctly hear Him saying, "You know you've been acting like a fool."

"Yes, Lord, You're right," was all I could say. But I thought to myself, "Anyway, Christmas is *Your* fault!"

As I drove on home I confessed my childish anger, and when I pulled into the driveway, guess who was still standing on the edge of the porch, holding on to the railing, eyes still huge and staring, wondering if his dad was going to get out of the car clothed and in his right mind?

I gently carried the Christmas tree to the porch, stood it up in the stand, and tightened the bolts. Then I got down on one knee to look my little son right in the eye and said, "Benjamin, your daddy was kind of mad, wasn't he?"

Benjamin looked right back at me and said, "Yeah, you sure were."

"Benjamin, I'm sorry. I didn't let Christ be on the throne of my life. Will you forgive me?"

I'll never forget Benjamin's response. He put his little arm around me, patted my shoulder, and said, "It's okay, Dad, everybody makes mistakes."

FORGIVENESS IS FREEING

Over the years I've admitted to just about everyone in our family that I've been wrong on many occasions, and of course Barbara has heard me say it more than anyone. It's liberating to admit you're wrong, and it's even more liberating when the other person forgives and says, "That's okay—everybody makes mistakes."

You can't improve on the way Paul put it when he said, "Be gentle and ready to forgive; never hold grudges. Remember, the Lord forgave you, so you must forgive others" (Colossians 3:13 TLB). To practice this advice means oneness and intimacy; to ignore it means loneliness and isolation.

The first step is the hardest—*admit you're wrong and ask forgiveness.* Both sexes can have trouble with this one, but in marriages I've seen or worked with, the edge goes to the men. The celebrated "male ego" is all too real and it's just hard for us husbands to say, "I was wrong. I'm sorry. Will you forgive me?"

During the first years of our marriage, I struggled to admit I was wrong. When I did I would often say, "If I was wrong when I did this, I'm sorry." I would admit there was a remote possibility I could have been wrong, but frank confession was out of the question.

After all, it seemed to me that there were really few times when I was *totally* wrong. Asking forgiveness when you're 100 percent wrong is one thing. But what about the times when you're 60 percent right and only 40 percent wrong? During the first years of our marriage, the 60/40 situations seemed to come up regularly and I seldom wanted to admit I was wrong.

My attitude was childish, of course, but I couldn't see it then. It's amazing how many spouses behave like little kids who try to weasel out after getting caught with their hands in the cookie jar.

At one of our conferences, a man boasted to me, "You know, I've been married for twenty-four years and I've never once apologized to my wife for anything I've done wrong."

"Oh, really?" I said, with a tone that urged him to tell me more.

"Yeah," he said with obvious pride. "Every time we get into a squabble or any kind of disagreement, I just tell her, 'I'm sorry you're mad at me.' I don't admit anything—I just tell her it's too bad she had to get so mad."

Then, with a "cheesy" grin, he admitted, "And all these years she's never realized that I have never once apologized."

I tactfully attempted to explain to this husband that he was dead wrong. Unfortunately, he wouldn't listen. He went on his way quite sure he was a very clever fellow, but I wonder if he really sleeps that well.

JOIN THE "SEVENTY-TIMES-SEVEN CLUB"

As difficult as it is to ask for forgiveness, it's equally hard to grant forgiveness when you have been wronged. If you can't forgive until your spouse asks you for forgiveness, your conflict may go on far longer than either of you wants it to.

I often advise married couples to take out a joint membership in the "Seventy-Times-Seven Club." Christ formed that club when Peter asked Him how many times we are to forgive one another. Peter wondered if seven times would be enough. Christ answered, "No—seventy times seven!" (Matthew 18:21–22).

In other words, forgive an infinite number of times, not just when you *feel* like it. By an act of your will, you must put away resentment and the desire to punish the person who has wronged you.

You can tell if you have forgiven your mate by asking one question: "Have I given up my desire to punish my mate?" When you lay that desire aside, let it go, and no longer seek revenge, you free your spouse—and yourself—from the bonds of your anger.

Every marriage operates on one basis or the other: the "Insult-for-Insult" relationship or the "Blessing-for-Insult" relationship. Husbands and wives can become extremely proficient at trading insults—about the way he looks, the way she cooks, or the way he drives, and the way she cleans house. Many couples don't seem to know any other way to relate to each other. Consider these:

Exhibit A: My friend and associate Dave Sunde heard a woman say, "The reason our marriage has worked is that my husband and I are both in love with the same man."

Exhibit B: And then there was the man who had his wedding ring on the wrong hand and his wife asked him why. He replied, "That's to remind me I married the wrong woman."

Exhibit C: Another wife complained to her husband, "You love football more than me."

"Maybe so," he admitted, "but I love you more than baseball."

Exhibit D: And you may have heard of the husband who asked his wife, "Why did God make you so beautiful but so dumb?"

She answered, "He made me beautiful so you would marry me and dumb so that I could love you!"

SPITTING IN THE SOUP

The insult-for-insult relationship is also well illustrated by a well-known story—supposedly true—that came out of the Korean War. Some G.I.s were living off-base in their own rented quarters and they hired a

Korean houseboy to do the cooking, cleaning, and other necessary chores. These soldiers loved to play tricks, so one day the Korean houseboy got up, slipped into his slippers, and started to take a step, but found that they had been nailed to the floor!

The young Korean just smiled and said nothing. Then he crawled into bed one night and found shaving cream under his pillow. On other occasions, he would find his bed short-sheeted or be victim to a bucket of water over the door. Through it all he just smiled and nodded and told his employers, "Everything OK."

This foolishness went on for quite a while until the G.I.s came to their senses and realized they were being inhumane. When they apologized, the Korean houseboy looked dubious and asked, "No more short sheets?"

"That's right, no more short sheets."

"No more nail shoes to floor?"

"Right."

"No more shave cream under pillow?"

"No more. We have been wrong and we're sorry."

The houseboy began to nod. A little smile crossed his lips and he said, "Then me no more spit in soup."

There are many ways to spit in each other's soup, and married couples find new ones all the time.

Long Day's Journey into Conflict

The insult-for-insult relationship is based on an unforgiving heart and finds each partner focusing on personal rights and feelings. Forgiveness is costly, but to refuse to forgive costs even more. As someone said, "The longer you carry a grudge, the heavier it gets." And I might add, "The lonelier it gets."

Yet it's easy to do when you focus on your own rights and feelings, as the following personal story illustrates.

I had spent a busy day wrapping up last-minute details before leaving for a conference. I came home to a wife who had spent a hard day with the kids—a very hard day. But I was preoccupied with the upcoming conference, and while I wanted to reach out and help Barbara, I was just too busy preparing to leave.

Just as I picked up the phone to make one last important call, she said, "Please don't get on the phone right now. I really want to talk to you, and if you get on that phone, I'm going upstairs."

I could tell she was hurting and needed to talk to me, but I *had* to make that call. So I hastily dialed the number. With disappointment on her face, Barbara disappeared upstairs. More than a few minutes went by before the phone conversation ended. And then my mother called and we talked another twenty minutes.

My mother and I finally hung up and I stayed a few more minutes, cleaning up the kitchen and watching a small TV set we have on the counter. The show was so interesting I sat for a moment to see how it would end.

So there I was, watching television, when Barbara walked in. Obviously, my stock didn't go to Blue Chip status at that moment. She didn't notice her kitchen was clean. All she saw was her husband glued to the TV set when he knew she had been waiting to talk to him.

By the time we got to our bedroom, the temperature seemed to be about forty degrees below zero. Our conversation opened on a note especially familiar to many married couples. With keen male insights, I said, "What's wrong?"

"Nothing!"

Then she added, "I hope this isn't going to be an illustration for that conference coming up."

"Sweetheart," I said, "you knew I was trying to get up here."

Barbara brushed that comment angrily away and said, "And you knew I wanted to talk because it has been a hard day."

"Well, do you want to talk or not?" I asked, getting a little perturbed.

No answer. By now my eyelids were getting heavy and I was doing my best to hold them open as she nursed our newborn baby, Laura. All this wasn't doing much to create deep intimacy in the relationship. Then, when Barbara finished feeding the baby, she put her in the crib, took a pillow, and hit me on top of the head!

SIMMERING WITH ANGER

It wasn't a very playful whack, and I got the message loud and clear. Smarting with anger, I took the pillow, propped it under my head, and rolled over to stare at the wall, dramatizing where our relationship was headed—straight toward isolation.

Then Barbara said, "Don't you want to talk?"

"I tried to talk a while ago," was all I could think of.

There was a long silence. Finally, I gathered enough presence of mind to say, "You know, sweetheart, neither one of us is doing real well in this relationship at the moment, and we should reschedule this conflict for tomorrow because we're not getting anywhere. Why don't we just go to sleep?"

"Okay," was all she said, and we turned out the lights and tried to make believe we had not let the sun go down on our anger. I'm not sure about Barbara, but I was still simmering. As I lay in bed facing the wall, I was consumed with thinking about how to get back at her.

And then I remembered. Tomorrow I would be speaking in a conference, and one of my messages was on giving a blessing rather than an insult! My anger turned to guilt. As I lay there sulking, God's truth reached into my heart, and I realized this kind of behavior was not building oneness.

I knew my attitude was wrong, and by an act of my will I asked God to take away my childish feelings of wanting to punish Barbara because she had hurt me. As I finally fell asleep, I was determined to make things right in the morning.

The next morning things were still a little tense when we sat down to talk, but before I left for the conference I admitted to Barbara that I had been insensitive by not coming upstairs when she had given me her first distress signal. "I should have seen you really meant it. I blew it, and I'm sorry."

"Well, I'm sorry too. It was pretty childish to whack you with a pillow, but I was hurt, and finding you watching TV was the last straw."

We talked a while longer, and then I had to leave to catch my plane. But by the time I left, we were both feeling a lot better because we had used a key principle regarding forgiveness: Even though we didn't feel all that loving and relaxed, we forgave each other anyway *by an act of the will.*

Forgiveness also should be unconditional. Some spouses often tell me this is impossible. They say, "I can't forgive him," or, "What she did is so rotten I can never forgive her for that."

When you say you can't forgive, what you really mean is "I *won't* forgive." The way to become willing is to trade the insult-for-insult relationship for a *blessing-for-insult* relationship. When Peter wrote to Christians who were being persecuted, he said, "Do not repay evil with evil or insult with insult, but with blessing . . . so that you may inherit a blessing" (1 Peter 3:9 NIV). First you stop adding fuel to the fire, and then you give a blessing. You find concrete, specific ways to do good to the other person.

THE BLESSING-FOR-INSULT THEORY IN ACTION

I knew a woman named Linda who was married to Lou, a fourth-year seminary student. They had four children and you can imagine their hectic schedule with Lou's studies and Linda trying to care for the kids. So they decided to take a break and plan a pleasant, romantic evening at home.

Lou was due home at 6 P.M. and Linda had gotten all the children ready for bed, picked up the baby-sitter, and was beautifully dressed and waiting at 6:30. As the minutes ticked by, what Linda didn't know was that Lou was back at the seminary library, feverishly studying his favorite subject, Hebrew. He had gotten so involved in a delicious verb-parsing exercise that he had simply forgotten the time. When he finally looked at his watch, it was 6:45.

Because more tantalizing Hebrew tidbits lay yet to be unearthed, Lou decided he'd "study a few more minutes" and then call. The next time Lou looked it was 7:30. He decided he'd better call home and tell Linda where he was. Linda took the baby-sitter back, and Lou finally got home at 8:45. He offered a perfunctory "I'm sorry," they ate the ruined meal in silence, and finally slipped into bed.

In a bit of brilliant perception, Lou asked, "Sweetheart, have I done anything to offend you? I told you I was sorry I didn't get back. What do you want me to do?"

Still facing the wall, Linda began to pour out her heart to Lou, telling how she had looked forward to the evening because it had been such a terrible semester. She went for several minutes, ending with, "And I was looking forward to this so much, don't you understand that, Honey? Honey . . ." and then Linda rolled over, and there was Lou, fast asleep.

When I tell this story in FamilyLife Conferences, I've had women come up afterward and say, "I would have put my foot in the small of his back and he would have been right on the floor. If I'm miserable, he's going to be miserable."

What did Linda do? She not only knew the truth of Scripture, but she also was the kind of woman who could practice it. She knew it would be far better to pay Lou back with a blessing and not an insult. The next morning she got up an hour early, put on his favorite negligee, and made breakfast for him, which she served him in bed. Then, to cap it off, she initiated making love!

How did Lou react to Linda's effort to pay back insult with blessing? For the next month, he couldn't do enough to serve her. Her actions had heaped coals of fire on his head, and he realized how wrong he had been. It was something of a turning point in their marriage—toward oneness and away from isolation.

How to Give Your Mate a Blessing

By not repaying Lou with insult for insult, Linda inherited a blessing for herself. She applied Peter's words, which give this advice: "Whoever would love life and see good days must keep his tongue from evil, and his lips from deceitful speech. He must turn from evil and do good; he must seek peace and pursue it" (1 Peter 3:10–11).

While Peter talks about keeping your "tongue from evil," he means you should change your natural tendency to lash out, fight back, or tell your mate off. Changing the natural tendency of tongue and lips is just about as easy as changing the course of the Mississippi. You can't do it without God's help, without yielding to the power of the Holy Spirit.

Peter goes on to say that being a blessing means turning away from evil and doing good. To apply this to marriage, picture stepping aside as your mate hurls an unkind comment at you, or simply refusing to retaliate if your partner gets angry. It may be the circumstances—the end of a tough day, or just too much hassle—that has your spouse feeling hostile. Instead of digging in to fight for your rights, step aside, "roll with the punches," and give back a blessing instead.

And how do you do that? Peter simply says, "Do good." Doing good depends on the situation. Sometimes doing good simply takes a few words spoken gently and kindly, or perhaps a touch, a hug, or a pat on the shoulder.

Finally, being a blessing means seeking peace, actually *pursuing* it. When you eagerly seek to forgive, you are pursuing oneness, not isolation.

I see many married couples getting mugged by the same old knotty problems that continue to lie in wait for them, much as a thug lies in wait in an alley. They continue to walk blindly into the same alleys and fall victim to the same irritations over and over.

But you don't have to keep walking into the same alley. When conflicts and problems come up, you can simply say together, "No, we're not going to respond like we usually do." You don't have to pursue isolation; instead, you can seek peace and oneness by giving a blessing instead.

HOMEBUILDERS PROJECTS

TO THINK ABOUT INDIVIDUALLY

1. Take your time and complete the following statements as honestly as you can:

   I forgive my spouse: always, sometimes, seldom, never.

   My spouse forgives me: always, sometimes, seldom, never.

2. Our marriage is characterized by:

   _____ An insult-for-insult relationship

   _____ A blessing-for-insult relationship

3. The last time I gave my spouse a blessing for an insult was

   _____.

FOR INTERACTION TOGETHER

1. Share your answers to the above questions. Discuss the concept of forgiving one another by an act of the will, even if you don't feel like doing so. Do you both think this is possible? Why or why not?

HOMEBUILDERS
PRINCIPLES

A mutually rewarding sexual
relationship demands that both
husband and wife deny "self"
and meet their mate's needs.

22

WHAT MAKES A GREAT LOVER?

God Himself invented sex for our delight. It was His gift to us—
intended for pleasure.

—ED WHEAT, M.D.[1]

A TV talk show host was interviewing one of Hollywood's biggest male stars, a man known for his prowess with the opposite sex. At one point, the host asked him, "What makes a great lover?"

"Two things," he said. "First of all, it is a man who can satisfy one woman over a lifetime. *And* it is a man who can be satisfied with one woman for a lifetime."

That was a great answer! To build an intimate marriage, husband and wife must be committed to meeting one another's physical and emotional needs. Because most men and women have differing ideas, standards, and expectations about sex, it's understandable that many marriages suffer isolation in this area. For many people, sex can be a lonely act.

USA Today told of how the late Ann Landers once put this question to her seventy million readers: "Would you be content to be held close and treated tenderly and forget about 'the act'?"

So many women wrote to answer Ann's question the letters started filling her office and mail room. Two months later she reported that 90,000 women had responded to her question and 64,000 said they preferred a warm hug or gentle touch to intercourse. Forty percent of those responding to Ann's information survey were under forty years of age!

267

One woman said, "I'm under forty and would be delighted to settle for tender words and more warm caresses. The rest of it is a bore and can be exhausting. I am sure the sex act was designed strictly for the pleasure of males."

A fifty-five-year-old woman wrote, "I . . . vote yes. The best part is the cuddling and the caressing and the tender words that come with caring."

But a pair of comments from those who prefer sex to cuddling brought a smile to my face:

"To say that touching and tender words is sufficient is like settling for the smell of freshly baked bread and ignoring the nourishment it provides. Such people must be crazy."

And a sixty-two-year-old woman said emphatically, "If my old man was over the hill, I would settle for high school necking. But as long as he is able to shake the walls and wake up the neighbors downstairs, I want to get in on the action. And I'll take an encore any time I can get it."[2]

Some therapists and "sexperts" thought Landers's question and the responses were misleading, but others believed she was very close to the truth. What her informal survey proved is that marriage is not either/or, it's both. It's two people coming together in the sexual act to communicate their caring and tenderness that says, "I love you; I care for you."

WHAT DOES GOD THINK ABOUT SEX?

I wonder how God might have answered Ann Landers's survey question. Since He created sex, He might have a few thoughts worth considering. First, sex is the divine process He gave us to multiply a godly heritage. He commanded us to "be fruitful and increase in number; fill the earth and subdue it" (Genesis 1:28).

But God also designed sex for our pleasure. In fact, Scripture talks a lot more about the pleasures of sex than it does about being fruitful and subduing the earth.

Although the Song of Solomon has spiritual meaning and application, it is considered by a large number of scholars as primarily God's description of what a sexual relationship between man and wife should be like. According to Solomon, the man has the freedom to enjoy his wife's body and the woman has the freedom to enjoy his. Here are just two samples of how the lover and his beloved expressed that freedom in The Song of Songs. The Lover (King Solomon himself) said:

How beautiful your sandaled feet, O prince's daughter! Your graceful legs are like jewels, the work of a craftsman's hands. Your navel is a rounded goblet that never lacks blended wine. Your waist is a mound of wheat encircled by lilies. Your breasts are like two fawns, twins of a gazelle . . . How beautiful you are and how pleasing, O love, with your delights! Your stature is like that of the palm, and your breasts like clusters of fruit. I said, "I will climb the palm tree; I will take hold of its fruit." May your breasts be like the clusters of the vine, the fragrance of your breath like apples, and your mouth like the best wine. (Song of Songs 7:1–3, 6–9)

These words tell us three things about being a great lover from a male point of view. *First, Solomon readily praised Shulamith, his beloved.* He told her how beautiful she was with vivid and picturesque language that communicated his admiration to her.

I often ask the husbands at our conferences, "When was the last time you wrote your wife a love letter? When was the last time you verbally praised her and told her how beautiful she is?" Solomon understood how important this is in communicating love.

Second, Solomon was a romantic. His poetic description of Shulamith pictures her whole body as a source of delight—a palm tree whose fruit is there to be taken gently into his hands, a goblet of fine wine whose bouquet and taste are to be enjoyed. Some husbands are creative romanticists, but many need help in this area, and we'll talk about that later in this chapter.

Third, Solomon's focus was physical. He zeroed in on what he saw, a classic male characteristic. A woman may be tempted to resent her husband's sex drive and physical focus, but she needs to remember that men are stimulated by sight more than women are. It's the way God made them as part of His plan to keep the human race going. Generally, the male sex drive pursues the female.

A LOVELY LOVER

And what about Shulamith's approach to sex? As we glance at some of her comments about her lover, we see that she also focused on what she saw:

> My lover is radiant and ruddy, outstanding among ten thousand. His head is purest gold; his hair is wavy and black as a raven. His eyes are like doves by the water's streams, washed in milk, mounted like jewels. His cheeks are like beds of spice yielding perfume, his lips are like lilies dripping with myrrh. His arms are rods of gold set with chrysolite. His body is like polished ivory decorated with sapphires. His legs are pillars of marble set on bases of pure gold. His appearance is like Lebanon, choice as the cedars. His mouth is sweetness itself; he is *altogether* lovely. This is my lover, this is my *friend*, O daughters of Jerusalem. (Song of Solomon 5:10–16)

But Shulamith also spoke of how she feels in her lover's arms. Obviously, she would have answered Ann Landers's survey by saying tender touching is an important part of the sexual dimension of marital love:

> May the wine go straight to my lover, flowing gently over lips and teeth. I belong to my lover, and his desire is for me. Come, my lover, let us go to the countryside, let us spend the night in the villages. Let us go early to the vineyards to see if the vines have budded, if their blossoms have opened, and if the pomegranates are in bloom—there I will give you my love. (Song of Solomon 7:9b–12)

Shulamith went on to speak of her lover's left arm under her head while his right arm embraces her:

Under the apple tree I roused you; . . . Place me like a seal over your
heart, like a seal over your arm; for love is as strong as death, its jealousy unyielding as the grave. It burns like blazing fire, like a mighty
flame. Many waters cannot quench love; rivers cannot wash it away.
(Song of Solomon 8:5b–7a)

More Than a Physical Act

These passages illustrate two sides of the female's approach to love.
There is a physical side, and Shulamith described her lover's body in words
every bit as picturesque and colorful as Solomon's description of her. But
Shulamith also *focused on the total person and their relationship.* This is
where men often make a mistake, focusing on the physical side of sex and
forgetting that the woman *needs* the relationship.

Shulamith mentioned her lover's arm under her head and his right
arm embracing her (8:3). Here we find snuggling and intercourse coming
together in total-person communication. Sex is much more than a physical act that is over in a few minutes. Sex actually brings two people
together in three dimensions: body, soul, and spirit. When the soul and
spirit are missing, sex leaves the woman feeling empty, not really wanted,
but only used.

One woman I counseled confessed that her husband approached her
only one night a month. "He never shares his life with me," she said. "He
slips into bed with the lights off, we make love, and that's it."

I will never forget her next comment: "Making love with him is like a
bread-and-water diet."

Sex is a thermometer that measures the depth of the relationship, and
for this woman the experience was leaving her lonely and longing for true
companionship. For sex to be truly satisfying to both partners, each has
to risk being totally open and vulnerable to the other. Each person in the
marriage relationship should feel needed, wanted, accepted, and loved
sacrificially.

Sex is a God-given desire that can bring a husband and wife together
in oneness. Some individuals might remain isolated permanently were it

not for the desire God gave us to come together with our mates in the merging of body, mind, and heart.

Throughout our marriage, Barbara has allowed me to know her fully (not just physically) and I, too, have risked letting her know me in the same way. But this was not something we just naturally started to do on our wedding night. It has taken years of sharing, adjusting—and yes, occasionally arguing—to make progress toward a total person communication of body, soul, and spirit that sex is designed to achieve. And we're still working on it. We wrestle with problems in three basic areas: spiritual, mental, and emotional.

A PERFECT NIGHT IN MAZATLAN UNTIL . . .

Sex therapists discuss "sexual dysfunction" in profound terms, analyzing why a husband and wife can't have an enjoyable relationship; but often, when you boil down all of the big words, they are describing selfishness. God designed sex to be a giving relationship, but selfishness is bent strictly on taking. Real love can't wait to give, while selfish lust can't wait to get.

I believe selfishness is, at its base, a spiritual problem. Early in our marriage I learned just how big a problem it can be.

At the end of that incredible year of catastrophes and crises that Barbara and I experienced between 1976 and 1977, a good friend heard about what we had gone through and telephoned us to say, "My wife and I want to fly you to Mazatlan, Mexico, with us. We'll go down and spend a few days and relax and have some fun together."

It was a much-needed refreshing break. Barbara and I had a suite with a balcony, and one evening we enjoyed a spectacular dinner on the beach with the balmy breezes blowing ever so gently over our table. Then we went back to our room where the candles were lit, the windows were open, and romantic music drifted up from below, with the muffled crash of the surf filling in the background.

There had been a brief thunder shower and the moon was peeking through the clouds over the ocean. It was a perfect evening. Barbara was spectacularly beautiful—the perfect woman. It was the perfect moment for love and romance, but there was one problem—an imperfect man. I tried to rush things physically while Barbara was focused on the relational. She wanted to be held tenderly and enjoy the beauty of the moment, while I was in a hurry.

When she didn't respond, I grew so angry that I threw a bottle of hand lotion through a window! Fortunately, it was a small window, but the damage was done. Romance evaporated, and the evening was ruined. We both shed tears and I confessed my selfishness and lack of sensitivity to her need. I vowed that in the future I would learn to do a better job of denying myself, quit making demands on her, and be more patient. As we both look back, it was a pivotal point in the development of our sexual relationship.

I have made tremendous strides in my battles with selfishness, but I still have work to do. I make the most progress when I yield myself to God and then to Barbara. One thing that has drawn us closer into oneness throughout our marriage has been our daily ritual of prayer. At the close of each day, we yield our lives and our rights to God, and when you do that, selfishness has no place to grow.

Loneliness and isolation are put to death when a husband and wife pray together regularly. An open, honest relationship with God, in the presence of your mate, is a prerequisite to a mutually satisfying sex life.

How Men and Women View Sex

Nothing will melt the icicles in many marriage beds faster than the husband realizing that women are built with a different sexual time clock and with different perspectives and expectations concerning sex. The "Differences in Sexuality" Chart on the next page is a *general* guide to how men and women can be so different in this area of sex. (Obviously, this chart cannot be 100 percent true. It compares the general tendencies and differences between men and women and how they view sex.) These differences cause certain expectations on the part of men and women which often lead to misunderstanding, frustration, and disappointment.

DIFFERENCES IN SEXUALITY

	♂ MEN	♀ WOMEN
ORIENTATION	Physical Compartmentalized Physical oneness Variety Sex is high priority	Relational Wholistic Emotional oneness Security Other priorities may be higher
STIMULATION	Sight Smell Body-centered	Touch Attitudes Actions Words Person-centered
NEEDS	Respect Admiration Physically needed Not to be put down	Understanding Love Emotionally needed Time
SEXUAL RESPONSE	Acyclical Quick excitement Initiates (usually) Difficult to distract	Cyclical Slow excitement Responder (usually) Easily distracted
ORGASM	Propagation of species Shorter, more intense Physically-oriented Orgasm usually needed for satisfaction	Propagation of oneness Longer, more in depth Emotionally-oriented Satisfaction possible without orgasm

These are *general tendencies,* and are not true in all cases.

Perhaps the biggest cause of problems is that husbands expect their wives to be every bit as interested in sex as they are. I ran across an article about a survey of 230 married couples by sociologists in Tallahassee, Florida. These couples were given a list of ninety-six possible leisure activities and asked to pick the five they enjoyed the most.

The list included watching TV, gardening, going to church, visiting friends, sex, athletic events, reading, and sewing, to name only a few.

Forty-five percent of the men picked "Engaging in sexual or affectionate activities" as their first choice, followed by attending athletic events and reading books. Thirty-seven percent of the women ranked reading first, with sex barely edging out sewing for pleasure by twenty-six percent to twenty-five percent!

What these percentages suggest is that men put a much higher priority on sex than women do and that women have a different orientation that demands a different approach. As the chart shows, and as we also saw with Solomon and his wife, the man's orientation is physical, a woman's is relational. A man wants physical oneness, the woman desires emotional oneness. The man is stimulated by sight, smell, and the body. The woman is stimulated by touch, attitudes, actions, words, and the whole person.

A man needs respect and admiration, to be physically needed, and not to be put down. The woman needs understanding, love, to be emotionally needed, and time to warm up to the sexual act.

The man's sexual response is acyclical, which means anytime, anywhere. The women's response is cyclical, which means she goes through times when she is more interested in sex than others. A man responds sexually by getting excited quickly, while the woman is much slower.

During sex, a man is single-minded, while a woman is easily distracted. The woman wants to know, "Are the kids all asleep?" "Have you checked to see if they're all covered?" "Is the door shut?" "Is it locked?" "Are the windows closed?" "Are the blinds down?" "I think I hear the bathroom faucet dripping."

In the old days, I suppose the wife used to ask if the drawbridge was up and the moat filled with alligators. *More than one lovemaking session has been ruined because the man didn't understand that the woman's distractions have no reflection on him.* It's just the way God designed her. Barbara can hear a dripping faucet two and a half floors away. I couldn't hear a dripping faucet if I were sitting next to it.

Understanding some of these basic differences between men and women is how you become a student of your mate. As you understand your mate's needs you can sacrificially act to meet those needs in a loving, caring way. What do you need to deny yourself to communicate love to your mate? What communicates that you care?

An excellent piece of advice is in the title of Kevin Leman's book *Sex Begins in the Kitchen*. Leman develops one basic idea: You don't begin to make love at 10:30 P.M. You begin in the morning when you have breakfast together and actually converse instead of being buried in the newspaper. That evening you continue "making love" as you help your wife clean up the kitchen and talk with her about her day and share your life with her.

Later, you continue to take some of the load off of her by getting the kids to bed, bringing them glasses of water, and all the other duties involved in closing the household down for the night. Then, when you finally get to bed, you don't face an exhausted, irritated partner who thinks you don't care; instead, she knows you do care and will be more likely to respond to your loving advances. All this assumes, of course, your motivations are correct and your helping and relating are genuine, not just ploys so you can have sex.

THE EMOTIONAL SIDE OF SEX

There are many reasons for emotional blocks to sexual fulfillment. Sometimes the block is a traumatic incident from the past, like rape or incest. A wife may be frigid or a husband impotent because of resentment, anger, fear, or guilt. When the block is severe, professional counseling or therapy is in order.

Many couples, however, could benefit sexually from simply developing a little more "freedom of expression," with verbal or nonverbal techniques to communicate warm affection. What appeals to one couple may sound silly to another. Barbara and I have a little system which says, "Three of anything means I love you." It might be three honks on the horn, three pats on the leg, or even three winks. We've come up with all kinds of creative ways to say "I love you" over the years. It keeps our relationship fresh.

Sex is affected by the mind and emotions, but it is also affected by your will. If you have some kind of emotional block, it will severely limit your sexual fulfillment. Keep in mind that your will is naturally driven by the desire for self-centered gratification.

I'll never forget a doctor's wife who came in for counseling. She had waited until age thirty-five to marry and had given up her own professional career to do so. Her husband would not come for counseling even though she shared with him she had never experienced much satisfaction during intercourse. Apparently the husband didn't care. The irony is he knew better. As a surgeon, he was well acquainted with basic information in the sex manuals, but in his own marriage he believed sex was supposed to be a "ten" for him and a "zero" for her. His stubbornness and pride kept him from seeking help.

As my FamilyLife Conference colleague and friend Bob Horner says, "The bedroom is a lousy place for a battle of wills." For sex to be the fulfilling experience God planned, both partners must submit to the other and commit themselves to a mutually rewarding sex life.

MUTUAL OWNERSHIP

The first commitment to mutually satisfying sex involves several parts. First, commit yourself to recognizing and confessing your own self-centeredness. Seeking to satisfy each other means yielding yourselves to one another completely.

Commit yourself to honor the spirit of mutual ownership described in Scripture. The apostle Paul had this to say about sex: "The husband should fulfill his marital duty to his wife, and likewise the wife to her husband. The wife's body does not belong to her alone, but also to her husband. In the same way, the husband's body does not belong to him alone but also to his wife" (1 Corinthians 7:3–4).

Paul's advice is possibly even more practical today than it was when he wrote it. When either mate is deprived of sexual satisfaction, the temptations of our culture become overpowering. Both spouses are in danger, but the husband is usually the most vulnerable because sexual release is such a basic need for him.

Sex is also a major element of a man's self-esteem. In an article called "Straight Talk to Wives," Barbara wrote:

> I'm realizing more and more with each year of marriage how crucial sex
> is to my husband's self-image. It is not merely a means of recreation or
> satisfying an appetite. It builds his confidence as a man. It makes him
> feel accepted. Fulfilling his sexual needs and desires not only builds a
> wonderful intimacy between a husband and wife, but it protects him
> from "wondering" about other women. Why would he want to? You
> are all he needs and wants. Without the physical affirmation of love, a
> man is left insecure and susceptible to another woman who may think
> he's wonderful.

Obviously, I appreciate Barbara's words, but I am also aware that a mutually satisfying sex life is a two-way street. One of the most liberating thoughts I have ever had in our marriage relationship is that I will never stop competing for Barbara's love. As a result of that commitment, I stay much more creative in how I communicate with her sexually.

I am well aware that if I start taking her for granted, someone else could walk into her life and catch her at a weak point. My constant goal is to strengthen her and have her know that she is still the woman I decided to carry off to the castle back in 1972.

TAKE TIME FOR CREATIVE ROMANCE

Husbands often tell me they're "too busy for that romantic stuff—besides, that isn't reality." I always respond by saying reality shouldn't preclude romance.

I know a man who planned a "scavenger hunt" for his wife. About two weeks before they were to leave on a romantic getaway, he began to scatter little hints around the house. Using clues he gave her, she would find these hints and collect them.

On the day before they were ready to leave, he had the baby-sitting lined up, all travel arrangements ready, and his wife still wasn't aware of what was going on. He held one more scavenger hunt throughout the yard, and his children helped him scatter more clues. His wife even had to climb a tree to find some of them.

Finally, she took all the clues and pieced together a map of New England. Then the husband told her what was happening and all she had time for was to pack and kiss the kids good-bye. They took off and spent their tenth wedding anniversary in New England—seven days of peace and quiet. They picked apples, ate lobster, and sat in a foggy harbor drinking hot cider. They explored places they had never been and just had a great adventure, along with plenty of leisurely romance. His wife still talks about that trip—and is ready for another one!

You don't have to plan scavenger hunts and trips to add a note of adventure and romance to your marriage. Start by making your own home a creative setting for sex. Your bedroom needs to be a private, secure, romantic hideaway, not a place where the husband rebuilds his motorcycle or the kids gather to sculpt Play-doh.

I know of one stockbroker husband who had a ticker-tape machine installed in his bedroom and kept it running twenty-four hours a day. He may have been able to watch the Dow Jones go up, but my guess is that the market for romance hit an all-time low.

Of course, wives can be guilty of de-romanticizing the bedroom too. Mounds of laundry that need to be washed or folded and ironed are a sure killer of romance. One wife had so many African violets in their bedroom that her husband was afraid he was going to die in an avalanche of plants one night!

SAVE SOME OF YOUR BEST FOR EACH OTHER

To make romance and adventure come alive, you must make your relationship a top priority. One reason so many marriage beds are frozen over or boring is that couples "just don't have time" for sex. Too many couples try to work sex in somewhere between the late-night news and David Letterman's show. I ran across a quote in *USA Today* that describes the problem with vivid accuracy.

> She gets home at 6:30. He gets home at 7:30. Both have had hard days at the office. They're tired. A quick dinner goes into the microwave. They eat, put the kids to bed, watch TV for an hour, and crawl in bed and go to sleep . . . The missing ingredient? Sex.[3]

One New York therapist believes, "Sheer exhaustion is the biggest problem affecting people's sex lives today."[4] Let's face it, today our jobs and businesses seem to get our best. Our children usually get our best. Even church work can get our best. But adding romance and adventure to our marriages seldom gets our best.

IF YOU HAVE AN UNRESPONSIVE MATE . . .

Sexual isolation occurs when two people withdraw and no longer progressively pursue meeting one another's needs. He or she may make what the other feels are unreasonable demands. Perhaps the wife has found responding difficult and the husband has become angry and bitter. What once was a tender act between two young lovers has slowly deteriorated into a physical necessity. Resentment replaces growth. Ultimately the union that God designed as the celebration of oneness erodes into sexual and emotional isolation. If you have an unresponsive mate:

• Consider that he or she may be going through a particularly stressful time, which could be caused by pressures at work, the birth of a child, an illness, loss of job, or any number of other problems. Any of these may be contributing to your mate's disinterest in sex or lack of response. Always be sensitive to your mate and what is going on in his or her life.

- Bitterness, worry, or fear are just a few causes of lack of sexual response. You may want to ask your mate:

  "Is there anything I have done or am doing to inhibit our enjoyment of sex together?"

  "Is there any problem or conflict between us that needs to be resolved?"

  "Is there anything in your background that is hard to talk about? Could you share it with me so I could try to help?"

- Should problems persist, don't be too proud to seek professional help.

- Find out what you can do that would really please your mate. Make a list of these things and then begin to do them.

- Do a long-term study of your mate to learn how to create the best possible environment for him or her to respond to sex or to initiate it.

- Set aside time for frequent get-aways to talk and share together. If you want romance to ignite you, you need to periodically devote large blocks of time to lighting the fire. Barbara and I try to get away for at least two consecutive nights, three or four times a year.

At the Rainey house, we work hard to save some of our best for each other. Our kids now know that Mom and Dad often like to have quiet evenings *alone.* Occasionally, we turn the kitchen into a famous big-time restaurant called "The Rainey Rainbow Room," and let each child order a special meal from a little menu that we provide.

Barbara and I serve as chef and waiter, and the kids have a great time learning a little bit about how to "eat out."

Later, they know they are to go to their rooms and stay there, not coming out for anything except bathroom runs. I jokingly tell our younger ones, Laura, Deborah, and Rebecca, "Kids, I have just released 233 alligators into the hall. You may have to leave your room to go potty, and, if you hurry right back, they are trained not to eat you. Anything else and you're in big trouble."

At 8 P.M., Barbara and I turn our bedroom into our own romantic café, complete with a small table, candles, and flowers (when I can remember to pick them up). There we eat, talk, and relax. We don't have to worry about a baby-sitter, and we don't have to leave the house to get away from home.

The point is that if you're going to make anything like this work, you must schedule it and then take the time. If I have learned anything in marriage, it is that *romance, our relationship, and sex all take time.*

At FamilyLife Conference we suggest that couples start that very night to take more time for each other by eating early and retiring to their rooms by 8:30 or 9:00 P.M. No TV. No newspaper. No radio. They should take an hour or two to relax and talk and then make love. It's amazing how we get in a rut, and just need a little encouragement to go to bed early.

"What Do I Do for an Hour?"

At one conference I was approached by a man who had been married for about two years. He said, "Dennis, my wife . . . she hasn't . . . ah . . . hasn't been able to . . . ah . . . be truly satisfied in our relationship."

"You mean she hasn't had an orgasm yet?" I asked.

"Yeah, yes, that's what I mean."

"Well, may I ask you a couple of questions? Would that be okay?"

"Sure—whatever you want, I'll tell you the truth."

"Okay," I said, "how much time are you taking to just kind of prepare her? You know, to warm her up a little bit."

"Oh, quite a while—a long time really."

"Well, can you give me an idea of how much time?"

"Oh, a long time."

"How long? How many minutes?"

"Oh, I'd say maybe two or three minutes," he said.

I smiled, put my arm around him, and asked, "Can I encourage you to do something tonight?"

"Sure, what is it?" he wanted to know.

"I want you to take an hour."

"An hour? What am I going to do for an hour?"

I looked at him and said, "Just ask your wife, my friend. You'll figure it out."

The next morning he was so excited his face seemed to light up the room when he walked in. Obviously, things had gone much better. Why? Because his wife needed time.

All of us need time. And when we take time to put our physical love for each other in its proper perspective, it can mean excitement, delight, joy, and an opportunity to just plain have fun.

One of the best feedback letters I ever received on a FamilyLife Conference came from a wife who wrote:

When you suggested last night for us to be more creative in our romance, you never gave us warning that it could be dangerous.

Rule #1: Always be prepared! At least with a spare key.

After dinner and the sunset, we decided to take your advice to add a little romance and be a little daring. Staying here at the hotel, we crept out onto our fourth floor balcony for an incredibly romantic view not to mention privacy. Unbeknown to us, while we were "communicating" and "learning more about each other," the maid was turning down our bed for us and leaving those ever scrumptious night mints.

She did not know we were on the balcony. We did not know she was in the room. Maybe you can guess the rest . . . she locked our sliding glass door! . . . Two lovers, romantic sky, and lots of privacy.

(Signed) Embarrassed from Alabama

I chuckled when I read her letter, wondering how they ever got in off that balcony. But as I put the letter down I realized they had discovered the formula: two lovers, romantic sky, lots of privacy—and enjoying oneness together.

There are no cookie cutter solutions for defeating isolation and achieving a fulfilling sexual relationship. Oneness can only occur as you remain teachable, willing to learn from and about the mate God has given you. Why not ask Him for some fresh understanding? Then turn off the lights early tonight!

HOMEBUILDERS PROJECTS

TO THINK ABOUT INDIVIDUALLY

1. How satisfied are you with your sex life together? Use the following statements to rate various aspects of your sexual relationship. Use a scale of 1 (strongly disagree) to 5 (strongly agree).

   _____ We view sex with positive anticipation.

   _____ We have no trouble deciding when and how to have sex together.

   _____ We both communicate during lovemaking (i.e., we tell each other what is most pleasing).

   _____ We make love often enough.

   _____ We both sufficiently understand each other's sexual needs and preferences.

   If you score 3 or lower on any of these questions, it may be pointing to a problem area you need to discuss with your mate.

2. List any fears you may have about sex or your sexual performance. How can you alleviate these fears?

3. Complete the following statements:

   When we are making love, I wish my mate would:

   _____.

   When we are making love, it discourages me if:

   _____.

1. If at all possible, schedule a good block of time—ideally a whole day and night, to get together for a special time of communication and intimacy. Go over your answers to the above questions and share your needs, fears, and questions. Be sure to interact with an attitude of understanding, sympathy, and forgiveness.

   If you believe you need some guidance in sexual technique, the following books offer excellent help:

   Ed Wheat, M.D., and Gloria Okes Perkins, *Love Life for Every Married Couple* (Grand Rapids: Zondervan Publishing House, 1987).

   Ed Wheat, M.D., and Gaye Wheat, *Intended for Pleasure* (Old Tappan, N.J.: Fleming H. Revell Company, 1997).

   William Cutrer, and Sandra Glahn, *Sexual Intimacy in Marriage* (Kregal Publications, 2001).

   Pray together and thank God for each other. Make a commitment to each other to improve communication and intimacy.

PART
SIX

....

A Final Challenge

....

HOMEBUILDERS
PRINCIPLES

The heritage you were handed is not
as important as the legacy
you will leave.

Your legacy will be seen in both your
physical and spiritual descendants.

23

YOUR FAMILY CAN MAKE
THE DIFFERENCE

Children are messengers we send to a time we will not see.
—AUTHOR UNKNOWN

It was the five-o'clock hour, and as I drove home from work I flipped on my radio to a favorite news program. As the host concluded his program, he wrapped up his show with a statement that reached out and grabbed my attention:

"I hope you did something of value. You just wasted a whole day of your life if you didn't."

That question sliced through my fog of fatigue and I thought about what I had done of value that day. Yes, I had been involved in things that changed the direction of families, but what had I done for my own family?

As I continued home, I pondered my game plan for the evening. What I really wanted to do was completely unplug, zone out, and watch TV. It had been a hard day. A full one. That's what *I* wanted, but what did that lovely lady and those six kids at home *need*?

"Just one night, Lord," I pleaded. "You know I need to relax." But already I knew He had me pinned. As I drove into the garage and the kids surrounded the car whooping and screaming with anticipation, I was glad I had made the right decision.

Over dinner that night, I said to the children, "I'll give you three choices: We can wrestle on the floor of the living room, we can read, or we can act out a Bible story."

289

I was hoping they would choose reading because that took the least amount of energy, but naturally they chose wrestling in the living room. Barbara rolled her eyes but good-naturedly cleared away some of her favorite knickknacks and we went at it.

Miniature Sumo wrestlers grabbed my legs and soon had me pinned. Even Mom got in the act and started tickling Dad. Kids literally flew (gently, of course) through the air for the next hour. Even our ten-month-old baby got in the act as she pounced on my stomach after observing her brothers and sisters tickling Dad.

After praying with the kids and putting them to bed, I headed that way myself, tired and exhausted. Yet I had a good feeling. I wasn't even sure any of our children would remember that night, but I still believed I did something of infinite value. It had not been a wasted day.[1]

I've thought of that radio show host's question many times since then. And I have realized that it is days of value added to days of value that make weeks of value. Weeks of value, linked with other weeks of value make a year of value. And, finally, after enough years of doing something of value, you have a lifetime of value—a legacy of love to leave your children.

WHAT TYPE OF LEGACY ARE YOU LEAVING?

As we conduct FamilyLife Conferences across the country, I find that the concept of leaving behind a "legacy" is a bit unfamiliar to many couples. Oh, they may be familiar with the idea of an inheritance, but leaving their kids with a legacy that reminds them of who they are and what is important is a bit unfamiliar.

According to the dictionary, a heritage and a legacy are virtually the same thing: something handed down from an ancestor, a predecessor, or from the past. Some families take their heritage very seriously. As one young lad approached his sixth birthday, he could tell something big was going to happen. A week before his birthday party, he noticed the garage door locked with a shiny new padlock. The day finally arrived, and he was awakened by an uncle who asked him to come downstairs to the kitchen where his parents, aunts, uncles, grandmother, and grandfather were waiting.

They all formed a line and went out the kitchen door, across the concrete porch, and then formed a semicircle in front of the garage door. Then the boy's father unlocked that shiny padlock and opened the door. Standing in front of the boy was a one-foot-thick section of a redwood tree, nearly five feet in diameter.

As the boy drew closer, he noticed the huge slice of wood had been carefully lacquered and polished, and then he saw little signs painted on the rings of the tree. One ring was labeled, "The Emancipation Proclamation, January 1, 1863." Another ring dated the founding of the first Black college. There was still another marker that signified when his mother and father had met and gotten married.

The more the boy studied the carefully labeled rings on that huge piece of redwood, the more he realized it not only contained a history of his family, but a history of his race. His parents and the rest of the family knew the importance of helping a young man understand his origins. It is no wonder that this little boy—Alex Haley—grew up to write the novel *Roots*, which became the most-watched television miniseries in history.

TWO WAYS TO LEAVE A LEGACY

There are two ways for Christian couples to leave a legacy that is uniquely their own. The closest and most immediate way is *through your physical descendants*, your children. You nurture them in Christ, seeking to develop their character so they become individually dependent on God. Then they carry their own Christian torch and hand it on to their children after them.

When you look around the dinner table, what do you see in your children's faces? Runny noses? Smudges streaked with spaghetti or the remains of an M & M orgy? Or do you see the next generation? The next mothers and fathers who will carry the torch to a needy world? There's no question that the family you are going to leave behind is far more important than the family you came from.

James Dobson was once asked, "What motivates you to do what you do?"

He replied, "My one purpose in living is to serve Jesus Christ to the best of my ability and to take as many people to heaven as I possibly can. And my first responsibility is to do everything in my power to include my own kids in that number."[2]

"Are We Going to Be a Family Now?"

Recently I heard a report of how another father discovered the importance of his own legacy and took steps to preserve and cherish it.

This man worked for a television studio, but, unlike so many in the TV industry who seldom watch television themselves, this man was addicted to it. He would come home from work, turn on the tube, and watch it all evening—usually until it went off the air. He spent little or no time with his two children or his wife. In fact, his kids hardly knew they had a dad. All they knew was that someone living there watched TV all the time.

Needless to say, his marriage was hurting and deeply immersed in isolation. For some reason, however, he and his wife decided to attend one of our FamilyLife Conferences, and that weekend literally changed his life. He realized his priorities were totally wrong and that he was setting a bad example for his children.

When the man got home on the evening following the conference, the first thing he did was take the television set from the family room and store it in the garage. Then he took a family portrait he had stuffed away in a closet and hung it on the wall where the television set used to be.

Next he called his wife and two children into the family room for a family council meeting. As he shared with them his new set of priorities and asked for their forgiveness, his twelve-year-old son interrupted him and said, "Daddy, now that there is a picture of our family where the television used to be, does this mean we are going to be a family now?"

This husband and wife had made a giant step, from spending night after night doing nothing of value, to deciding to be a dad who cared about his family. That's what a legacy is all about.

A Legacy That Reaches Beyond Itself

When she was asked, "Is there anything worse than being blind?" Helen Keller replied, "Yes, the most pathetic thing in all the world is someone who has sight but has no vision."

A second and just as important way to leave your own legacy behind is through the investments you make while on planet earth to *change people's lives for Christ.* Your spiritual descendants—those persons you influence through the use of your talents, gifts, abilities, finances, and prayers—are the second component of your legacy.

One of your major goals at every FamilyLife Conference is to help people see beyond the problems they are facing in their own families and look outside to a world that desperately needs the peace offered only by Jesus Christ. One of God's primary purposes for your family is that you be a part of fulfilling the Great Commission.

When Jesus said, ". . . go and make disciples of all nations" (Matthew 28:19), He was talking to His disciples, common men like you and me. God is never dependent on paid professionals or highly trained technicians to do His work. Of course, He can use well-trained professionals, but He usually works through the average, available person.

Many Christians feel they can do nothing for their culture—that they are caught in a vast tidal wave of pagan unbelief and immorality, and all they can hope for is to barely stay afloat themselves. The result is we get used to seeing friends end their marriages, used to the girl pregnant before wedlock, and used to "no-fault divorces."

A few years ago, national news wires carried the story of a California couple who were in a hot tub when the thermostat got stuck and the temperature rose from 100 to 110 and finally to 120 degrees. They didn't notice the increase in heat and both of them dozed off. They literally cooked to death after going into a coma. Our culture is like a giant hot tub that is slowly boiling us to death. But it doesn't have to be. You, your spouse, and your family *can* make a difference.

THE COMMON PEOPLE MAKE THE DIFFERENCE

Some of the best advice I ever received was given by a good friend as we were driving home from a fishing trip. I asked him, "What would you do if you had a fast-growing family ministry and were trying to help the church strengthen families?"

I'll never forget his words spoken in the darkness of the car: "I would take the message and ministry out of the hands of the professionals and put them into the hands of the people."

That's exactly what the Family Ministry is doing. All over America, husbands and wives are meeting in the HomeBuilders Couples Series, small group Bible studies dedicated to making your family all that God intended. And it's working. Led by lay men and women, this couples study aims to strengthen marriages through creative sessions and practical application of the biblical blueprints for building a home.

I'm sometimes asked if depending on volunteer lay people is a good idea, and I respond by saying that history is full of examples of lay people who stepped forward at critical times to make a difference. For me, there is no better example than Dunkirk, a name forever linked with heroic tales of World War II—and men who left a legacy of courage.

It was the spring of 1940 and the tide was running against the Allies. The French army was reeling from the onslaught of Hitler's panzer divisions. The Dutch and Belgians had surrendered and the Allied forces were trapped in the channel port of Dunkirk with no way to escape.

Among the Allied forces caught on the beaches at Dunkirk were 220,000 of Britain's finest young men. Hitler's panzer divisions, only miles away in the hills of France, were ready to slash forward, turning the English Channel red with their blood.

The king was powerless. The Royal Navy did not have the ships to rescue more than 17,000 men and the House of Commons was told to prepare itself for "hard and heavy tidings." In his biography of Winston

Churchill, *The Last Lion: Visions of Glory,* William Manchester describes what happened next:

> Then, from the streams and estuaries of Kent and Dover, a strange fleet appeared: travelers and tugs, scows and fishing sloops, lifeboats and pleasure craft, smacks and coasters; the island ferry "Gracie Fields"; Tom Sopwith's America's Cup challenger "Endeavour"; even the London fire brigade's fire-float "Massey Shaw"—all of them manned by civilian volunteers; English fathers sailing to rescue England's exhausted, bleeding sons.[3]

From May 29 to June 4, it was one of the most remarkable naval operations of all time, and it went on in the face of an incredible artillery bombardment. In the skies overhead, the tiny Royal Air Force held off the Luftwaffe, shooting down four German planes for every one of theirs, as the evacuation went on in the waters below. Original estimates suggested only a comparative handful of Allied troops might be rescued at Dunkirk, but in the end the ragtag civilian armada brought 338,682 men safe to the shores of England!

Dunkirk was a critical turning point in the war. The men who were evacuated represented three-fourths of the Allied forces at that time. And the job was not done by the experts or the professionals. Common people had made the difference!

THE FAMILY FACES ITS OWN DUNKIRK

Today there is a war being waged against the family. Our nation's marriages, specifically our children, face their own particular Dunkirk, but families can hope for little help from Washington or the legislators of their state capitals—the problem is too large for them. Trained psychologists and counselors can assist only a comparative handful of the thousands of families that need guidance and direction. Mighty voices in church pulpits and on television and radio can provide influence, but if the war is to be won, *it must happen with lay people like you and me.*

Our nation's families hang in the balance. With over five billion people inhabiting our planet today, your family, like mine, needs to feel it is significant. Everyone in your family should realize it is part of something that will outlive all of them. What greater investment could there be than to learn to make your own marriage and family work, and then begin to reach out to help others do the same? That's how you can build a heritage of destiny.

The choice is yours. I want to challenge you to help rescue America's broken and bleeding families.

When Nehemiah directed the rebuilding of the wall at Jerusalem, he made each man responsible for the section of wall that was in front of his own home. Nehemiah's strategy was brilliant. Each man was highly motivated to rebuild the wall high and well fortified in front of his own home. Why? If the wall were low or weak, that would be the first place where enemies would burst through to overwhelm everyone in their path.

The parallel for today is clear. The family is for a nation what the wall represented for Jerusalem—our country's protection. We need Christian families who will first begin building strong walls for themselves. Then we need you to reach out to help your neighbors build.

As I stated in the beginning, one of the reasons this book was written was to *enlist you* as a couple to reach out and make a difference in the marriages of others. In the next chapter I'll explain how you can experience a new level of growth in your marriage by teaching others what you've learned.

The world is full of people erecting monuments to themselves, but leaving nothing of real value behind. Why not determine that with God's help you will leave behind a legacy that will last forever!

HOMEBUILDERS
PRINCIPLES

Jesus Christ did not go to the
Cross just so we could have happy
marriages, but so that we would
love Him, love one another, and go
to the world with the greatest news
ever announced.

24

HOW TO BECOME A HOMEBUILDER

The first reformation put the
word of God *in the hands of*
laymen and women.
The second reformation must put the
work of God *in the hands of*
laymen and women.

—ROBERT SLOCUM

Armand and Linda Dauplaise live in a suburb of Washington, D.C., and they are HomeBuilders.

Steve and Dianne Robinson make their home in Marietta, Georgia, and they are HomeBuilders.

Warran and Sharry Milanowski reside in Boise, Idaho, and they are HomeBuilders.

Who are these HomeBuilders? What do they do? What makes them unique?

As I mentioned in the last chapter, the needs of the family today will not be met by professionals—counselors, government officials, ministers, or parachurch organizations. The need is for Christians who have growing marriages to begin to reach out and influence other families. That's exactly what each of these couples has done—the couples have used their gifts and abilities to reach out to marriages in their communities by starting and leading HomeBuilders Groups.

WHAT IS THE HOMEBUILDERS COUPLES SERIES?

This marriage enrichment series is designed for either a couple to complete on their own, or a small number of couples (four to seven) to go through as a group. When completed, this series of four Bible study books will answer one question for couples: *How do you build a distinctly Christian marriage?*

These HomeBuilders Groups, while led by lay couples, are designed to be a blend of the biblical blueprints for building a marriage, open and honest interaction, and practical application. HomeBuilders Groups are structured to see a couple defeat isolation and build oneness in their marriage.

Armand and Linda first taught the HomeBuilders Couple Series in a Sunday school class three years ago. Now their church has a permanent HomeBuilders Class (attended by seventy to ninety people every week), and Armand and Linda have seen their vision for starting other HomeBuilders Groups grow. They have made a ministry to couples and families their focus in ministry together.

Not only have Armand and Linda helped give leadership to our FamilyLife Conference, influencing several thousand marriages in the Washington, D.C., area, but they have helped start HomeBuilders Groups throughout our nation's capital. Over seventy groups have been formed with more than six hundred people involved in small group accountability for their marriages.

One man who attended one of the HomeBuilders Groups was a workaholic, who almost always missed meals at night. But as a result of the practical application with his wife, he changed his work habits and now makes it a point to be home every night for meals and spending time with his family.

What our ministry to families is seeing is that couples are in deep need of intimacy not only with one another, but also with a group of peers. We have lost our sense of community and need a group who knows us well—a group who'll challenge us even to change our work habits if our family needs it.

WHY ARE HOME BIBLE STUDIES SO IMPORTANT?

There are three reasons why a home study is effective:

1. *The relaxed surroundings of a home study lend themselves well to the informal interaction of a small group.* People are more inclined to open up in the nonthreatening environment of a home.

2. *Most home studies result in concentrated learning and increased growth in people's lives.* Jim Diffee, a lay leader in the Evangelical Community Church of Jackson, Tennessee, wrote in *Discipleship Journal* about the HomeBuilders Couples Series. "This study is both provocative and challenging. Even though I've been a Christian for sixteen years and have been married for more than eight, I found myself being challenged to ask some hard questions and to reevaluate my marriage in light of what Scripture has to say."

3. *A home group can be a place where people slow down and experience "community" with others.* We cannot only find out what is going on in one another's lives, but we can also be affirmed and experience intimacy with others.

Craig Havener of Cumming, Iowa, reported, "We've become very close knit over the last year—we can hardly wait to get our hands on the next study when it becomes available." And Sharry Milanowski in Boise said, "Our group wants it to go on and on. It is such a diverse group of people—but we have really bonded—a lot of them are saying they could go on for the rest of their lives."

WHO IS BEST SUITED TO ATTEND A HOMEBUILDERS GROUP?

A HomeBuilders Group is good for any couple who wants to improve their marriage. Gene Koepfler, from Regalsville, Pennsylvania, told us:

We had resistance to starting a HomeBuilders Group at first because people think it's for rotten marriages. But I encourage them to attend because it's for good marriages that need to be better. You change the oil in your car before it becomes a problem—you don't wait until the engine blows up. A HomeBuilders Group is good marriage maintenance.

300

Many couples have started right in their own neighborhoods and invited people they would otherwise only occasionally see. People who have no religious affiliation or background feel comfortable in these groups because they are formed around the felt need of marriages. People are hungry for real solutions to their problems.

Steve and Dianne Robinson started a HomeBuilders Group in their neighborhood in Marietta. For some time they had been troubled by the needs of families in their neighborhood. Going door to door they passed out nearly three hundred flyers inviting neighbors to come to their home for a dessert and to hear about the study. Ten of the fifteen couples who showed up decided to participate. At least half of them started attending church with Steve while attending the HomeBuilders Study.

Steve has since volunteered his time to us and become instrumental in helping formulate our strategy for launching our FamilyLife Conferences and HomeBuilders Groups around the United States.

What Are the Benefits of Starting a HomeBuilders Group?

When Warren and Sharry Milanowski came all the way from Boise, Idaho, to Little Rock just to find out about the HomeBuilders Couples Series, I was surprised. But they had a vision for seeing marriages and families in Idaho strengthened through small groups. Since that time Warren and Sharry have become so excited about this new series that they have become city coordinators for beginning HomeBuilders Groups throughout Boise.

At the Boise FamilyLife Conference about nine hundred attended and the Milanowskis saw over eighty HomeBuilders Groups form after the conference. One church started fifteen HomeBuilders Groups just for its own people. The Milanowskis have seen couples cancel divorces and defeat isolation. They've seen new Christians grow, and communication strengthened. And they've also seen several persons become Christians through attending HomeBuilders Groups they've started.

Look at these comments from other couples around the country who have benefited from HomeBuilders Groups:

I've seen a much happier group of children from these parents.

Not only does it increase the communication between husband and wife, but it brings you in touch with others. You realize every couple has the same problems. We no longer *feel alone* in our problems.

A man who had been married for thirteen years said this:

It forces you into areas of discussion with your spouse where you've never ventured before. Things you've only thought about talking about. There were questions that I had regarding our sex life that I'd always wanted to ask her and never really thought it was appropriate. But when it became a private project for just the two of use, a lesson we had to do—Boom— there it was. It knocks down a lot of barriers.

A pair of veteran Sunday school teachers commented:

The greatest benefit was the growth in the two couples who taught the sessions. The time spent in preparation together as a couple was priceless. A special closeness and excitement developed between us as couples as we saw how God's Word built acceptance, understanding, and goal-directed sharing into each marriage that we taught.

A lay church leader, Tim McKinsey of Little Rock, compared the warnings he received in the HomeBuilders to receiving a warning for a traffic violation:

If I do not heed the warnings, later on I will be pulled over and pay a substantial fine. The warnings I received during the HomeBuilders study are a minor embarrassment compared to the long-range savings in cost to my marriage later on!

Robert Lewis, a pastor who has seen more than eleven hundred adults involved in HomeBuilders Groups, said this:

The HomeBuilders has probably been the most exciting small group series we have ever used in my ten years at Fellowship Bible Church. The biggest encouragement to me was the number of people who have mentioned the simplicity of the series. It has defined simply and clearly what a Christian marriage is. Couples are able to related all that goes on in their own marriages back to that basic blueprint.

How Much Time Does Each Session Take?

Usually, these sessions last for ninety minutes, although some groups go longer. You'll find there's so much to talk about that couples will leave each session wishing they had more time.

There is a HomeBuilders Project at the end of the session. It's been fun to see couples carrying their study guides into restaurants to do their HomeBuilders Project (a sixty- to ninety-minute practical project to help couples apply what they've interacted over in their small group). This is where the *real* application occurs.

Do I Need Any Specialized Training to Start a HomeBuilders Group?

Obviously some experience in small groups would help, but if you have basic conversational skills, then you'll do just fine. One leader shares, "We have now led HomeBuilders Groups for three years and you don't lead the group as much as you 'guide it.' You're not a counselor, but you're just another married couple that wants to see marriages work."

The Leader's Guide that accompanies each study will help you prepare for lessons, and the Family Ministry also can send you information or help train you in leading a Bible study.

Will It Take Much Preparation Time?

No, just an hour or two for each session. Couples who have led the discussion in these HomeBuilders Groups say that the Leader's Guide is the best part—it walks you through the entire session and shows you how to facilitate interaction during the group. One leader shared, "The leader's guide was the best I've ever come across. You really have to be a dolt not to be able to lead one of these groups."

WILL THIS MATERIAL WORK IN A SUNDAY SCHOOL FORMAT?

Yes, this material is easily adaptable into a sixty-minute format. You'll need to divide each session in half—it will take two Sundays to complete each lesson.

"It's by far the most practical material we have ever used in our Sunday school—it forces couples to open up," said Jim and June Yoder in Beavercreek, Ohio. Their class had over seventy different people involved at one time or another.

Bill Galliger shared that his Sunday school class doubled and then tripled in size. "I was strictly a male chauvinist pig—we didn't have oneness in our marriage. The study made a phenomenal impact on me, improving my life and my relationship with my wife. It also helped me develop relationships with other Christians. Our group finally became so large we broke into five different groups. And now we plan on breaking those into seven to ten groups."

WHAT'S THE IDEAL SIZE?

The most effective groups have three to seven couples—if it gets larger than that it's best to break out in smaller groups. The sessions are designed for interaction and a large group defeats the strength of the study.

WHAT'S SO UNIQUE ABOUT THE HOMEBUILDERS COUPLES SERIES?

There are four unique features of this Couples Series:

1. It's a fun study just for couples. There are many fine studies available today, but nearly all are for individuals.

2. The "Make-A-Date" is an enjoyable structured date (a HomeBuilders Project) that has couples get together between sessions to work through and apply what they've learned.

3. There is a healthy accountability within the group that encourages

people to make decisions and then follow through in making lifestyle changes.

4. No homework—no preparation for the next session—just a date with your mate! We promise more intimate conversations than when you dated!

WOULD THOSE WHO AREN'T RELIGIOUS FEEL COMFORTABLE IN THE STUDY?

We've seen several individuals make commitments to Christ as a result of the study. One man and woman who were unmarried but living together attended a HomeBuilders Group. As a result, he moved out and became a Christian. Eventually they were married and *then* he moved back in!

It's especially good for couples who are not all that spiritually committed. In fact, we've heard story after story of individuals and marriages that are finding new spiritual vitality through these groups. Steve Hanes runs an automotive speed shop, but said nothing goes faster than a HomeBuilders Group. "We started with eight attending, and before long, many of those who had been on the fringe in our church were inviting others. We ended with twenty in our group."

WHAT MATERIAL IS AVAILABLE TO TEACH?

Each of the following studies features attractive plastic spiral-bound study guides. Leader's Guides are also available for each study.

Building Teamwork in Your Marriage, by Robert Lewis, defines our God-given roles and responsibilities as husbands and wives. Topics include: comprehending your mate's differentness, meeting special needs in your wife/husband, role responsibilities for the man/woman, and succeeding in the Spirit.

My study, *Building Your Marriage,* covers the basic blueprints for building a distinctly Christian marriage. The subjects covered are overcoming isolation, creating oneness, receiving your mate, and building a legacy. This study follows closely the material in this book.

Building Your Mate's Self-Esteem, which I wrote with Barbara, reinforces the importance of building up one another. Major topics include: planting positive words, allowing the freedom to fail, valuing your wife/securing your man, and managing pressure in marriage.

In *Mastering Your Money in Marriage*, by Ron Blue, you will gain a new perspective into the often-controversial area of finances. By learning biblical concepts of handling money, you'll gain a handle on how you can solidify your financial situation.

Growing Together in Christ, by David Sunde, emphasizes the importance of practicing the basics of Christ's teachings daily. It'll be ideal for showing anyone how to grow in his or her faith, and it's especially helpful for new Christians. Learn about prayer, obedience, fellowship, and walking in the power of the Holy Spirit.

Resolving Conflict in Your Marriage, by Bob and Jan Horner, permeates beneath the surface of the marriage relationship. Learn that understanding one another requires communication, that communication and commitment are synonymous, and discover the privilege and responsibility of transparency.

Other studies in the HomeBuilders Series include *Improving Communication in Your Marriage*, by Dr. Gary Rosberg and Barbara Rosberg; *Making Your Remarriage Last*, by Jim Keller; *Stress in Your Marriage*, by Doug Daily; *Raising Children of Faith*, by Barbara and myself; and *Defending the Military Marriage*, by Lt. Col. Jim Fishback and Bea Fishback.

HOW DO I START A HOMEBUILDERS GROUP?

Step One: Go to your Christian bookstore and get a copy of the HomeBuilders study you want to lead. You'll need to buy a copy for both you and your spouse, plus a copy of the Leader's Guide. If none are available you can ask your bookstore to order, or you can call our customer service at 1-800-FL-TODAY or visit our Website: www.familylife.com.

Step Two: Prayerfully make a list of those you'd like to invite to join your group (four to seven couples) and then ask them. Keep in mind you may need to ask more than the number of couples you hope will come.

Don't just think of those in your church, but those in your neighborhood or associates at work who would benefit from your time together.

Step Three: Set your first meeting date, get the participant's materials, and begin.

So, there you have it. I hope this book has strengthened your marriage—it has certainly been a challenge for us.

As Barbara and a team of friends helped me finish this manuscript, they have witnessed the realities of our marriage and family operating under stress. In the final editing process there were four computers humming along at our house. Our dryer and dishwasher quit. Samuel broke his arm. Rebecca broke her finger. Ashley had a bunking party of teenagers. Our roof developed a leak. Report cards came in. An intestinal infection invaded the *entire* family. And our cocker spaniel, Abby, still has fleas.

Somehow, we manage to maintain oneness—a real miracle. May God grant you the same type of unity as you build your marriage and family. Happy HomeBuilding!

NOTES

CHAPTER 1

1. David R. Johnson, *The Light Behind the Star* (Sisters, Oreg.: Questar Publishers, 1989), 13–15.

CHAPTER 2

1. Dr. James Lynch, *The Broken Heart: The Medical Consequences of Loneliness* (New York: Basic Book Publishers, 1977), 8, 14.
2. Dr. Philip Zimbardo, *Psychology Today*, August 1980, 71–76.
3. Ibid.
4. Dr. Willard F. Harley Jr., *His Needs, Her Needs* (Old Tappan, N.J.: Fleming H. Revell Co., 1986), 11.

CHAPTER 3

1. "Dear Abby," *Dallas Times Herald*, 2 April 1989, K-2.
2. *Forbes*, 17 December 1984, 19.
3. Quoted by Dr. James C. Dobson, *Straight Talk to Men and Their Wives* (Waco: Word Books, 1978), 44–45. Used by permission from *American Girl*, published by Girl Scouts of the U.S.A.

CHAPTER 4

1. Brian Moorehead, *The Luck of Ginger Coffee* (Boston: Little, Brown and Company, 1960), 267.

CHAPTER 7

1. Christopher Lasch, *The Culture of Narcissism* (New York: W. W. Norton and Co., Inc., 1979), 72, 22.
2. Ibid., 141.
3. Ibid., 5.
4. Ibid., 67.
5. C. S. Lewis, *The Four Loves* (New York: Harcourt, Brace and World, Inc., 1960), 169.

CHAPTER 8

1. Malcolm Muggeridge, *A Twentieth Century Testimony* (New York: Ballantine Epiphany Books, 1988), 72.

CHAPTER 9

1. Harley, 25.
2. Ruth Senter, "Rick," *Partnership* Magazine, January/February 1988, 30–34, 60, 61.
3. Harley, 162, 163.
4. Stephen Arterburn and Fred Stoeker, *Every Man's Battle* (Colorado Springs: Waterbrook Press, 2000).

CHAPTER 10

1. "Hello, Columbia! Man Soars Three Miles up in a Chair," *The Denver Post*, 3 July 1982, 1A.
2. Statistics provided by Dave Stoop, *Self Talk: Key to Personal Growth* (Old Tappan: Fleming H. Revell Company, 1982), 12.
3. Hans Selye, *The Stress of Life* (New York: McGraw-Hill Book Company, 1956), 62, 63.
4. See Keith W. Sehnert, *Stress/Unstress* (Minneapolis: Augsburg Publishing House, 1981), 27, 28.
5. Max Lucado, *No Wonder They Call Him the Savior* (Portland: Multnomah Press, 1986), 31, 32.

CHAPTER 11

1. "When I Get Married," edited by Bill Adler, *McCall's*, June 1979, 107.
2. Dr. Joyce Brothers, *What Every Woman Should Know About Men*, (New York: Random House, 1981).
3. John and Sylvia Van Regenmorter and Joseph S. McIlhaney Jr., M.D., *Dear God, Why Can't We Have a Baby?* (Grand Rapids: Baker Book House, 1986), 9.
4. William Barclay, *The Letters to the Corinthians* (Edinburgh: The St. Andrew Press, 1954), 107.

CHAPTER 13

1. Wilbur Reese, "$3 Worth of God," quoted by Tim Hansel in *When I Relax I Feel Guilty* (Elgin: David C. Cook, 1979), 49.

CHAPTER 14

1. *The Tulsa World*, 26 February 1988, 2A.
2. William Hendriksen, *New Testament Commentary on Ephesians* (Grand Rapids: Baker Book House, 1967), 248.
3. Harley, 10.
4. Richard Selzer, M.D., *Mortal Lessons: Notes in the Art of Surgery* (New York: Simon & Schuster, 1976), 45, 46.

CHAPTER 15

1. Robert Lewis, *Building Teamwork in Marriage,* The HomeBuilders Series (Dallas: Word Publishers, Inc., 1989), 84.

2. Jeanne Hendricks, *A Mother's Legacy* (Colorado Springs: NavPress, 1988), 88.

3. James Dobson, *Love Must Be Tough* (Waco, Tex.: Word Publishing, 1983).

CHAPTER 16

1. James Dobson, *What Wives Wish Their Husbands Knew About Women* (Wheaton: Tyndale House Publishers, 1975), 55–56.

2. David Elkind, *The Hurried Child* (Reading, Mass.: Addison-Wesley Publishing Co., 1981), 188.

3. Burton White, "Should You Stay Home with Your Baby?", *Young Children,* November 1981, 3–5.

4. For a complete account of this story, see Henry Hurt, "From the Jaws of Death," *The Reader's Digest,* April 1987, 117.

5. Anne Morrow Lindbergh, *Gift from the Sea* (New York: Pantheon Books, 1955, 1975), 49, 50.

6. E. M. Bounds, *Prayer and Praying Men* (Grand Rapids: Baker Book House, 1977), 36.

CHAPTER 17

1. Charlie Shedd, *You Can Be a Great Parent* (Waco, Tex.: Word Publishing, 1970), 63.

2. Keith J. Leenhouts, *A Father . . . A Son . . . and a Three-Mile Run* (Grand Rapids: Zondervan Publishing House, 1975), 126–129.

3. This story also appeared in my book, *Pulling Weeds, Planting Seeds* (San Bernardino, Calif.: Here's Life Publishers, Inc., 1989), 76–79.

CHAPTER 18

1. Ken Durham, *Speaking from the Heart* (Fort Worth: Sweet Publishing Company, Inc., 1986), 17.

2. The full account of Red McDaniel's experience can be found in *Scars and Stripes,* American Defense Institute, P.O. Box 2497, Washington, D.C., 20013.

3. John Powell, *Why Am I Afraid to Tell You Who I Am?* (Chicago: Argus Communications, 1969), 55–61.

CHAPTER 19

1. Reprinted by permission from Ann Landers, *Los Angeles Times* Syndicate.

2. "Second Acts," *People* Magazine, 6 March 1989, 121.
3. *The Greenville News,* 26 April 1981, 19A.

CHAPTER 22
1. Ed Wheat, M.D., and Gaye Wheat, *Intended for Pleasure* (Old Tappan: Fleming H. Revell Company, 1977), 16.
2. Mei-Mei Chan and Michelle Healy, "Lot of Women Grinning and Bearing It," *USA Today,* 8 May 1985.
3. Steven Findlay, "Jobs Sap Couples Craving for Sex," *USA Today,* 8 May 1985.
4. Ibid.

CHAPTER 23
1. This story appears in slightly different form in the book by Dennis Rainey, *Pulling Weeds, Planting Seeds* (San Bernardino, Calif.: Here's Life Publishers, Inc., 1989), 19.
2. *FamilyLife Today,* March 1982, 14.
3. William Manchester, *The Last Lion* (New York: Dell Publishing Company, 1984), 3.

APPENDIX

THE FOUR SPIRITUAL LAWS

Just as there are physical laws that govern the physical universe, so are there spiritual laws which govern your relationship with God.

LAW ONE

God loves you, and offers a wonderful plan for your life.

GOD'S LOVE

"For God so loved the world, that He gave His only begotten Son, that whoever believes in Him should not perish, but have eternal life" (John 3:16).

GOD'S PLAN

(Christ speaking) "I came that they might have life, and might have it abundantly" (that it might be full and meaningful) (John 10:10).

Why is it that most people are not experiencing the abundant life? Because . . .

LAW TWO

Man is sinful and separated from God, therefore, he cannot know and experience God's love and plan for his life.

MAN IS SINFUL

"For all have sinned and fall short of the Glory of God" (Romans 3:23). Man was created to have fellowship with God; but, because of his stubborn self-will, he chose to go his own independent way and fellowship with God was broken. This self-will, characterized by an attitude of active rebellion or passive indifference, is evidence of what the Bible calls sin.

MAN IS SEPARATED

"For the wages of sin is death" (spiritual separation from God) (Romans 6:23).

This diagram illustrates that God is holy and man is sinful. A great gulf separates the two. The arrows illustrate that man is continually trying to reach God and the abundant life through his own efforts, such as a good life, philosophy, or religion.

The third law explains the only way to bridge this gulf . . .

LAW THREE

Jesus Christ is God's only provision for man's sin. Through Him you can know and experience God's love and plan for your life.

HE DIED IN OUR PLACE

"But God demonstrates His own love toward us, in that while we were yet sinners, Christ died for us" (Romans 5:8).

HE ROSE FROM THE DEAD

"Christ died for our sins . . . He was buried . . . He was raised on the third day, according to the Scriptures . . . He appeared to Peter, then to the twelve. After that He appeared to more than five hundred" (1 Corinthians 15:3–6).

HE IS THE ONLY WAY TO GOD

"Jesus said to him, 'I am the way, and the truth, and the life; no one comes to the Father, but through Me'" (John 14:6).

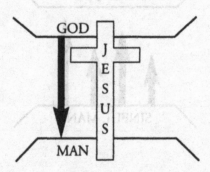

This diagram illustrates that God has bridged the gulf which separates us from God by sending His Son, Jesus Christ, to die on the cross in our place to pay the penalty for our sins.

It is not enough just to know these three laws . . .

LAW FOUR

We must individually receive Jesus Christ as Savior and Lord; then we can know and experience God's love and plan for our lives.

We Must Receive Christ

"But as many as received Him, to them He gave the right to become children of God, even to those who believe in His name" (John 1:12).

We Receive Christ Through Faith

"For by grace you have been saved through faith; and that not of yourselves, it is the gift of God; not as a result of works, that no one should boast" (Ephesians 2:8–9).

When We Receive Christ, We Experience a New Birth

(Read John 3:1–8.)

We Receive Christ by Personal Invitation

(Christ is speaking.) "Behold, I stand at the door and knock; if anyone hears My voice and opens the door, I will come in to him" (Revelation 3:20).

Receiving Christ involves turning from self to God (repentance) and trusting Christ to come into our lives to forgive our sins and to make us the kind of person He wants us to be. Just to agree intellectually that Jesus Christ is the Son of God and that He died on the cross for our sins is not enough. Nor is it enough to have an emotional experience. We receive Jesus Christ by faith, as an act of the will.

These two circles represent two kinds of lives:

SELF-DIRECTED LIFE

S—Self on the throne

✝—Christ is outside the life

●—Interests are directed by self, often resulting in discord and frustration

CHRIST-DIRECTED LIFE

†—Christ is in the life

S—Self is yielding to Christ

●—Interests are directed by Christ, resulting in
harmony with God's plan

Which circle best represents your life?

Which circle would you like to have represent your life?

The following explains how you can receive Christ:

YOU CAN RECEIVE CHRIST RIGHT NOW BY FAITH THROUGH PRAYER

Prayer is talking with God. God knows your heart and is not so concerned with your words as He is with the attitude of your heart. The following is a suggested prayer:

> Lord Jesus, I need You. Thank You for dying on the cross for my sins. I open the door of my life and receive You as my Savior and Lord. Thank You for forgiving my sins and giving me eternal life. Make me the kind of person You want me to be.

Does this prayer express the desire of your heart? If it does, pray this prayer right now, and Christ will come into your life, as He promised.

ACKNOWLEDGMENTS

Fritz and Jackie Ridenour shaped and gave life to these pages and a book that would otherwise have not been written. Your commitment to excellence, organization skills, and work on this manuscript get a "perfect 10" in our book. Bubba, the Roadrunner thinks you're terrific!

Dave Boehi has been an angel sent from heaven. Thanks for giving us truthful feedback and a quality sharpening of these pages. You are truly a gifted writer and editor. We're looking forward to editing *your* book next time—we promise you will be able to read *our* edits.

Brenda Schulte and Tami Melling were incredible with our younger children when it became necessary for Barbara to help on the book for a few weeks. Thanks for loving us and our tribe. And, Brenda, thanks also for your initial editing. Tami, you may be the highest-qualified baby-sitter ever!

Jeff Schulte, Sue Stinson, and Pat Orton ran interference and juggled the demands of our office as no other trio of professionals could. Thanks for loving us when we were dazed by the deadlines and frazzled by a full spring schedule. You three pitched in and contributed significantly to the most productive year yet. You deserve a special award for being so diverse, excellent, and encouraging.

Fred Hitchcock deserves kudos for naming this book and for the strong work he did on tracking down all the quotes and needed permissions. We're glad you're on the team. Julie Denker, once again, came through in the clutch. Thanks for your faithful smile and cooperative spirit. Thanks to Elizabeth Reha, again, for typing the raw manuscript—we sure hope you can find a man.

Jane Anne Smith, thanks for pitching in, again, and helping with this book.

To the leadership team at Word—Gary Ingersoll, Byron Williamson, and Kip Jordon—you men are a great encouragement as we launch The HomeBuilders. Thanks for your partnership and long-haul commitment to a concept which *will* be used by God to strengthen hundreds of thousands of families.

To Al Bryant and the editorial team at Word, a hearty thanks for sharpening these pages and their message. By now you know I (Dennis) barely passed seventh-grade grammar.

Joey Paul, you are one in five billion. Thanks for taking the time to listen to that message on tape as you drove through Dallas. Our partnership with Word, Inc., this book, and The HomeBuilders would not have occurred without you. Thanks for championing the cause of strengthening marriages and families.

And finally, to our family who sacrificed so that this book could help others. Ashley was understanding, Benjamin was helpful, Samuel was encouraging, Rebecca kept me laughing, Deborah was sweet, and Laura's hugs and kisses lifted my spirits. You are all terrific!

ABOUT THE AUTHORS

DENNIS and BARBARA RAINEY are the cofounders of FamilyLife, and frequent speakers at FamilyLife's Weekend to Remember and Rekindling the Romance arena events. Dennis is the President of FamilyLife and the host of the radio program *FamilyLife Today*. He is the creator of the HomeBuilders Couples Series®, which has sold more than 1.5 million copies worldwide. Dennis and Barbara, have coauthored several best-selling books, including *The New Building Your Mate's Self-Esteem, Moments Together for Couples, Starting Your Marriage Right, We Still Do, Parenting Today's Adolescent,* and *Two Hearts Praying As One.* They have six children, one son-in-law, two daughters-in-law, and five grandchildren. The Raineys live near Little Rock, Arkansas.

*F*amilyLife has been presenting couples with the wonderful news of God's blueprints for marriage since 1976. Today we are strengthening hundreds of thousands of homes each year in the United States and around the world through:

- ◆ Weekend to Remember™ conferences

- ◆ One-day arena events for couples

- ◆ HomeBuilders Couples Series® and HomeBuilders Parenting Series™ small-group Bible studies

- ◆ "FamilyLife Today," the daily, half-hour radio program, and four other nationally syndicated broadcasts

- ◆ A comprehensive Web site, www.familylife.com, featuring marriage and parenting tips, daily devotions, conference information, and a wide range of resources for strengthening families

- ◆ Unique marriage and family connecting resources

Through these outreaches, FamilyLife is effectively developing godly families who reach the world one home at a time.

FAMILYLIFE™
Bringing Timeless Principles Home

Dennis Rainey, President
1-800-FL-TODAY
(358-6329)
www.familylife.com

A division of
Campus Crusade for Christ